Donald Trump's Circus Maximus

AND

Joe Biden's Excellent Adventure

Donald Trump's Circus Maximus

=== AND ===

Joe Biden's Excellent Adventure

Live from Two Elections – 2016 and 2020

*Scenes from primaries, caucuses, debates, conventions,
and other electoral rituals that illustrate and explain
America's electoral descent*

by Matthew Mills Stevenson

Odysseus Books

DONALD TRUMP'S CIRCUS MAXIMUS AND
JOE BIDEN'S EXCELLENT ADVENTURE.
Copyright©2024 by Matthew Mills Stevenson.

ISBN-13: 978-0-9970580-9-3 (e-book)
ISBN-13: 979-8-9896654-0-2 (paperback)

Manufactured in the United States.
This book was printed on acid-free paper in the United States.
This paper meets the requirements of ANSI/NISO Z39.48-1992

Much of the enclosed book appeared previously in *CounterPunch*,
in slightly different forms.

For fulfillment information, address: Odysseus Books c/o Pathway Book Service,
34 Production Avenue, Keene New Hampshire 03431.
Toll free: 1-800-345-6665. Email: pbs@pathwaybook.com

Please visit the book's website: www.odysseusbooks.com To contact the author
on any matter, such as to arrange a speaking engagement,
please use: matthewstevenson@sunrise.ch.
Author website is: www.matthewmstevenson.com

Edited by David Aretha.
Jacket and book design by Nanette Stevenson.

Library of Congress Cataloging-in-Publication Data

Stevenson, Matthew Mills, 1954–author.
Donald Trump's Circus Maximus and Joe Biden's Excellent Adventure /
by Matthew Mills Stevenson.
p. cm. (Odysseus Books)
ISBN-13: 979-8-9896654-0-2 (paperback)
1. Stevenson, Matthew Mills, 1954—U.S Presidential Elections 2016-20.
2. Donald Trump. 3. Joe Biden.

10 9 8 7 6 5 4 3 2 1
First edition

This book is dedicated to my friend of 40 years

Rob Schmoll

I am glad that life put us in the same peloton

To

Jeffrey St. Clair

CounterPunch's editor and writer extraordinaire

And to

Erroll Allen Rhodes II & III

Who launched me in New Hampshire

on these electoral roads

Contents

BOOK ONE

2016: DONALD TRUMP'S CIRCUS MAXIMUS   1

PRIMARY COLORS   3

Open Season in New Hampshire   5

CONFESSIONS OF A PRIMARY INSIDER   41

The Candidate Wears Prada   43

Hillary's Self-Server   56

Bernie Soldiers On   76

Making Trump Presidential?   96

Who Owns the 2016 Election?   113

SEX, LIES, AND VIDEOTAPED
IMPEACHMENTS   125

Sex and the Presidential City   127

Getting the Word on Election Day   135

BOOK TWO

2020: JOE BIDEN'S EXCELLENT ADVENTURE   141

LIVE FROM THE IOWA CAUCUSES   143

Requiem for a Lightweight: Pete Buttigieg   145

A Crooning Biden Takes the Stage   153

A Des Moines Trump Rally   161

Candidates "R" Us   171

Iowa's Lost Votes   200

The Morning After: The Coming Democratic Wave   208

LIVE FROM THE NEW HAMPSHIRE PRIMARY   215

Retail Politics   217

The Last Weekend   235

Trump Rallies Manchester   244

The Super Tuesday Sting   248

A COUPLE OF 70-YEAR-OLD GUYS SITTING AROUND TALKING   255

Can Biden Beat Trump?   257

Will Trump Cancel the Election?   265

THE GREAT DEMOCRATIC INFOMERCIAL   275

Conventional Thinking   277

The Dems Zoom It In   282

Day Three of the Great Democratic Jamboree   289

Closing Acts   296

TRUMP'S REPUBLICAN NATIONAL CONVENTION:
CASINO ROYALE   303

God's a Republican   305

Holy Log Rolling   318

Scaring Americans to Life   328

All the President's Caddies   338

A PRESIDENTIAL DEBATE PRIMER   349

Don and Joe Play Talk Radio   351

Pence v. Harris Debate: Synchronized Robocalls   366

DEMOCRACY'S END   381

Trump's Reichstag Fire   383

The Lost Art of the Steal   391

America Installs a Pope   397

Who Won the Impeachment?   406

CODA   419

Trump Is Guilty, Biden Should Resign   421

Preface

PRESIDENTIAL ELECTIONS ARE A LOT EASIER TO COVER through the rear-view mirror, when you know that Mayor Pete Buttigieg will fade into obscurity or that Joe Biden will snatch nomination victory from the jaws of defeat after Iowa and New Hampshire.

As events, primaries, debates, conventions, and mob attacks are unfolding, it is harder to know how things will end. At the same time what is lost, by the rewriting of history into a neat package of predestination, is the immediacy of the campaigns and, often, the mad hattery associated with many runs for the presidency.

Here it would be easy to white out my many errors of prognostication and give the reader the sense that, all along, I knew that Trump would defeat Hillary in 2016, or that Joe Biden, emerging from the wreckage of his campaign, would win in 2020. But no pundit on the planet made all those calls, beginning in autumn 2015.

The political soothsayers had the Trump candidacy driving a clown car in 2015-16, Hillary bestriding the earth after her election, Bernie Sanders or Elizabeth Warren winning the Democratic nomination in 2020, and, after all that, in the 2020 general election, Trump getting reelected on the strength of Wall Street's and the economy's runaway successes—none of which remotely matched reality.

Rather than clean up my errant forecasts in this account, I have let them stand, if only to recall what I was thinking, seeing, or hearing as the events themselves unfolded. Many of these chapters were literally written on the night of a particular event, or maybe the morning after, when I didn't have the luxury, which all have today, of knowing what would happen. At the same time, by letting these observations stand, I want to convey the turbulence of American democracy—its aspects of carnival barking and randomness, all of which defies prediction, but which contribute to the dramas.

Keep in mind too that in presidential politics I am a citizen-soldier. I was not embedded in any campaign, and I was not beholden to the dictates of any news organization. I paid my own expenses and attended the events as best I could. I didn't ride on candidate press planes or eat meals with Washington pollsters. I was free to come and go as I pleased, as is any voter following any campaign. I confess I was persistent, and I was lucky to see and hear as much as I did, testament that American politics, for all its shortcomings, remains an outdoor sport. So don't think of this as an insider's account, yet another "making of" the president; it is not. Think of it more as diary notes from a cruise gone wrong (yet another ship of fools?) or perhaps something similar to what Daniel Defoe called, in 1722, his *Journal of the Plague Year.*

—M.M.S.

Book One

2016
Donald Trump's
Circus Maximus

"The government you elect is the government you deserve."

—THOMAS JEFFERSON

Primary Colors

"Apparently, a democracy is a place where numerous elections are held at great cost without issues and with interchangeable candidates."

—Gore Vidal

Open Season in New Hampshire

FACED WITH 14 REPUBLICAN POTENTIAL NOMINEES for president in 2016 and three on the Democratic side, I did what any sensible person would not do: I borrowed my sister's car, stayed with a friend in New Hampshire, and for 10 days stalked presidential candidates across the Granite State.

Most days I found myself commuting between places such as Lebanon, Keene, and Plymouth. Invariably I would pull up in front of an elementary school, an Elks club, or an American Legion hall to hear a candidate play what Huck Finn called The Royal Nonesuch—the flimflam that passed for intellectual currency along the Mississippi River.

According to cable news pundits, as New Hampshire goes, so will go the nation in choosing candidates for the 2016 election. In a state of 1.3 million people, there are roughly 750,000 eligible voters, of whom there are about 240,000 registered Democrats and 260,000 Republicans.

If the pundits are right, and if Donald Trump wins the New Hampshire primary with about 70,000 votes (27 percent), he will be launched toward the Republican candidacy with the votes of less than one percent of the American populace. So much for the storyboard that proclaims the United States the "greatest democracy in the world."

At least politics in New Hampshire is still a retail business, and with a set of wheels it is possible over 10 days to meet and greet most of the candidates. I saw all the frontrunners—Hillary Clinton, Bernie Sanders, and Donald Trump—and many of the soon-to-be also-rans, such as Republicans Lindsey Graham and James Gilmore. I had to leave the state before Rand Paul showed up, and candidates such as Ben Carson and Mike Huckabee might as well be on (organic, locally produced) milk cartons, as they never made it on to my radar, not even with surrogate speakers at events.

In general, I tried to see each candidate at least twice, to be sure I got the intended paid political messages, which among most Republican candidates could be summarized by paraphrasing World War II Navy Admiral Bull Halsey, "Kill Arabs! Kill Arabs! Kill more Arabs!" By contrast, the Democrats want to win hearts and minds with paid family leave and fewer gas pipelines.

Who will win in New Hampshire? I pick Donald Trump among the Republicans and Bernie Sanders among the Democrats. Whether that will carry them to their respective nominations is another question.

I did leave New Hampshire day dreaming about a national election between Donald and Bernie, which would pit the two extremes of their parties in a contest as stark as that in 1896 between William Jennings Bryan (cross of gold) and William McKinley (higher tariffs). I doubt it will happen, as voters are less extreme when confronted with a ballot box than when they are pollster respondents two months before a vote.

At least for now in New Hampshire—until the vote on February 9—extremism in the defense of liberty is no vice.

Ground Zero: Manchester Airport Diner

Although I missed the covered wagon pulling former Virginia Governor James Gilmore (Republican) around the state, I began my campaign at the Manchester Airport Diner, where many presidential hopefuls stage their events in the early days, when the event room off the back is perfect for a hesitant crowd of 20. It also serves well those candidates who want to leave the engines running on their private jets and still make the evening news clasping the hands of men in Caterpillar caps.

The diner is straight out of a Norman Rockwell illustration, and perfect for showing a candidate shaking hands with crusty Granite Staters seated in booths or at the counter, frugally nursing their coffee and hash browns. As it should be, the diner's exterior is corrugated tin. What neither the evening news nor press reports tell you is that the Manchester Airport Diner is a full-service Potemkin village, sitting in a suburban parking lot, grafted to the lobby of a modern 1990s Holiday Inn.

Calvin Coolidge could be alive and well in the diner. In the parking lot or the hotel, however, New Hampshire is less a state of granite and more an SUV commuter nation, on its way to Boston or Home Depot. And the reason that the New Hampshire primary plays out in fading remnants of Populist America—Grange halls, elementary school gyms, etc.—is because it transmits the preferred message that American democracy remains a descendant of the New England town hall, not a creature that has crawled out of a pollster's sewer or the bank account of the Koch brothers.

Hillary Clinton: Eye of the Tiger

I HAD TO DRIVE THROUGH MANCHESTER to Southern New Hampshire University to get to my first event with Hillary Clinton. A retired mill town, Manchester is doing its best to seed the downtown with quaint cafés, needlepoint boutiques, red-brick condominiums, and a tarot shop, which have better signage than the tattoo parlors and the gun stores.

Just north of the downtown, on Elm Street, Victorian houses take over from the rehabbed storefronts (it looks like a neighborhood of funeral homes), and they lead to the campus that started life in 1932 as the New Hampshire School of Accounting and Secretarial Science. Since then it has gotten a stadium, dorms, and university accreditation, and Hillary was there to attend a symposium on women in the workplace, although, truth be told, it was a campaign whistlestop dressed up with a panel of loyalists, maybe there to gin up some college credits.

My briefcase passed the inspection of a sniffer dog at the front door (for a moment, my breakfast muffin took on terrorist odors), and I took my seat in the Banquet Hall, which had the air of a college gym, one the Clinton campaign worked hard to fill with extras (in this case college sophomore boys, with hats on backwards, who spent part of the conference watching replays of Sunday football on their phones).

Hillary was late, so we had lots of state senators warm up the crowd with a recitation of her commitment to "fighting." Clearly that's the market-tested slogan of Hillary 2016. Her "brand" is an H crossed with an arrow. It probably cost her campaign about $500K worth of brand consulting and test marketing, although to me it looks like it belongs on the back end of Ben Cartwright's cattle (he was the prime-time owner of the Ponderosa, on the TV series *Bonanza*).

There were huge screens (like in an airport departure lounge) over the lectern to remind the audience that women in New Hampshire are exploited and ripped off, and that in response Hillary will "fight" against those injustices. One picture on a loop showed an American flag draped over a beachside fence post, as though the Cartwrights had moved their herd to New Hampshire's Rye Beach.

Hillary entered not through the adoring crowd but from stage right, as if on the *Tonight Show*, and waved in the manner of someone striding toward Jimmy Fallon's couch. One of her entrance "fight" songs is "Eye of the Tiger" (go figure, it's about an ex-con) although the remix made it sound like a version put out by the Mormon Tabernacle Choir. In person, she looks exactly as you imagine Hillary looking, although maybe a little warmer than the newspaper photo version. Her elegant gray pants suit was unmistakably expensive, which spared her from looking like the doorman at an Indian hotel.

Hillary's wrists and neck were loaded with bling, of NBA proportions, and all very nice stuff. I would say it came from Bill, over many Christmases, but since all Monica got from the Black Dog was a sweat shirt, I am guessing the campaign has a jewelry consultant. Her hair has been tamed into an anchorwoman bouffant, and given that she loves to host political events that have the feel of daytime television, I came to think of Hillary as the White Oprah.

At Southern New Hampshire University, Hillary read the perfect speech, complete with soundbites for the local television market, but at most of her events she holds forth in a conversation pit (think of the audiences that adore the Ellen DeGeneres show) and takes questions from the studio. No one I heard on the campaign trail can do empathy as well as Hillary. Whatever the question, Hillary's answer confirms that this issue (Syrian refugees, equal pay for women, climate change, or gay marriage) is one that she has been "fighting for" since at least the late 1970s, when she was first lady of Arkansas.

No matter how obscure the subject, as a senator Hillary introduced legislation to correct this tragedy (only three of her bills passed, and one was to rename a bridge), and if elected president, on her "first day" (a favorite metaphor for everyone running) she will ban assault rifles, shut down air polluters, and raise the minimum wage.

Since many of those in her audiences come with some grievance (many of them about men), Hillary can share a lot of pain during an hour-long campaign stop. It makes for great political TV (*"Next on Hillary, a coal miner's daughter and her struggle for freedom. . ."*), and it plays to her campaign strategy of putting together a coalition of older women and minorities, and fighting for them into the White House. Will it work? It can, especially if the Republicans nominate an abortion-hating, anti-gay, Bible-belt, tub-thumping candidate, and the center coalition is there for Hillary and her girl band.

The more I listened to Hillary speak, the more I came to the conclusion that her persona is that of a corporate lawyer. She sounds like a lawyer, thinks like a lawyer, and speaks like a lawyer. All her speeches sound like summations to a jury. I am sure that many American men, watching her running for president, will be reminded of the smart lawyer their wife dragged into divorce court and who took away their BMW.

On many occasions, Hillary is the class action lawyer for an aggrieved group of women, telling them, in patient lawyerly language, how she plans to improve their childcare, get them a raise, boot out their NFL-loving husbands, and tell off their boss at CVS pharmacy. In that role, she's effective and persuasive, and she could ride such a plaintive class into the White House.

The reason she loses, however, is because she is playing it safe, and her campaign feels more like a coronation than an election. Even her devoted supporters can hardly muster much enthusiasm for her. I have heard more cheering for a third-grade pageant than Hillary got in two events. And keep this mind: Bernie gets 2,000 supporters at his appearances, while Hillary is lucky to get 300.

The Nixon Trust Issue

There is also the Nixon-trust issue. Not all that many voters believe Hillary, for this reason: she is almost pathological in her empathy for everyone and every issue. You name the problem, and she has a five-point program on her website and has been fighting for it since 1974.

I can see why even the emotionally challenged Barack Obama beat her in 2008. At least his campaign had some buzz. Her campaign feels like a real estate open house ("and over here we have the breakfast nook, Iraqi foreign policy, and the den").

I listened and listened to see if I could figure out Hillary's theory of government, and mostly it eluded me. Basically, I think she's a 1960s liberal, of the LBJ mold, for whom every human, political, or international problem can be solved with tax credits and another federal agency (*"When I was in the Senate, I supported the Paycheck Fairness Act. . ."*). Women beaten by their husbands, Kurds run off their reservations, and unemployed miners all just need Our Lady of Perpetual Concern in the White House, there to convene another conference or "dialogue," so that she can "fight" for them.

Hillary has very little feel for economics and none for business, and so falls back on DC platitudes (*"I want to give America a raise"*) about the inequalities of the U.S. economic system (the same that has netted Hill and Bill $160 million in "speaking fees"). Her economic theories sound like someone faking it during a college oral exam on marginal utility.

Otherwise, the invented self that Hillary has chosen for her public persona is that of a bedraggled single mom, maybe someone working at Target or Walmart (not on the board, as she was in the 1980s), who is trying to make rent on a double-wide and at the same time care for her dying parents. (*"People like you and me, like those people shot down dead at their Christmas party in California. . ."*)

The eerie thing I picked up, along the way, was this: between events in the car, I listened to public radio, and thus heard Obama endlessly mourning the dead in the San Bernardino shooting. Four hours later Hillary was using exactly the same phrases about gun control and terrorism. (Cue the *Twilight Zone* music, and then flash the *Manchurian Candidate* on the big screens.)

For a '60 liberal, however, Hillary is deeply in the tank for the FBI, local police, and the intelligence services, and did a tap dance for the no-fly list being extended to gun buyers and others who would harm "the Homeland." (It makes America sound like a savings bank.)

Intellectually, Hillary has an ordinary mind—pedestrian even. Does she read? I doubt it. She never mentioned a book during the entire day. Does she write? Little people do that. What she's a genius at is remembering and digesting the issue books and legal briefs, and she has a Washington insider, wonk view of the world. Only Jeb Bush can match her detailed knowledge of government programs.

Nor is Hillary a natural politician and at times on stage she can stand frozen, looking a bit like Barbie on her yacht. She is more like the scripted Reagan (standing on the taped footprints his aides would mark out for his appearances), but with a liberal, feminist agenda, and with a chip on her shoulder that America owes her the presidency for all the crap she has had to absorb with Whitewater, Monica, Benghazi, etc. ("*It's our time.*")

She never talks about being secretary of state, and all she did in the Senate is champion whatever populist cause is mentioned in a question. The amazing thing about Hillary-speak is how she can transform even a perfunctory campaign stop into a "woman's forum" with dialogue, panel discussions, and democracy in action.

As best I can determine, American politics is a game show, with a live, in-studio "audience," a host (the candidate), and applause cue cards. There's no debate, no intellectual exchange, and little eloquence. Lincoln and Douglas at least had to speak for five hours on slavery. All Hillary has to do is take (perhaps) planted questions from a studio audience, and then the White Oprah can share America's pain, giving little tips about how to rein in terrorism, apply for a small business loan, or deal with a cheating husband.

In case you are wondering, she's a pro at waving away the gotcha questions (there was one about "believing rape victims" and not believing Paula Jones and Jennifer Flowers), and deals with them, throwing in a Lady Macbeth smile, as if swatting flies. Part of her appeal is that she's a survivor (*"It's the eye of the tiger/It's the thrill of the fight. . ."*).

The Bill Clinton administration might as well have predated the second term of Grover Cleveland. No one remembers it; no one cares. In her own right Hillary's a celebrity, and she's blessed us here with her visit—the arrival of a wounded saint on the road to Assisi or Durham, New Hampshire.

Marco Rubio: Country Club Republican

I found Marco Rubio at the Portsmouth Country Club, surrounded by the luncheon remains of a ladies auxiliary group. I had gotten stuck in traffic—yes, even in the Granite State—and Marco had finished his brief prepared remarks and was answering questions, most of them wanting to know "How can we get the federal government out of our lives?"

I took a seat at one of the tables in the dining room (about 80 people were present), and listened while he deftly answered questions, mixing in anecdotes about his family (his mother is on Social Security, so he will never cut any of that) and his conservative values (set the political philosophy of William F. Buckley Jr. to a Latin swing band).

Not all the candidates in New Hampshire wear suits and ties, but Marco had on both. For a Floridian, he looked pale—with what in college we used to call a library tan, although in Marco's case I don't think he's spending his time in the stacks. He's taller than I thought from television appearances, and seemed older than his 44 years, because, in person, the comb-over part to his hair is more obvious, giving him the vain look of "Bob from Accounting."

Compared to Hillary, Marco speaks quickly and, one might say, more off the cuff. He is quick with his answers (practiced as I am sure they are) and can manage to put humor into the equation, although his wit is always in the service of the conservative cause.

In condemning the Veterans Administration, for example, he told a story about his brother, who lost his front teeth while an airborne Green Beret in the Vietnam War era. Much later, the brother went to the VA for some treatment to his mouth, and they challenged him to document that his condition was tied to his government service. According to Marco, his brother said, "It was only while I was in the Army that I ever jumped out of an airplane."

When he gets warmed up, Rubio knows all the lyrics to every hymn about the virtues of small government. The only function he would assign to the federal government is that of national security (*"not the reason we have high national debt"*). As for other services, such as the Environmental Protection Agency or the Department of Commerce, Rubio—as a spiritual air to Ronald Reagan—would do his best (on his "first day in office") to consign them to oblivion.

Government benefits are "a safety net, not a lifestyle," and while he would not touch Social Security—to the relief of the older country club women—he would turn other government departments into business-like corporations or get rid of them. When government is chasing bad guys around the Middle East or searching the Internet for metadata, it's a force of light; when it's funding abortion or supporting gay marriage, it's a public menace.

Apparently one of the local newspapers criticized Marco as a "fly-in, fly-out" New Hampshire candidate and made fun of the fact that he was always too busy to shake hands with his supporters. Today, to prove that he was listening, he stuck around the dining room while swarms of auxiliary women posed with him for selfies or shook his hand.

As the room was fairly small, I joined the claque, shook his hand (for those measuring these things, his handshake is fairly unimpressive, what in grade school we used to call a "dead fish"), and asked him a question about Cuba and Castro. When he saw I was press, he said he would answer that question "afterward" in a small "green room" set up for journalists to ask questions.

His "press avail" (from availability) took place downstairs in the country club, at the end of a hall, overlooking what I assume is the 18th green. Marco stood in front of a makeshift "Marco Rubio for President" banner and watchful aides orchestrated just how "available" Marco would be for the press.

For anyone campaigning in New Hampshire the press only means local television. Print journalists might as well be wearing the upturned fedoras featured in the 1928 Broadway show *The Front Page* (Ben Hecht and Charles MacArthur) about reporters angling for scoops. In 2015, the "real" press comes with a movie camera, and the questions they ask are limited to the most recent news cycle.

No one at a press availability with Marco Rubio would ask him about Cuban foreign policy or his ideas for monetary reform. Instead all the questions were about Donald Trump's latest outrage or insult and what he thought of the shootings in San Bernardino, all events that were less than 24 hours old.

The Marco upstairs with the ladies auxiliary group was their charming grandson, back home from college in Washington, telling funny stories about the people mismanaging the faculty or the country. He was wry (*"even if I retired from the Senate at age 68, I would still be the youngest there"*) or outraged (*"no gun laws would have prevented this attack*"), but still a handsome poster boy for the *National Review*.

Marco in the basement, however, struck me as an angry Miami Cuban, mistrustful of the press, contemptuous of their questions, and annoyed that running for president meant wasting his time with people who earned their living waiting around in country clubs to pick up a soundbite. He was dismissive of anyone who questioned the wisdom of going to war with ISIS, and scoffed at the idea that the San Bernardino murders should have prompted any calls for gun control. ("*It had nothing to do with that.*") He spoke about "ideological terrorism" and put the boot into Hillary for her "radical" views on late-term abortion, implying that Hillary would allow for a pregnancy to be terminated one day before the due date. (It sounded like she was capable of selling fetus body parts from the back of her campaign bus.) He railed against Obamacare ("*his ideas don't work*"), and anyone who would ban assault rifles, sounding a lot like some NRA bumper sticker ("*Guns don't kill people. . .*").

It was during the "press avail" that I figured out that Marco is a direct descendant of the YAF (Young Americans for Freedom), that group of campus politicians who all slept with posters of William F. Buckley, Jr. over their headboards. When I was in college, they wore suits and ties and mouthed cliches about getting government "out of our lives." They read *Witness* by Whittaker Chambers or the novels of Ayn Rand, and talked about privatizing most government departments. From a distance they were easy to mistake for Jehovah's Witnesses, although when you got closer they were usually talking about Ronald Reagan rather than Armageddon. Listening to Marco behind the cordon, I could hear the call to prayer of a disciple.

I wish I had a new necktie for every time Marco managed to use the word "radicalize" in his speech and briefing. Although he used it to describe Hillary Clinton's views on abortion, he mostly saved it to describe the epidemic of "home-grown terrorism," which threatened the American way of life, much the way "radicals" had attacked the concert hall and restaurants in Paris.

Anyone who went to the Syrian front lines or ISIS training centers was probably "radicalized," and if they were allowed to come back to America, they threatened to infect the body politic. The only solution, according to Marco, was to beef up metadata sweeps, if not turn loose the "well regulated Militia" that is protected in the Second Amendment. We needed both to round up their pipe bombs as well as their social media, although, unlike Hillary, he did not celebrate the TSA's "no-fly" list, calling it just another government intrusion into the lives of the citizenry. (*"Good luck trying to get your name removed from it. There is no recourse. We have tried for constituents. It's impossible."*)

Most impressive in Marco's tango behind the rope was how he managed to absolve gun ownership from any involvement in mass American shootings, and pin nearly every mall attack on "Islamo-fascist terrorists." Gun owners enjoy Constitutional protection while Islamic terrorists are sworn enemies of the state, on whom the national security apparatus needs to take its revenge.

A man who can handle such political gymnastics ought to go far. But can he win? Ideally Rubio would like to be the candidate from the center-right of the Republican Party—because of his good looks, ability to speak on his feet, and youth; its John F. Kennedy, so to speak. Unfortunately for Rubio, that is a busy electoral intersection. Waiting for the same bus are at least Chris Christie, Jeb Bush, and John Kasich.

While in mid-sentence, going on about radicalization, Marco ghosted. One minute he was ridiculing Obama's feckless foreign policies, and then in the next he was gone. Not even could Emmuska Orczy's Scarlet Pimpernel have vanished faster. From Marco there was no thank you, no goodbye, just a last "radicalize" from his lips, and then the country club Republican was climbing into his shiny, white SUV, and he was back on the trail.

Lindsey Graham: Senator Strangelove

It was two hours to my next event, late in the day at the Lebanon Elks lodge. Again I was stuck in traffic driving there. Lebanon is literally across the state from Portsmouth, and I was lucky to get there on time. I took I-89 northwest toward Dartmouth College, and off the highway in Lebanon I found the Elks lodge (formally BPOE or the Benevolent and Protective Order of Elks, who my grandmother jokingly called the "best people on earth").

Upstairs on the main auditorium floor I found a group (maybe a hundred?) of crusty old Granite Staters and a few campaign volunteers with bumper stickers for Jeb or Rand Paul set up on a long table. There were a few women and wives in the crowd, but mostly this was a gathering of older, get-off-my-lawn Republican men, many wearing blazers, all of whom (judging from their later questions) want "to get the government out of their lives."

The Republican Party had invited all of the candidates to address the gathering, and three—Senator Lindsey Graham (R-South Carolina), Ohio Governor John Kasich, and former New York Governor George Pataki—had promised to show up. Some others—Jeb, Marco Rubio, and Ted Cruz—agreed to send surrogates.

Near the buffet I chatted briefly with Senator Lindsey Graham, who has staked his all on the New Hampshire primary and has made 170 appearances in the state (Trump's number is 25, while Hillary's is 38). I asked him how many votes he needed to do well, and he said about 30,000, and he thinks in his glad-handing across the state he has met about 3,000 people. When

I asked him how he liked the state, he said, "I have enjoyed the New Hampshire experience," which made it sound like an IMAX movie.

If he was wearing a white lab coat, Graham would look like a CVS pharmacist. Sixty years old with a modest personality, Graham ever so slightly resembles David Brent, the cringe-worthy boss in the English version of *The Office*. (Brent: "*I haven't got a sign on the door that says 'white people only'. I don't care if you're black, brown, yellow—Orientals make very good workers.*")

Only when the self-effacing Graham addresses a crowd does he turn into General Buck Turgidson, played by George C. Scott in *Dr. Strangelove* ("*Gee, I wish we had one of them doomsday machines*"). A colonel in the Air Force reserve until recently, Graham wants to do with ISIS what Buck would do to the Ruskies, which is to accommodate them in their dreams of martyrdom.

Graham's sister, Darline, introduced him to the Elks and spoke about him in tear-jerking terms. They grew up in one room, behind their parents' pool hall and saloon in rural South Carolina. In the 2016 campaign saloons are the new long cabins; many candidates grew up in them. The Graham parents died when Darline was 13 and Lindsey was 21. He was steadfast in his support for her, coming home from college on the weekends to work in the bar and pool hall, and to look after his sister. Darline: "He was always there for me."

In foreign affairs, however, Graham is less modest, calling for an all-out war against ISIS. He said that since 2003 he and his Senate soulmate, John McCain, have made 36 trips to Iraq and Afghanistan, and that President Obama "just doesn't know what the hell he's doing. . . . We don't have a plan to destroy the caliphate." He gave a ringing endorsement for the surge in Iraq ("*it worked*") and called for sending 5,000 ground troops to the front lines against ISIS ("*for command and control*").

Simplifying the conflict for the Elks, Graham said, "This will make it easier for you. In a World War II context, ISIS is Germany; Assad is Japan." He advocates supporting the Free Syrian Army against the Assad government and predicted that with American boots on the ground, Raqqa (the capital of the Islamic State) "would fall like a cheap suit."

When I heard him speak on other occasions—once about the local New Hampshire heroin epidemic and women's rights, and then about Social Security—he always managed to turn the conversation back to ISIS. On the subject of battered women in Manchester, he talked about radical Islam's treatment of women, as though ISIS was running New England shooting galleries.

Fundamental to Graham's bid to be president is the proclamation that now is not the time to rely on amateur leadership. He would rebuild the Army and the Navy ("*the smallest it has been since 1915*"). Otherwise, "they" (radical Islam, broadly defined) will "hit us, and hit us hard." Against this threat Colonel Graham would mobilize the armed forces and grind ISIS into the desert sands ("*I understand the threat*"). His candidacy is a call to arms, and no one I heard in New Hampshire is more hawkish than Graham. (Barry Goldwater comes to mind.) His bad luck, in attracting militarist support, is that other candidates—Donald Trump and Chris Christie among them—have more traction as war-mongers.

Trump put it in terms that the courtly Graham would never use, saying he wanted to "bomb the [bleep] out of ISIS," and the blustery Christie sounds like the front man for the national surveillance state. Meanwhile Graham continues his odyssey across New Hampshire, drawing a dozen supporters here and there, stopping as randomly as Robert Frost's horse on that famous snowy evening.

Coach John Kasich Takes One for the Team

Ohio Governor John Kasich followed Lindsey Graham in addressing the Elks. Seeing all the empty chairs at the front of the room, he said, "I am going to speak right here." He was wearing slacks and a black North Face windbreaker and, as he walked to the front of the room, looked like someone buying a shovel at Lowe's.

Fairly tall, he reminded me of Gene Hackman in *Hoosiers* ("*Five players on the floor functioning as one single unit: team, team, team—no one more important than the other.*") An optimistic man, Kasich decided against laying out his economic plan or reviewing his time as Ohio governor ("*it's on the website, if you want to look it up*") and instead talked about his family and values.

The father of 16-year-old twins, Coach Kasich spoke about how his fantastic travels across the country (Iowa, South Carolina, New Hampshire, South Dakota, etc.) contrasted with their lives in the 10th grade (they had just made cookies with his wife, Karen Waldbillig Kasich). The Elks probably wanted him to denounce the IRS or Obamacare, but he carried on with his family homily until he turned the subject to Iraq, a long way from Westerville, Ohio (near Columbus), where he lives.

I had read articles about Kasich trying to be a moderate Republican—and liberal on social issues, such as gay marriage. He seems warm and generous when speaking about his daughters, but all that vanished when the subject turned to San Bernardino and ISIS. Many Ohio presidential candidates of earlier eras, such as Robert A. Taft and Warren Harding, made their reputations as isolationists. (Harding had a slogan, "*League us not into temptation.*") Instead of being wary of foreign entanglements, Kasich wants to win the big game against ISIS.

"They despise our way of living," he said, calling radical Islam and ISIS "a cult of death" and adding, "They want to wipe us out."

He urged a coalition of Middle Eastern powers to "take care of business," but did not explain how those now funding ISIS (many Gulf states) would suddenly change sides at halftime. Kasich went on to state there is "a battle of ideals" being waged in the Middle East, and that many Westerners had gone over to the "dark side." These were otherwise normal and accomplished individuals, who had found something missing in their lives. They had lost "faith and hope" and decided to fill the void with Allah and extremism. "They are looking for something to be part of," the coach explained. ISIS was starting to sound like a Big Ten booster club.

Not wanting to end his talk on such a Manichaean schism, Kasich came back to his children, explaining that each day, even while running for president all around the country, he took time out to tell them that they were special, unique people with much to offer the world, which is his strategy to keep them away from drugs and ISIS.

Later, at Saint Anselm College's Life of the Party series (unscripted roundtables with the candidates at which among other questions they are asked to describe their favorite party, music, and books), Kasich owned up to liking Pink Floyd, getting some of his "daily information" from the Golf Channel, reading a lot of books about faith, loving Glacier National Park and the Sistine Chapel for travel destinations, and wanting to give a state dinner (as did the Kennedys) at George Washington's estate, Mount Vernon. Then, unprompted by a question, he told the students gathered at the event that if they found things in their emotional life out of balance, "you should seek out help." He added, "Everyone has a sock or two in their drawer that doesn't quite fit."

If Kasich were a front runner, his call for group therapy might have been front page. Instead, the unfitting socks passed directly in the 24-news rinse cycle, and none of the press reports I read about the session included the phrase "Dr. Freud, call your media guy." I later told a friend that if I had to hire one of the candidates to baby sit my children, I might choose Kasich, who at least would feed them pizza and let them watch a movie. Bernie might belittle their knowledge of the proletariat, and I am not sure Trump or Hillary would know they were there.

After the session ended Kasich returned to his enormous bus, the only one I saw on the campaign. On the side, instead of Lucky Star or Fung Wah, it reads, "John Kasich For Us." Leaving Saint Anselm's, for an instant he had that bemused look of Harrison Ford in the film *Air Force One* (they bear resemblance), although who can imagine a thriller becoming memorable for the line, "Get off my bus."

Governor George Pataki: Mad as Hell

There was a little break in the action before former New York Governor George Pataki's driver found the Elks hall, although I am sure the wealthy gov's car has GPS.

Pataki is very tall, and wore a New York pinstripe investment banking business suit, and when he started talking, all I could think of was some wealthy guy at the far end of a New York club bar, on his third martini, railing about how the Jews or ISIS or the Micks are "taking over this country."

George didn't so much speak to the Elks as suffer an emotional breakdown behind the mic, shouting that we're "at war" with ISIS and declaring that he'd turn Raqqa into a dust bowl. ("*Congress should declare war on radical Islam.*") His sons were in the military, he was New York's governor on 9/11, and goddammit, we need to hit ISIS hard, before they "hit us." They were behind the shooting in California, and the only response of the bedwetting Obama ("*this horrible administration*") was to have his attorney general warn Americans not to say bad things about Muslims. Otherwise they would be arrested for hate crimes.

"Well, goddammit," he said, "he can arrest me today, because I am telling you that we're at war with Islamo-fascist terrorists." I almost expected that at the end of his talk he would flip out of his chair, in the style of John Belushi on SNL's *Weekend Update* in the 1970s, screaming "Oh, they love their mothers. . ."

William Jennings Bernie

I listened twice to Senator Bernie Sanders, for the first time on the campus of Keene State University, in the west of the state, and next at Plymouth State University, in a fold of the White Mountains. On both occasions, the audience was a mix of college students (who help to pad out the numbers) and an older crowd (all of whom, I am sure, devote much time and energy to recycling). On each occasion Bernie drew more than a thousand supporters, to the point of standing room only in the halls, while his chief rival, Hillary, struggles to fill up elementary school auditoriums for her holiday pageants.

Bernie gives set speeches. Sometimes he will answer questions or mix with his audience, but my sense is that he's most comfortable behind a lectern, reading his speech in his Brooklyn, senatorial voice. As it turned out, I drove halfway across New Hampshire (from Keene to Plymouth) to hear Bernie give exactly the same speech (almost word for word) at the second appearance: same pauses for applause, same attempts at humor, same outrage at the corporations and billionaire democracy ripping off the people.

Nor do I think Bernie has much interest in changing his fixed ideas, honed over many decades of outrage. In no particular order, he is for gay marriage, single-payer medical insurance, sowing salt on Wall Street, free tuition for public universities, drive-thru abortion on demand, kumbaya for the unions, group therapy with ISIS, paycheck equity, overturning Citizens United and the billionaire democracy, public funding for elections, an end to super PACs, shock therapy for the "rigged" economy, youth job programs, comprehensive immigration reform, a tax on Wall Street "speculation," caps on climate change, decriminalization of pot, and a grand coalition of Muslim and onward Christian soldiers to take down ISIS. He speaks well, or maybe I should say he reads his set speech very well. Most senators do.

In Plymouth, Bernie took a few questions, but playing to the crowd really isn't his thing. He's more Savonarola, denouncing, if not bonfires of the vanities, then at least the Koch Brothers. One thing I have learned in all these political speeches is that every candidate has their particular fear list of dragons under the bed. Listening to Bernie, I was reminded of a New School professor of sociology, of Brooklyn-Polish origin, beating the table about injustice and imperialism—be it that of the Russian tsar or Bismarck's partitions. Easy to imagine him in a Lviv or Krakow cafe surrounded by a lot of newspapers and young university students, eager to hear him put the boot into the Austrian emperor.

Can Bernie win? I do think he can win the New Hampshire primary (he's peaking at the right time) or certainly get very close to winning it. His problem is that his appeal (that of a favorite son Vermont senator) could be regional. Also, he has a college team, and he's running against the Green Bay Packers (the Clintons).

Hillary has already launched her 50-state campaign, for which she has the money to endure through primaries in remote, rural states. Yes, the students in New Hampshire prefer Bernie to Hillary, but in more conservative states he might not make the same positive impression. Shop steward Bernie, with a few well-placed negative TV ads, can be made to look like a cross between Marx and Engels. I am sure Hillary's media types are cueing up the soundbites that have him calling for a "political revolution" or show pictures of the Unabomber-like cabin where he lived for a while in Vermont in the 1960s.

One thing that became clear to me in listening to William Jennings Bernie is that the San Bernardino shooting and the rise of ISIS are a gift for two otherwise powerful lobbies—the National Rifle Association and Israel, both of whom are now getting a free electoral pass on gun violence.

According to virtually everyone's campaign script, the problem in the Middle East isn't Mossad or Bibi but ISIS, which is "a Sunni Arab problem," which Saudi Arabia and Qatar, among others, must solve. No mention in that equation about Israel changing any of its ways.

The same too with declaring the San Bernardino shooting a "terrorist event." In a gift to the candidates, the evil couple firing the guns had earlier downloaded some rage porn from Raqqa or "liked" some beheadings in Mosul. That frees up Obama, Bernie, Donald, Carly, everyone, from having to denounce what Hillary calls "responsible gun owners" or blame the NRA board for these random mall shootings. How convenient: no more brooding in press conferences about assault weapons. The American gun problem has its origins along the Euphrates River, not in God-fearing gun shows. Blame Eye-raq, if not Eye-ran. Case closed. Even Bernie sings a hymn in this amen corner.

So far, Bernie's warm-up music track most closely matches my own. Hillary's pre-game music sounds like a Pilates class. Bernie is more a Mamas & Papas man, or he's Dylan, blowin' in the wind. I would imagine Donald's soundtrack will resemble a Vegas floor-show with Wayne Newton.

Jeb Bush: Going Nowhere in a Big Hurry

I am sad to report that Jeb Bush (Jeb! on his bumperstickers) is articulate and personable, the complete anti-W. Yes, they look fairly similar, although Jeb is taller and more comfortable in a political setting. I heard him twice: once at a Social Security summit (we shook hands as he worked the room) and that evening at the American Legion Post 37 hall in Hooksett, New Hampshire, which is near Manchester. The mystery to me of the New Hampshire primary is that he's about 5 percent in the polls, and sinking.

Both Jeb's domestic and foreign policy are conservative, although on economic issues he makes more sense than he does when speaking about "Eye-ran." I actually agree with his prescription for fixing Social Security (increase the age of eligibility and charge wealthy people more for their premiums than the needy). He might almost be a traitor to his class.

Aside from that, however, the Jeb of the town halls is far removed from the Jeb of the TV debates. On screen, he's just this side of a robot—hesitant and awkward—while in person he works a room with grace and with interest in those he's meeting. He speaks effortlessly about all sorts of wonkish subjects. He is well read on and clearly loves public policy, and he can speak persuasively about Social Security reform, Medicaid, the space program—you name it.

If W adopted the persona of a Texas sheriff, Jeb's the headmaster of a private New England boarding school (Mr. Chips, if you will), exhorting his students to study harder and make better decisions. (*"The Left thinks life is not fair. It's deeply pessimistic. We have to believe that life is divinely inspired."*)

The odd part about the Jeb campaign is that he's at 5 percent in the New Hampshire primary polls, while Donald Trump is at almost 30 percent. Politically, Jeb is more mainstream Republican than Trump, and on foreign policy he's equally nativist. (Take it on faith that all Republican candidates want a ground war with ISIS.) So why is the well-funded Bush brand doing so poorly in the local market, one that in the past it has owned?

I can only surmise that Bush in New Hampshire is suffering from bad luck and timing. In 1988 Bush the Elder won

Reagan's third term, and W was elected in 2000 because he faced weak challengers in the primaries (John McCain) and because a Bush restoration seemed an antidote to the stains of the Clinton scandals.

Bush 2016, however, looks like a model (something like a Dodge Charger) that went out of fashion in 1990s, and New Hampshire must have the impression that Jeb is trying to sell them a used car. Maybe in a smaller field of candidates—after all, there are 14 Republicans left in New Hampshire and they all sound about the same—Jeb would stand out. Instead, all that distinguishes him in the field is his trademark name, although I get the impression he might be losing the copyright.

Nor does it seem to be helping Jeb that he's a policy wonk, of Hillary Clinton proportions. (If these two were ever to marry, they could talk to each other for decades and never run out of government programs to dissect.) Clearly Jeb loved being Governor of Florida (in the White House, W always looked as if his club membership was temporary), and in those eight years he learned a lot about immigration, Social Security, Medicare, Medicaid, and unemployment.

Most of his prescriptions to improve the economy are a mix of government benevolence and free-market economics, but his social positions would work equally well in the Democratic as the Republican party. Jeb's first term would look a lot like Bill Clinton's second, and its economic model would be Jeb's dynamic Florida economy, with its AAA bond rating and happy immigrants launching tech start ups.

Only on foreign affairs does Jeb show the extent to which all Republican candidates believe they have to run on a declare-war platform: "Our friends can no longer count on us. Our enemies no longer fear us." Jeb wants to rebuild the military, start a war against ISIS, embed troops with the Iraqi army, sandbag the Homeland, re-arm the Kurds, reawaken the Anbar Sunnis, establish a no-fly zone in Syria, mine metadata, and round up the usual Islamo-fascist suspects. In tone and substance, he sounds like one of the Dulles brothers (John Foster or Allen), getting ready to unleash Chiang Kai-shek.

With Jeb in charge, government would look like a charitable corporation, with enlightened board members and noble goals—the ASPCA comes to mind. Instead the government we have is Obamacare and the EPA, a hopeless despond. Bush's slogan, "Jeb can fix it," picks him as the handyman-in-chief.

The only *Twilight Zone* moment in my Bush day came at the Hooksett American Legion post, when a college kid stated that he would respect Jeb more if he would stop talking about God in the context of government. (Actually, I didn't find Jeb very religious in his talks.) The Governor went off on the kid, at one point puffing up his chest and facing him directly. (I thought of a howler monkey, getting ready to fight.) He ended the question and answer by testily saying he refused to hide his beliefs (*"I am informed by my faith"*) and then, putting his hand in his pocket, confessed that he always carries around "a little baby Jesus. It's my strength."

It was all a bit creepy. I almost expected him to start humming:

> *I don't care if it*
> *Rains or freezes*
> *As long as I've got my*
> *Plastic Jesus*
> *Ridin' on the dashboard*
> *Of my car*

Otherwise—even though I don't agree with whole sections of the Bush canon and maybe because he is losing—I warmed to

Jeb personally. He is clearly the smartest Bush, and absent much vanity. At the same time, he's going nowhere, although in a big hurry and on a huge budget ($113 million and counting). But as one Republican friend of mine in New York likes to ask: "How do you spin 5 percent?"

Virginia Governor James Gilmore: Retirement Project

Former Virginia Governor James Gilmore, who I had missed at the Manchester Airport Diner, showed up at Saint Anselm College in Manchester, which is ground zero for many primary events. It has its New Hampshire Institute of Politics & Political Library, and a venue that is perfect for candidate events. Had I known more about it, I might have spent all my time there, and waited for the candidates to find me.

I had never heard of Governor Gilmore (in his mid-60s) until reading up on the campaign, and even then he made little impression on me. In person, I liked him as well, although that may be because, for a change, he tracked me down and gave me some time to interview him. Normally I went to the candidates, but Gilmore's staff is dedicated to his cause.

With the mien of an insurance executive (somber suit and shoes), Gilmore talked about living in Europe in the early 1970s, and serving as an intelligence officer in the Army during the cold war. He later went to law school at the University of Virginia, and was elected governor of the state in 1997. He served one term, until 2002, and his signature issue was repealing the property tax on automobiles. After leaving office, he served on various boards, including some dealing with terrorism. He was also a commentator for Fox News and a board member of the NRA.

Unlike Jeb, he is opposed to "means testing" for Social Security, and made the point that the quick fixes to the system (increasing the age of retirement or "scrapping the cap") are feel-good solutions, not remedies for a pending bankruptcy. Instead, he proposes lifting the economy with a flat tax for individuals (10, 15 or 25 percent, depending on income), and revamping the corporate tax code by having one tax (15 percent) and eliminating so-called double taxation. He would strip away much Obama regulation, including Dodd-Frank, and calls the Affordable Care Act "a drag on the economy." He would end inheritance taxes. All those changes would put more full-time employees into the economy, lessening the burdens on Social Security funding.

Gilmore is the only Republican I heard, except for Carly Fiorina, who denounced Donald Trump. He said, "I reject Donald Trump's approach to politics. That's not who I am." On foreign affairs, however, his views may be even more hawkish than Trump's, as he spoke of rebuilding the military, adding another brigade to the Marine Corps, and striking out against ISIS.

I didn't have the heart to ask Gilmore why he was persisting with his uphill climb of running for president when no one knew who he was. But when I asked him how he was liking New Hampshire, he mentioned going to a local college football game. He went up and down the grandstand, greeting the fans, who, he said, appreciated that a candidate for president—even a long shot—was taking in the game. Finally a fan rushed down the stadium steps and started pumping his hand, saying how much he admired the governor and how pleased he was to meet him. A bit startled, Gilmore thanked him, and then the fan said, "You are Governor O'Malley, aren't you?"

Later I had the idea that Gilmore should be running as a Democrat (even though he's a dyed-in-the-wool Republican). Party labels mean almost nothing these days (Trump used to be a Democrat, and Bernie is a socialist), and as a conservative Democratic candidate, and former southern governor, Gilmore would be well positioned to follow in the footsteps of Jimmy Carter and Bill Clinton. Plus his views would contrast sharply with those of Bernie and Hillary, and his slogan, "I am not an amateur" might play well among Democrats. Instead he's off the grid in the New Hampshire polling, with less than the 0.3 percent of George Pataki. That said, Gilmore seemed to be enjoying himself, another reason I came to think of presidential politics—many candidates this year are over age 65, as are those attending their speeches—as an ideal activity for senior living.

Christie, Cruz, and O'Malley: They Also Ran

Among those candidates not campaigning in New Hampshire while I was there, several sent surrogates to events or taped prerecorded messages to certain groups. In this way I got secondhand access to Chris Christie, Martin O'Malley, and Ted Cruz, but surrogates, in general, all sound like college reference letters. Name the candidate, and the surrogate will talk about his or her love of country and family, hatred of ISIS, shock at San Bernardino, kindness toward children and animals, and, finally, their faith in God.

Actually, I learned more about the campaigns that never sent surrogates to any events. Ben Carson and Rand Paul, for example, missed many chances to have a wing man or woman speak on their behalf. I can only assume, from these absences that the campaigns are short of funding or friends, or both. Paul, in particular, needs to do well in New Hampshire, but he prefers to go it alone on the campaign trail and, in my estimate, will struggle to break 5 percent in the polls.

Carson may be betting his ranch (that with the informal hallway painting that has Jesus with an arm around the neurosurgeon) on Iowa and South Carolina. In New Hampshire his presence, as best I could tell, is limited to front yard placards (of which there are plenty). Such penetration might allow him to say he's "doing well on the ground," although he's fallen behind Rubio and Cruz in the polls, and more drops are to follow.

Chris Christie has invested a lot of his time and energy, in the early campaign cycle, in playing the tough cop to New Hampshire voters. It won him the editorial endorsement of the influential (among Republicans) New Hampshire Union Leader, and after San Bernardino, when people in New Hampshire caused traffic jams around gun ranges, he has benefited from his prosecutorial demeanor. Christie appeals to 9/11 Republicans who share some of Trump's outrage but can't quite fathom voting for a gold-plated casino owner.

Cruz's hope in New Hampshire is that he expects to do well in Iowa (possibly winning there). Then he could come into New Hampshire a week later with street cred and ample TV coverage. Cruz's risk in New Hampshire is his perceived weakness in talking tough to terrorism and ISIS, preferring to concentrate on other conservative hot buttons than the Allah menace. For the moment all New Hampshire Republicans want to hear is how to keep ISIS or active shooters out of their parking lots.

All I picked up in New Hampshire about Martin O'Malley is what an aide told me (and a few others in a small room): the former Maryland governor gets involved in drafting his own position papers and he "likes talking to other politicians." (Neither item is of a stop-press nature.) He does not see Social Security in crisis (Christie has it broke in seven years), and he would not increase the retirement age.

He is also perhaps the only candidate in New Hampshire who is calling for outright gun control. (Hillary is close, but has a way of talking nice about "responsible gun owners" and promising never to take away their heat. And Bernie has his Vermont hunting constituents.) I also learned from an O'Malley aide that, as governor, Martin liked inviting both Democrats (his party) and Republicans to a weekly pizza night at the governor's mansion. Once that led to him inviting a vitriolic Republican opponent, but when a member of O'Malley's staff protested the invitation, the governor responded: "Hey, it's only pepperoni." Unfortunately he's only making one New Hampshire appearance in December, and maybe for that he's trying to raise Greyhound bus fare.

Carly Fiorina Lays Off America

I caught up with Republican Carly Fiorina, the former CEO of Hewlett-Packard, at The Common Man in Concord. It's a chain of faux diners or country kitchens, meant to evoke the family-style dining of the 1950s (when ketchup saved a lot of bad cooking). The New Hampshire bankers association had booked out the event room, and Carly spoke for almost an hour to a group of money men and women, who, needless to say, warmed to her messages in praise of entrepreneurship, capitalism, and innovation—although this wasn't a cheer-on-the-table crowd.

Carly showed up 45 minutes late (very un-corporate on her part), but she shook hands with everyone in the room and thanked them personally, using their name, for coming. Her dress was executive sober, although it had lace covering her décolletage and a nearby jewel-encrusted cross (a tiny version of something the Crusaders might have carried aloft to Jerusalem).

Carly's a corporate titan, not a rock star, so a hush covered the room as she went around it, giving her appearance the feel of a budget review, at which everyone knew the boss would not be happy.

Carly's also a force. After graduating from Stanford University, she worked in a real estate office, "typing and filing," until the two partners asked her if she "wanted to do more." An MBA and some jobs later, she was appointed CEO of Hewlett-Packard, the tech giant that paid her well enough for her to throw millions of her own money, in 2010, on a failed U.S. Senate bid in California. (She lost to Barbara Boxer when it turned out she had not one, but two yachts and a possible net worth in excess of $100 million.)

She married her second husband, Frank, in 1985, and together they raised his two daughters (until one was "taken by the demons of addiction"). She never had children of her own and survived "a long battle with cancer." In her standard stump speech, she describes America as a failing company (with heavy union rules, lots of red tape, lazy executives, and no strategic plan), and she's the turnaround expert that shareholders need to put in the top job. Looking at her, you can tell that the one part of the job (HR director-in-chief) she would love is laying off the entire staff of the EPA.

A vote for Carly is a vote for ruthless corporate efficiency, if you think those words go together. She hates the inefficiency of the Homeland Security folks, Obamacare, the tax code, Dodd-Frank, compliance regs, metadata sweeps (as a tech exec, she'd do them better), coal regulations, and government waste. She'd bring back zero-based budgeting and give citizens the chance to vote weekly on their smartphones, by posing questions to the populace and asking them to click on a "democracy" app.

On her mythical "first day" in office, she would call her "good friend" Benjamin Netanyahu, the prime minister of Israel, and tell him he finally had a friend back in the White House. Then she would call the president of Iran and let him know that "Personnel" had some "issues" with his "file." Perhaps later that day she would return to the active military list what she calls "the Warrior Class," the likes of generals David Petraeus and Stanley McChrystal ("*my good friends*") and unleash them in the war against ISIS. She would let the world know, especially the many leaders with whom she is personally acquainted, that the United States "is back in the leadership business."

At one point she spoke confidently about wanting to survive long enough in the presidential race to debate Hillary Clinton. Now that would be a catfight: a tough corporate executive versus a class action lawyer, and a believer in the corporate gods versus an architect and au pair of the nanny state. I am not sure on whom I would bet in such a melee. Believe it or not, Hillary has a little more personal warmth than Carly (think of the supervisor that fired your spouse and only left a month of severance on the table), but Fiorina has the unwavering conviction of a medieval saint (something she studied as an undergraduate at Stanford before "typing and filing").

Although Carly is well under 10 percent in all of the primary polling, she has done better since the summer (thanks to all her retail appearances in New Hampshire) and now will remain a fixture in Republican debates, where her only five minutes of fame came when Trump said, "Look at that face. Would anyone vote for that?" Later she cut back at him, noting he had been "forced to file for bankruptcy not once, not twice, four times—why should we trust you to manage the finances of our nation any differently?"

My guess is that she has staying power in the race—both because of her own money and because she's a no-nonsense candidate of the Richard Nixon variety (and a woman), who might be the perfect vice presidential candidate, as an attack dog against Hillary. She has enough humor (although I would put it in the single digits) to maintain some rapport with voters, but maybe too much money or too many yachts to charm working-class women. Under national media attention, she might show a little too much pink slip for a populace already nervous about keeping their jobs.

Donald Trump Packs Heat in Portsmouth

My swing through the New Hampshire primary ended in Portsmouth, at the Sheraton Portsmouth Harborside Hotel, where Donald Trump was accepting the endorsement of the executive council of the New England Police Benevolent Association.

Trump showed up more than an hour late for the event, which featured—in front of the hotel—several hundred demonstrators (some from Bernie World) against what their signs described as Trump's xenophobia and racism. The protesters even brought along a marching band, which gave the demonstration the air of a football halftime.

Waiting inside the Sheraton ballroom was a phalanx of police from Massachusetts, Maine, and New Hampshire, seemingly all keen to give their political blessings to The Donald. I waited with the cops from York, Maine, and enjoyed their company more than I did their descriptions, firsthand, of New England's heroin epidemic. The drug is cheap, comes from everywhere into Maine, and sometimes hospitals treat the same patient three times in a day for an overdose.

Before Trump arrived, his personal security agents made a sweep of the ballroom (actually we were all packed into a smaller part of the bigger room). Unlike the Secret Service, who also protect him and who have a non-nonsense look about them, Trump's home army reminded me of department store detectives, and every time I saw them eyeing the crowd suspiciously I got the feeling they were watching the lingerie racks for shoplifters.

From where I stood at the back of the room, Donald was hard to see coming into the ballroom. At first all I could make out, bobbing along the stage over the heads of the adoring cops, was his trapezoidal hair, which is the color of marmalade and turns on more angles than the track of the Daytona Speedway. That his "do" stays in place is a marvel of Western spray technology.

Trump's remarks were a salute to the gathered police, whom he praised by blowing his own trumpet and hoping that some of the high notes might fall on his hosts. Donald praised his own wisdom and judgment for having always admired and liked police, and he singled out his own sagacity, even before San Bernardino, for believing that the police deserved their own tanks and heavy weapons. (*"Let them have the finest equipment available."*) He quoted his earlier critics as now saying "You know, he's right" on immigration, and he bragged about monopolizing the national conversation after he said that Muslims should be banned from coming to America. He patted himself on the back (the sound of one hand flapping) for coming up with the idea of a Great Wall of Trump along the Mexican border, and he emphasized that it would be a "real wall," not some temporary barrier like those set up inside skating rinks. He shared with the audience his prescience in year 2000 for having doubts about Osama bin Laden and wanting him to be killed—almost two years before 9/11. He wished the current administration had been as skeptical about the bombers at the Boston Marathon or the shooters in San Bernardino. Many of Trump's homilies about the current state of affairs ended with prayers for relief—something that often involves some kind of death wish or demand for capital punishment.

Listening to Trump's New York accent, I was reminded of the boxing promoters who floated through my childhood on Saturday afternoons on ABC's *Wide World of Sports*. After Trump paused a few times for applause, I half expected heavyweight Mike Tyson to come out and weigh himself.

The other side of Trump's personality reminded me of a Catskills entertainer, those who mug the crowd with exaggerated facial expressions and seem a little too eager for laughs or applause.

(*"Did I tell you the one about the HP executive running for president?"*) If only he had worn a checked tweed jacket, the persona would have been complete.

I left the event with Donald posing for various pictures with the New England cops, many of whom were sporting Kojak's buzz haircut. In such company Trump had the look of a giddy boy dreaming of growing up and becoming a policeman. With his beefy look he could well have been mistaken for a homicide detective, except for his casino bouffant and speech pattern that at times has him sounding like Police Squad's Lieutenant Frank Drebin ("*. . .'blowing away a fleeing suspect with my .44 magnum used to mean everything to me. I enjoyed it. Well, who wouldn't?"*).

The less comical side of the evening and Trump's emergence as a serious candidate (the clear frontrunner in the polling) is that it speaks—to paraphrase a popular campaign construction—to homegrown fascism, perhaps a bigger threat to the democracy than the mall gunners.

At the events of most candidates in New Hampshire, I could still imagine I was at a town hall meeting, even if the citizens were reduced to asking talk show questions (*"How do you feel about San Bernardino?"*). But a Trump event, at least this one, is a variation on Mussolini shouting from his balcony overlooking the Piazza Venezia. Just to get into the Sheraton, I had to run a gauntlet of armed guards and sniffer dogs, and once inside the political platform called for detention, wire taps, barbed wire and walls, more guns, a heavier police presence, municipal tanks, and death penalties.

For now, Trump may have a more amusing personality than Il Duce, but he looks like someone who would be very comfortable carrying out his state duties in a trooper's uniform, complete with the jackboots. He already has down the guise of a buffoon.

Confessions of
a Primary Insider

*"Democracy is the art of running the circus from
the monkey cage."*

—H.L. Mencken

The Candidate Wears Prada

Trying to make sense of the primaries, I reached out to someone on the inside and got the enclosed reply:

"I AM FLATTERED that you think I have any insight into the mud wrestling that is our primary season. The fact is, if I were doing lines with Bill at Studio 54 ('70s allusion, so you might not get it) or cutting Melania's hair, I wouldn't know much more about the election than Carly's stay-at-home husband.

"Okay, I have changed planes in Vegas (more slot machines than security scanners in the airport) and looked at some of the polling numbers in South Carolina (no, not brain surgery). But I have no more insight than you do at what makes Jeb! run (must be a mommy thing?) or why everyone bailed after Don & Ted's excellent adventure in Iowa and New Hampshire.

"Since you asked for my take, here it is. All I ask, if you use any of this material, is that you make me more anonymous than either Deep Throat or some mob informer. I am like everyone else in this Marriott Courtyard—what I want for all these nights on the road is one of those assistant secretary positions that comes with a car, credit card, and personal assistant who can get me a table at The Palm that doesn't have an unobstructed view of the swinging door to the kitchen. Instead of a Christmas bonus, I will take face time with Megyn Kelly, talking the talk about ISIS or gun control. So please don't turn me in.

It All Starts with Hillary

"It all starts with Hillary. For the Republicans she's their worst nightmare—Obama in a pants suit or Bill back in the White House, chasing down their votes (remember triangulation?) and interns.

"The reason the GOP had all those strategy sessions back in 2012 was to come up with a plan and a candidate to drive a knife in her back and, while they were at it, throw some dirt in Bill's legacy direction.

"For that all they needed was someone like Christie or Jeb!, someone with good right-wing street cred, but not a tub-thumper on immigration, God, or the Fed, and someone to attract enough moderates or atheists to win in swing states such as Florida, Ohio, and North Carolina. They would even have taken Rubio as a vice presidential candidate, if he could deliver the goods in Florida and stopped looking like a bystander on *Girls Gone Wild.*

"That was the winning ticket until Trump showed up with his unscripted reality show, which, by comparison, made the partnership of Bush & Christie look like a funeral home.

"Mind you, the Republicans would take Trump in a heartbeat if they thought he could beat Hillary and drop off some swag bags in DC, but the fact is that not many in the corridors of power think Trump is anything more than a promoter of professional wrestling. And they fear that if nominated he will make the electoral votes of Barry Goldwater or Alf Landon look like landslides.

The Candidate Wears Prada

"Fortunately for the Republicans, Hillary 2016 is the 1962 New York Mets of presidential campaigns. (You may not remember them, but in one game 'Marvelous' Marv Throneberry hit a triple but was called out, on appeal, for missing first base. When manager Casey Stengel went out to argue the call with the umpire, a coach stopped him and said, 'Forget it, Case, he didn't touch second either.')

"If ever you wanted to see a campaign in a death spiral, look no further than Hillary's. Remember 'it's our time' and all that, and then it turns out she's even losing the women's vote in New Hampshire.

"At the last minute the Clintons summoned the graven image of former Secretary of State Madeleine Albright so that she could send all those female Bernie supporters down a walk of shame.

"Here's Hill losing in all categories (women, kids, men, you name it) to a Brooklyn socialist who for a while lived in a Unabomber cabin in Vermont, and all she can think of doing, to deliver 'her message,' is to drag out a few has-been careerists from DC or Hollywood.

"It speaks to the bigger problem that Hillary's staff is cut off from 'the family.' They want her to 'stand for something' other than Bill's Risorgimento or Chelsea's foundation inheritance, but every time they give her a speech that outlines the future of America, she is back in 1992, with that couple from *Cheers* or dancing the Macarena with some state senators.

"For all I know she's even happy having The Devil and Miss Paula Jones back in her life (you saw the Paula selfie with Donald, I assume?). Nothing like a good, safe menace, is there?

"I would tell you that Bill is the 800-pound gorilla in the Hillary campaign, except that he looks like a ghost and sounds like the nostalgic Joe Namath, talking about glory days. The staff hated having to bring him into New Hampshire. (Think of the

Yankees going to Mariano Rivera in the fifth inning.) Bill wasn't on the trail for 15 minutes when he was caught in a Twitterstorm about 'his past,' and suddenly Hillary looked like she was running as Mrs. Bill Cosby. Heck of a job.

"Don't believe for a minute that the loss in New Hampshire was a bump in the road on the way to her coronation. It was worse than Cam's beatdown in the Super Bowl. It showed her base is limited to cat ladies, and you have to wonder how many of those there are in South Carolina and Nevada.

"Yes, they are more conservative states, but Hillary goes into them looking like a younger version of Gloria Steinem (bet that will turn out the bubbas in SC), who can't beat a professional outsider whose resume is limited to Burlington bike lanes.

"Politically, besides being tied to Bill, Maddy, and reruns of *Cheers*, Hillary is caught in something of a political straight-jacket, even if it is one of beautiful, hand-crafted worsted wool. (At least she no longer looks like she's clothes shopping at Target.)

"If Hillary tacks left into Bernie's brave new world order, she will look like an opportunist, especially with all those canceled checks from Goldman Sachs in her handbag. If she turns to the right and says, 'Okay, I give up. I love banks and giving speeches for a million bucks,' she's a warmed-over, Democratic Nixon, with a message that could work for VA Gov Jim Gilmore (12 votes in Iowa, but he's still in the race). At the very least, she might think of changing her campaign fight song from 'Eye of the Tiger' to 'Stuck in the Middle With You.'

"Finally, she can't exactly run against Obama, now can she? Her fingerprints are all over the Osama snuff film, the Syrian mess, Obamacare, and Benghazi. Hell, she probably drove him over to the bowling alley when he rolled that 37, costing her the votes of all those Little Lebowski Urban Achievers now voting for the first time.

Bernie in Plato's Cave

"If the Republicans had their flanks covered (with Tea Partiers and Rockefeller Republicans both happily inside the GOP tent), they would be celebrating the decline and fall of the Clinton empire as if they had shares in Visigoth Inc. But just when they thought it was safe to go back in the presidential waters, Bernie turns up with his populist campaign, which, in its way, is as implausible as Trump's, and just as unpredictable.

"Inside-the-Beltway Democrats hate the idea of Bernie as much as country club Republicans despair over Trump (think of Rodney Dangerfield as Al Czervik in *Caddyshack*, shouting, *"Hey everybody, we're all gonna get laid!"*).

"Keep in mind that Bernie is an ideological purist who is living in Plato's cave, not the real political world. Free tuition might pack in the student vote at Keene State, and dissing Wall Street is an easy soundbite in primaries when most voters are not hedge fund owners. But Bernie is an outlier, as much of a shock jock talk-show host as is Donald with his Fox and friends.

"If there was a national primary on one day, Bernie would be a 7 percent guy, maybe, but now he has these advantages over Hillary: he's raking in piles of money, and his campaign team doesn't make a lot of mistakes. They're pros.

"Even people who, on normal days, would hate a socialist agenda (turning America into East Germany, complete with Trabants instead of Teslas) admire Bernie for his 'refreshing honesty' and the impression that he's there to turn out the money changers from the political temples.

"I would also ignore the polling figures that have Hillary way ahead in South Carolina and Nevada, and in the Super Tuesday states. That was when she was still breathing or, as the accountants say, Clinton Inc. was still a 'going concern.' Now it's in receivership, and Bernie's the only one in the field who is a declared creditor. Will that change?

White Knight: Joe Biden

"Playing the role of a white knight could be Joe Biden, who dreams about being summoned by his party, on a warm convention night, to carry the fallen, tattered Obama-Clinton escutcheon into battle with the evil Republicans, especially if they are led by the errant Sir Donald Trump.

"Despite all those articles you read about Joe grieving and working out a cure for cancer, he'd love nothing more than to jump into the presidential race, even if his political staff was limited to a few out-of-work Amtrak train conductors at the Wilmington station.

"Here are the problems with all the Biden-to-the-rescue scenarios. It only works for him if Hillary is out of the race, and she only leaves the campaign trail if she quits in disgust (dream on), gets sick, or is run out of town with a few indictments downloaded from her Best Buy server. Are any of these options possible?

"Nothing is impossible to imagine in 2016, but most likely the only way Hillary gives up is if Barack frogmarches her to the Justice Department, so that she can hang from a cross of Petraeus thorns. (Remember the amorous general? His crime was to preen to a mistress-biographer about his surging accomplishments in Afghanistan, and he mailed her some classified documents and, presumably, a few buffed-up selfies.)

"For the moment, no one thinks Obama is ready to feed Hillary to the Committee of Public Safety. The frenzy would make him look bad, as well. But imagine if the storyline of the 2016 general election turns out to be a fight inside the Obama administration about whether the FBI ought to be allowed to throw the book at nominee Hillary for server-ing up state secrets to Russian and Chinese hackers.

"In that food fight, Obama gets a lot of pie, and, instead, he might choose first to throw Hillary to the Justice wolves (*'we're a nation of laws...'*) and to replace her at the head of the ticket with the compliant Biden, especially if Axelrodworld convinces O that only Uncle Joe can beat a full house in Atlantic City.

Bloomberg's Waiting Game

"Another option being floated is that Mike Bloomberg, the former mayor of New York and a wolf of Wall Street, might jump into a race that may only have the extremes of Trump and Bernie.

"As you know, Bloomberg has his own billion-dollar fortune, and an ego to match-fund it. Under this scenario he can pay for an independent run for the presidency as easily as Trump can add gold trim to some of his New York towers.

"Would Bloomberg have a chance? I don't think so, for these reasons. The race already has a New York billionaire and a liberal Brooklyn politician, both with claims of ideological purity similar to those on which Bloomberg would run.

"In a race between two already successful New Yorkers, could the savior possibly be another New York master-of-the-universe who is already a hybrid of the two in the race?

"Besides, Bloomberg would be forced to run as a third-party candidate (Bull Moose? Know-Nothing? Free Soil?), and I think he would be lucky to get 5 percent of the vote.

"Would a Bloomberg candidacy throw the race to one party? It might, if he got between Hillary and Trump, and drained off Hillary supporters.

"Bloomberg says he will only jump into the race if the choice is between the extremes of Bernie and Trump. But the nominees might not be known for months (Cruz could well win some Western primaries, and Jeb! might recover his B or C game), which would force Bloomberg to wait on the sidelines.

"Then if he jumps in, it would at the last minute, and his impact could be that of James B. Weaver (FYI, the Greenback Party candidate in 1892, but you knew that).

South Carolina on My Mind

"So what happens now? In South Carolina, the Trump ground game is clear. He wants to knock Jeb! out of the race, and to weaken Cruz by bucking up Rubio, much as one might—in a French foreign legion movie—prop up a corpse on the ramparts of a desert fort under siege.

"Rubio is useful to Trump if he can divide the young, articulate, Tea Party senatorial vote, depriving Cruz of key far-right support. Trump's people think Rubio is the perfect, made-to-order stalking horse. He's angry at being played for the Christie fool in New Hampshire, and his goal is to push Cruz from the race, so he becomes the One No Trump.

"The Trump people, however, believe that if the final contest is between Donald and Rubio, 'make America great again' will sound a lot better than 'I didn't know they were GOP credit cards.'

Jeb: Trump Snake Poison

"Jeb! is also auditioning for the role of Trump snake poison. His problem is that he shook the Bush money tree for $113 million (or thereabouts), and all he has to show for it is a fourth in New Hampshire and sixth in Iowa, which isn't exactly what the insiders thought they were buying.

"Now Jeb! can go back to the money orchard and make the claim that only the Bush brand stands between the Republican establishment and a casino operator with tilted wheels. But campaign donors aren't there for capital gains (they're day traders), and I think they are weighing their in-the-money options between Trump and Cruz.

"If Jeb! was a racehorse (which I can assure you he is not; think of one of those carriages in Central Park), they would say he's no good in the mud.

Kasich Channels Warren Harding

"How about John Kasich? I hear you asking. *What are his chances?* Before anointing him the next Ohio president (Warren Harding was the last in that line), keep a few things in mind.

"Kasich did well in New Hampshire because instead of running for president of the United States, he was standing as the mayor of Manchester. He practically moved to the state (so did Carly and some others) and tooled around in his campaign bus to more than a hundred events, preaching a gospel of Midwest optimism based on family values and moral leadership (while waving the bloody shirt over the specter of ISIS).

"The rap on Kasich is that, under the patina of George Babbitt, there's a politician as angry as Richard Nixon yearning to break free and tell the world his mother was a saint. (As a college kid, Kasich managed to talk his way into Nixon's Oval Office, where he stood for one of those Elvis photos with the bowler-in-chief.)

"His relatively strong performance in New Hampshire was because many voters had met him, heard his halftime homilies about teamwork and love, and figured at least he wasn't as far 'out there' as many others. But Super Tuesday is about TV, and his cable plan is basic.

"John's not as vitriolic as some others about immigration or Obamacare—a moderate even—although as a Czech-Croatian Catholic (now Anglican) he can sound like the pope on abortion, and with ISIS, as singer Randy Newman might twang, he'd 'drop the big one now.'

"Please don't kid yourself that Kasich would be Mr. Smith going to Washington, although for now he's been taking enough chill pills for some voters to think he could be the next Garfield, McKinley, or Hayes, decent men from Ohio who the machine lifted to the presidency.

"And remember: you know more people in South Carolina or Nevada than he does. As I write, his bus is heading south on I-95, with aides in the back clicking on eHow websites, 'How to win the South Carolina primary.'

Vice President Marco Rubio?

"What about Rubio? Is he gaffe toast? I think he is. He's good on his feet (sometimes, at least when it's just a room full of wealthy donors or adoring women), but with the bright lights on, Marco's deep passes tend to wobble like Peyton Manning's. (Did you see the awful Super Bowl? Imagine winning the big game and all you want to do is to shill for Bud Light and Disneyland? This guy will be governor of Indiana before you can figure out how to pronounce Ndamukong Suh.)

"Rubio's problem is self-loathing, in that he despises the current administration, yet he's the Republican Obama doppelgänger—a first-term, celebrity-obsessed senator whose claim for the presidency can be found in the flickering verse of a teleprompter.

"Voters want to like Marco, as he's good-looking (in a Joseph A. Bank window mannequin kind of way) and occasionally glib, while mounting the bully pulpit for the National Security, lock-down state. But when asked to vote for him, all the voters see in front of their hand on the lever is, to use Nicholas von Hoffman's droll phrase, The Last Encampment of the Grand Army of the Bay of Pigs or maybe a grown-up Elián González.

"Marco would love to cut a deal with one of the winning candidates (probably not with Bernie, but who knows?), in which he delivers millennials and Florida in exchange for the vice presidency. I don't think he has enough high-test in his jet ski tank for such a deal. Carly hung around to be the GOP antidote to Hillary venom and to rally the women's vote against her. But she gave up when it was clear that Hillary only had the backing of a Richard Simmons exercise class.

Ted Cruz Loses Control

"Cruz is harder to write off, I must say, as he's heir to the political fortunes of Senator Joe McCarthy, and his head is as full of dirty tricks as the Watergate Plumbers.

"Yes, he apologized to Ben Carson over the 'he's-leaving-the-race' e-blast, but only after Tail-Gunner Ted had won in Iowa, and Cruz hid his own canceled checks from Goldman Sachs (the real winners here, with all their bases covered in IOUs!), while serving up Tea Party outrage over corporate greed.

"Next up, I am sure, is that his Keep the Promise PAC will give him a puppy, which he will name Checkers. (*According to the First, Fourth, and Fifth Amendments, I don't have to explain how and why I named my dog as I did.*)

"I am not convinced that Cruz is all that fussed about Donald's birther attacks—yeah, he's born in Canada and maybe he's the lost Hanson brother in *Slap Shot*—because the charge is easy to deflect, points up Cruz's background as a constitutional law and

Supreme Court expert, and reminds people that many of Trump's political positions come from call-in radio programs. (*'Hi, this is Donnie, from Queens. I have a question about D-Fish, Mrs. Barnes, and Syria...'*)

"South Carolina, however, is a must-win state for Cruz, because if he loses by 20 points to Trump or places behind Jeb!, he will quickly run out of non-PAC funding and get marginalized on Super Tuesday.

"A win in South Carolina or Nevada might turn the Republican contest into a battle between Trump and Cruz. In that run-off, Cruz's bet would be on his ideological faithfulness to the Tea Party and the strong odds that Donald Trump will go down in the flames of some casino scandal. (*Report: Escorts Frequented Trump Atlantic City...*)

"Not helping Cruz in the primaries, however, is his reputation for playing poorly in the Republican sandbox. He's perceived by his peers as nasty and defined only by naked ambition. Because he speaks in the grammatically correct sentences of Princeton and Harvard Law School, his sharp elbows are less pronounced in the debates, but in the smoke-filled rooms, I can assure you, Cruz always has to sit with his back to the corners.

"I almost forgot Dr. Ben, but then I wonder if he will even make it to South Carolina, Nevada, or Super Tuesday. He was a summer flower, and they rarely last through the winter frost. I haven't met him, but everyone says he's a nice and thoughtful man, and a good doctor (assuming you don't have to talk politics with him in post-op). In his house there's even a painting of him with Jesus, both in bathrobes, like two guys heading to the pool at the Breakers. Carson reminds me of a wealthy friend who was always getting into costly, expensive deals that had no chance of succeeding. After one of them, a mutual friend said, 'Well, he's had his $20 million of fun.'

Trump Über Alles

"So where does all this leave us? I think Trump wins in South Carolina, big-time, and also Nevada. He should be a favorite son in a gambling state. What will change hearts and minds between now and then? Not a lot, and certainly not another debate with Rubio and Cruz. Jeb!? He folds his tent after Nevada, before Super Tuesday, but don't tell his mother.

"Hillary? I think her problems will continue, on all fronts, until the Biden option is being openly discussed. There's a new expression in politics: 'It ain't over until Madeleine Albright speaks.' One way or another, Hill will leave the race, and don't rule out the possibility of some court orders.

"Meanwhile, Republicans will begin to think they can win it all with Trump, who will slowly evolve from a gong-show TV host to someone who 'isn't so bad' and then someone 'we can work with.'

"I think Bernie will have a good primary campaign—less so in the general, when negative ads would paint him as Lenin's lost poster child. Bloomberg is a no-go, if you ask me. Too many stars would need to align for him, despite all those billions sitting in his savings bank, to make a run of it.

"Finally, as they used to say in the 1970s, the only thing that could stop Trump is if he is found in bed with 'a dead woman or live boy,' although Cruz is probably capable of providing him with both options, which should make the Republican race close until the springtime.

"Keep in touch. I'm off early to Vegas. I am hoping David Copperfield can make all this go away. Best. . ."

Hillary's Self-Server

Someone close to the presidential campaigns sent this to me:

"The reason I can write to you now is because I am spared having to attend Nancy Reagan's funeral. (I just said no.) It made no sense anyway, because I never spent any quality time with her. We were just together at some events. But any candidate today who can nail down the Reagan endorsement, even from the grave, is a surefire winner.

"Even those septuagenarians Hillary Clinton and Bernie Sanders are hoping that some sawdust from Reagan's stables floats in their direction and confers on them some of the Gipper's bounce and vitality. Otherwise, come September, people may start asking, 'Have we become China, run by a bunch of old people?' Even Trump will soon be 70.

"I know, I know, the real question is whether Donald can be stopped before he turns the White House into something resembling the Bellagio. (Apparently there are already plans for a Trump White House in Atlantic City, with a roulette wheel the size of the Oval Office.)

"Jeb! tried to stop Trump, but all he got for his 150 million bucks were some great memories of the American Legion hall in

Hooksett, New Hampshire. As fall foliage package tours go, Jeb's cost more than most, but the Bushes do like to travel first class.

"Nor did Mitt Romney have much luck derailing the Trump Express. Why? For the same reason that he lost to Dr. Spock-Obama in 2012. The speech Mitt was handed to read in Utah hit all the highlights of Trump's hucksterism writ large—and his speechwriters even managed some nice allusions to confidence men and Trump U (not exactly Harvard, is it?).

"Sadly, Mitt delivered the speech while smirking, as if he were hosting the *Newlywed Game*. His body language made no sense, any more than it did when, in 2012, he would go on about economic fairness, and then in the next day's newspaper you'd find out that Mitt was installing, at one of his summer homes, an elevator for his car.

"Anyway, Trump bitch-slapped at Mitt, saying: 'Once a choker, always a choker.' He added: 'He's an elite. You see, to me I don't consider him elite. But hey, I don't consider him elite because I'm much richer than he is. I have a store—I have a store—that's worth more money than him. I jokingly said that because I don't like Romney.' And so it was goodbye, Mitt—from Cy Young to Sayonara. He says he's available for a draft at the convention, but then so are Rick Santorum and Jim Gilmore.

"In this exchange, you have an emerging truth of the 2016 election. In 2012 voters were uncomfortable with Elder Mitt because of his $400 million fortune and country club demeanor. By contrast, Landlord Trump apparently has $7 billion (so he says), but because he sounds like Don King (the boxing promoter) no one cares about his wealth.

"Just the opposite: Trump has managed to turn the election into a cable TV infomercial, in which voters seemingly judge the candidates on their abilities to flip condos in south Florida. (And then at the end of show, while walking around his swimming pool,

Donald makes the pitch for viewers to buy his DVD series, *Trump's Ways to Wealth,* 'for $49.99, plus postage and handling.')

"So what happens now?

Rubio's Last Stand

"The next order of business in the campaign is for Marco Rubio to get out of the race. He's been on life support for weeks, ever since Chris Christie compared him to a wind-up toy that comes with a Happy Meal.

"Okay, Marco won the primary in Puerto Rico, but, quite frankly, I work in this business, and I had no idea Puerto Rico even had a primary. Can Puerto Ricans vote? I don't think so, except maybe for Miss America, at least if the pageant is in San Juan.

"Aside from that win, and another in the Minnesota caucus (who knew Minnesota had Republicans?), Marco's only contribution to American political history has been to come up with positive soundbites for a series of fourth-place finishes.

"No matter how far down the voting table Marco lands, he's out there the next day explaining that he alone can defeat Donald Trump (except in the other 25 states already contested) or that he represents a purer form of conservatism than does Ted Cruz (the suggestion in some of these spins is that Cruz is getting his political opinions from the entrails of dead chickens).

"Mind you, the real reason Marco is hanging on in the race is because none of his political handlers have figured out a sensible way for him to quit. If he drops out now, before his hometown Florida primary (March 15), Trump will grind him into dust with prime-time insults about his manhood deficiencies. (*The guy's a loser. He couldn't get elected dog catcher in a Miami subdivision. . .*')

"If Marco waits until Trump beats him in Florida, he might well be saying goodbye to the rest of his political career. A loss in Florida means he will have no chance as a vice presidential candidate (*'Who needs a guy who can't carry his home state?'*), and such a loss might, in the future, doom him from standing for governor or even running again for the president in four or eight years. (My own take? He'd better start applying for his lobbyist license.)

"Rubio's hatred of Cruz is another reason he can't leave the race. Each of them has a lot of Cuban blood, and neither wants to fold his hand while the other is in the game. (I take it you saw the two of them, in one of the debates, arguing in Spanish. And then the camera panned to the smug Trump, who had the look of a Texas sheriff, getting ready to throw some illegals in the back of his squad car.)

"Nor can Marco bargain away his Puerto Rican delegates for anything more than a cold plate of *arroz con pollo*. His only possible deal could be with Ohio Governor John Kasich, but each is asking the other to quit the race, in exchange for that person becoming the vice presidential candidate of the successful nominee. On paper, Kasich could use Rubio in Florida, assuming he can swing it, and Rubio could use Kasich in Ohio, assuming Trump doesn't blow the doors off him in his home state.

"Anyway, it all sounds like a promising deal in the making, except Marco's not a deal guy. He's the kind of politician—a bit like Nixon—who really doesn't believe what anyone tells him and who thinks he can always get a better deal from the next candidate. He will only deal with Kasich after he, Marco, wins in Florida, or after the governor stumbles in Ohio.

"Chances are, however, that after Florida and Ohio, Trump's security guards will be hustling both men to the exit while Sultan Donald gloats to a crowd calling for blood: 'I gotta tell you. I never liked those guys. They're nasty, nasty guys.'

Kasich's Long Game

"What keeps Governor Kasich in the race? I ask because he has few delegates, no money (in the hole for about $4 million), and dismal name recognition despite running hard for a year.

"Kasich's dream is that Rubio and Cruz will somehow cancel each other out (as when you jumpstart a car and cross the wrong cables) and that he—the centrist governor from a necessary swing state—will look like a sane alternative to Trump's gilded gong show.

"If the presidential contest were simply between Kasich and Trump, it is possible that the governor's hopes might come true, although for the moment the 2016 campaign is one of extremes, and few Republicans (at least those voting in primaries) want a GOP Michael Dukakis at the head of their ticket. (In case you've forgotten, he was Willie Horton's parole officer who in 1988 ran against Pappy Bush.)

"In New Hampshire, Nevada, and South Carolina, Republicans didn't want Jeb, Christie, Kasich, or Rubio—the centrists, of a kind—and even if the Ohio governor, late in the campaign, becomes the last man standing, I doubt he will generate much enthusiasm.

"For the moment, Trump is the hot reality show, while Kasich looks like a black-and-white rerun of *Leave It to Beaver*. On the trail, he even sounds like Ward Cleaver. Meanwhile, all the Republican electorate wants is face time with The Fonz ('*Heyyyyyyyy. . .*').

Survivor: Ted Cruz Edition

"Without Kasich and Rubio in the race, would Cruz have a chance to take down The Donald?

"It's the only question anyone asks me, and every time I reply: 'Without Citizens United and its tsunami of slush funds in presidential politics, Ted would be in one of those right-wing Washington think tanks, tilting at windmills, churning out monographs on how only guns can keep us safe from Muslim gay marriage.'

"To date Ted's only genius on the campaign trail (you've heard the debates: he sounds like *Dragnet*'s Joe Friday reading out an indictment) is sweet-talking various millionaires and billionaires to fund his campaign.

"In raising over $100 million, much of it from tech titans and hedge funders, Ted has done well in the most important early primary—that in the great state of Wealth—and to date has pulled down more than all the other candidates, except for Jeb and Hillary Clinton.

"Nor, like Hillary or Jeb, has Cruz felt the need to blow his campaign fortune all at the beginning. In Ted's mind, he has spent enough to stay competitive in the race and to survive the scrum of other Republican candidates. But he has not spent so much that he cannot now stay in the race until the others have departed and he becomes the Lone Ranger, there to track down the Donald Gang.

"To be sure, Cruz never anticipated that Trump would turn into a lottery-ticket frenzy. Ted figured he would go into the semifinals against, perhaps, Jeb, Christie, or Marco, and that he would emerge from the GOP pole dance as the only true conservative—the Earl Grey of the tea party.

"Instead, the political center collapsed almost immediately, and he's been forced to share his ideological purity with Carson and Rubio, among others, which explains all those primary returns where he only pulls down 24 percent of the vote.

"As a contestant on *Political Survivor*, Cruz makes a strong case for staying on the island, at least over Rubio and Kasich. Neither of them is budging, however, probably because they find Ted personally unpleasant and because neither thinks that Ted can defeat Trump. (Remember what Dr. Evil said in *Austin Powers* to his son Scotty: *"You're semi-evil. You're quasi-evil. You're the margarine of evil. You're the Diet Coke of evil. Just one calorie, not evil enough."*)

"Nor is Cruz proving to be the 1984 Reagan, when it comes to winning his own primary elections. Granted, he won in his home state of Texas, and beat Trump in Iowa, Idaho, Oklahoma, Alaska, and Kansas. But for a fundamentalist tub-thumper inclined to rapture, his losses define his candidacy more than his wins. (Churchill might say of the Republicans, *"Never have so few said so much after losing so many."*)

"Ted got nowhere in the Deep South, a natural constituency for him, losing from South Carolina to Louisiana. He's only done better away from his comfort zone, in places like Idaho and Kansas, where Republican primary voters hate Trump and don't think Rubio can win. Maybe he should have left that porn star in his TV ads?

"Cruz does not do well in open primaries, which bodes poorly for how he would do in a general election. In Florida and Ohio— key states for the nomination and the presidency—he's not breaking 20 percent. But he can keep running a long time so long as he keeps his $10 million friends happy.

Trump Emerges

"By now everyone has an opinion about Donald J. Trump, and most of them are wrong. For starters he's not as stupid as he sounds, and you can't make $1, $3, or $7 billion in the New York real estate shark tank without having some competence as a manager.

"He has also run a thrifty campaign—mostly his big donors are the TV networks, giving him free airtime—that has broad national appeal in a party to which he's a stranger.

"Admittedly, he surrounds himself with mail-order storm-troopers, and, on Twitter, he often sounds like Mussolini. But he's less an aberration than most wish to believe, at least in presidential politics.

"Many Republicans, starting with one-term congressman Abraham Lincoln, have run for the highest office with little or no political experience on their records. Reagan spent most of his adult life as an actor, Harding had been a lieutenant governor and senator, and Benjamin Harrison was a white-shoe lawyer. The man with the best resume to be president, Herbert Hoover, failed miserably in office. (He's the case that businessmen don't make it in politics.)

"Despite what you might hear from the other candidates, at this point Trump has a lock on the Republican nomination. He has won primaries, by large margins, in all regions of the country (among them, New Hampshire, Mississippi, Michigan, and Nevada), and, if need be, he can draw on his unlimited personal wealth to fund the last round of primaries (when the likes of Kasich, if still around, will be tapped out).

"Get this: Trump has only 'lent' his personal money to his campaign. It's an old real estate trick—to stay ahead of the other creditors. Make that *ka-ching* sound. Overall, he's done a terrible job fundraising in the primaries (on a level with Carly and Kasich). Good thing he has overdraft checking.

"My guess is that the end game will come a lot sooner than anyone has predicted. For example, if Trump were to sweep the March 15 primaries (Florida, Illinois, Missouri, North Carolina, and Ohio), he would be right in calling the race over.

"Even if he drops a few of these primaries, I cannot see him massively losing on April 26 to Cruz or Kasich when the races move to Connecticut, Delaware, Maryland, Pennsylvania, and Rhode Island. Even if Trump splits the remaining primaries, he would still win the nomination.

"At this point all Trump has to fear is if, in the next few days, both Cruz and Rubio were to drop out and the race (in places like

Pennsylvania, Ohio, and New Jersey) were to come down to a choice between Donald and a surging, middle-of-the-road John Kasich. Then he might wobble. But this won't happen.

"A safer bet would be on the vanity of Rubio, Cruz, or both to stay at the masquerade ball long after their dance cards are empty, dividing the Trump opposition and giving him the nomination well before the Republicans gather in Cleveland July 18-21.

Trump vs. Clinton?

"Among the pros, all anyone can discuss, if the general election comes down to Trump and Clinton, is whether Donald can redraw the map of the electoral college and do well in new swing states (Pennsylvania, New Jersey, etc.) that traditionally have been Democratic.

"Since Bill Clinton was elected in 1992, Democrats have won the White House by carrying New England, California, and certain mid-Atlantic states (plus Minnesota, Ohio, and/or Florida). That coalition, which is the electoral map of Barack Obama, is the template for any Democratic victory. (When a Democrat loses Ohio or Florida or both, as Al Gore and John Kerry did, they tend to lose everything.)

"So how does the electoral map get redrawn? Because Trump (to use shorthand) appeals to angry, white, marginalized males, in a general election he might do well in the Rustbelt—for example, in New Hampshire, Ohio, Michigan, and Iowa, which have been largely Democratic in recent elections. By contrast, I could see Trump losing in traditional Republican states that have large populations of Latino voters or African Americans, say, Louisiana, Arizona, or North Carolina.

"In other words, the 2016 general election could well break in this manner: Trump could run strongly among Nixon's Silent

Majority, lapsed evangelicals, Homelanders, and fundamentalists, while a Democrat—say Hillary Clinton—would have in her corner older women, African Americans, Latinos, and some left-leaning men. If so, who wins?

"The Internet has lots of do-it-yourself electoral college maps, where you can assign a state to the Democratic or Republican column. I have spent hours running my own elections. Payoffs are kept to a minimum, and I am spared debates with the Rt. Rev. Anderson Cooper.

"How does the game come out? When I assign North Carolina, Virginia, and Colorado to the Clinton Democrats, and when I add Florida to that mix, they win big in the general election.

"Conversely, when the Trump Republicans win in Michigan, Pennsylvania, or New York (Trump's home city, and upstate is conservative), the Republicans win in a walk, no matter what happens in Florida or Ohio.

"I cannot see Trump-led Republicans winning Florida, Nevada, or North Carolina, but I can imagine him doing well in New York, which has had a Republican governor many times, but last voted Republican in a presidential election in 1984.

"Will the map get redrawn? I think it will. If Trump is the Republican nominee, my guess is that a new electoral alignment will emerge. (The last big shifts were in 1968 and 1980.) Among those states on the move could be Pennsylvania, New Hampshire, and Iowa.

The Future of the Electoral Map

"Here's another hot-stove topic: Will the looming electoral map change who Trump may consider for a vice presidential running mate? Actually, I could see Trump picking Jesse Ventura, Herman Cain, or Tom Brady sooner than I can imagine him selecting some career Republican senator or governor, based on 1960s demographics. Why cater to a political establishment that has done nothing but run you down?

"Trump will probably pick a woman as his running mate, and possibly a minority. (We know he's good at mating; the *New York Post* recently ran a campaign headline: 'Ex-lover says Donald Trump was great in bed.' The source was a *Penthouse* model, so presumably reliable.)

"Three vice presidential names that could be attractive to him are Condoleezza Rice (W's national security advisor and secretary of state, who could, so to speak, trump Hillary with women voters), South Carolina Governor Nikki Haley (although she endorsed Rubio in the primary, and Donald has a prickly memory), and Susana Martinez, the Hispanic Republican governor of New Mexico.

"Among men, he will never pick Rubio but could warm up to Cruz, to unify the right wing of the party. Kasich? I doubt it. Carson? At least he meets the bland test.

"For now my money is on Condi. It placates the Bush wing, she has 9/11 street cred on foreign policy, and she might do a good job negating Hillary's appeal among African Americans. Besides, anyone who could spend every Sunday night watching movies with W could certainly deal with Syria or the Russians.

Is the Democratic Race Over?

"Is the Democratic race over? Well, it should be. After all, Bernie is a socialist mayor and independent senator from the nowhere state of Vermont, with only food co-ops on his CV, who preaches revolution as often as he sneers at corporations. How can PAC-Woman Hillary, with her $200 million war chest, not put him away? After all, the Democratic Party isn't entirely in the thrall of

Nordic socialism, and she has every officer holder in nearly every state, except for Congresswoman Tulsi Gabbard from Hawaii.

"Bernie's like those characters in horror movies, who after having been chained and buried (see all those Southern primaries, if not the he'll-never-win headlines in the *New York Times*), manages to break out of the crypt (Michigan) and win in a bunch of centrist states (Oklahoma, Nebraska). Now he's looking ahead to a favorable run of primaries in places like Wisconsin, Washington state, and Pennsylvania.

"At this point in the Clinton campaign film, she thought she would be mulling over her cabinet or making one of those diplomatic preelection swings through the three I's (Ireland, Italy, and Israel). Instead, she is chasing the ghosts of 2008 and rereading *Washington Post* headlines: 'What should worry Clinton about Sanders's Michigan win.'

"Give Bernie and his handlers credit for running a terrific campaign. As best I can determine, he has one set campaign speech (free tuition, death to capitalism, etc.) and a handful of debate soundbites (most have the words 'special interests' as nouns or adjectives). He has no PAC money, and has never given a speech on Wall Street.

"Nevertheless, Bernie is fourth in the money sweepstakes—although gaining fast—despite taking contributions in amounts more familiar to the bearers of food stamps than corporate bonds. And while Hillary has a lock on superdelegates and African American voters, Bernie continues to win in states across the landscape.

"As impressive, for someone 74 years old, he refuses to give up, despite the long odds of winning the nomination. It speaks to his will and determination, if not Hillary's campaign incompetence, that this is still a race.

"Can he win? I don't see how. Hillary can plod along—winning in the South, losing everywhere else—but then she will hit a series of friendly, non-socialist states (Florida, New York, and California come to mind), and they should put her over the top. But if the race remains close for a long time, Hillary only has herself to blame, for failing to rally a core constituency besides African Americans and older women.

Clinton: Take a Chance on Me

"I think the bigger question is not whether Hillary will win the Democratic nomination, but if the drawn-out primary campaign will erode her chances in the general election. Candidates who struggle in the primaries often lose in the fall.

"The interesting aspect about the Sanders campaign is that he has rarely gone negative against Hillary. Remember his line that 'no one cares about your damn emails' and the other about no one caring that her husband was a sexual predator? In that sense Hillary remains untested on what might be called the Benghazi side of her campaign—all the negative dirt that the Republicans have been collecting since 1993.

"Sanders has stuck to economic inequality, and it has worked for him. By contrast, in the general election, Hillary will get it from all sides. She will be the redistributionist, not just the figurehead on the good ship Goldman Sachs, and much else besides. Get ready for Vince Foster's autopsy, Travelgate, Paula Jones, Monica, Marc Rich, Bosnian snipers, Libya, the Clinton Foundation, and Servergate, all coming soon to a negative ad near you.

"What Bernie has made clear to the voters is how isolated Hillary remains as a candidate. She might have large majorities among placemen Dems and African Americans (look at all those landslides in places like Mississippi, where they must think Bernie is Colonel Sanders), but the low turnout in the Democratic races speaks to Clinton fatigue syndrome.

"In a general election, Clinton needs to attract enough men to go with her pluralities among women and minorities, and to extend that coalition into the new swing states.

"In November, with favorable conditions, she could win most of New England, Illinois and Minnesota, the West Coast, and, I think, Florida, North Carolina, and Virginia. If the old electoral paradigm held, she would also win in places like New York (where she was senator) and Pennsylvania (part of the Clinton heartland), and become the 45th president.

"The problem with this forecast is that it assumes she is running against a Republican walking corpse (McCain and Dole come to mind), and not Hurricane Donald, who will be making landfall wherever voters have their doubts about the get-rich-quick schemes of Clinton Inc.

Who Runs with Hillary?

"For a vice presidential pick, Hillary would have fewer options than will Trump, who owes nothing to the political establishment. (I could see him skipping the convention, if Megyn Kelly plans to attend.) By contrast, with all those superdelegates lining their pockets with IOUs, nominee Hillary will have more chits to cash than one of Trump's tellers in Atlantic City.

"NPR types would love it if Hillary chose as her running mate Secretary of Housing and Urban Development Julian Castro, the former mayor of San Antonio. But she probably would need him to help out among Latinos only if Rubio were the nominee, which isn't going to happen.

"Against Trump, she might need less a Washington boy toy and more someone who can appeal to so-called Reagan Democrats (working-class men who feel the party has given itself over to Sioux dance troops and transgender restrooms).

"Tom Kaine from Virginia (ex-governor and now a senator) might give Hillary stroke in a swing state and gravitas among men, although he hardly has a national following. She would never pick Bernie (he only gets a prime-time speech at the convention, and then on an "off" night) or Senator Elizabeth Warren (who needs another internal auditor going through her files?).

"I could see her going for a Babbitt Midwesterner, such as Ohio Senator Sherrod Brown (an anti-Trumper, with aw-shucks, Lake Wobegon appeal), with the hope that she could save the Rustbelt from a Trump-NAFTA defection. And there are others out there who have similar stripes. But anyone voting for Hillary knows that Bill is her co-pilot.

Hillary's Self-Server

"All this vice presidential speculation presupposes that Hillary tap dances her way out of an indictment over her home-brew basement server, and all those classified emails that, by golly, just happened to show up in her inbox.

"The Clinton spinsters even went so far as to 'welcome' the development that the tech installation man for the server had gotten immunity from the Justice Department, in exchange for dropping a dime on Clinton's staff, if not the Secretary. How's that for hubris? The IT guy is now singing to the feds, and Hillary's media people are saying, 'Great. It's means we're finally getting this pesky subject out of the way.'

"Without any privy information, I suspect that the Obama crowd will try to ice the puck on the email investigation—to drag it out, without much that is conclusive, until after the election when everyone can go home.

"Having to decide before the election would be a nightmare for Obama: meaning, he either goes full Nixon and covers up the malfeasance of Hillary and her team in the State Department, or he lets the Justice Department book Clinton and her staff much as he did with the amorous general, David Petraeus.

"More than once Hillary has said she neither sent nor received classified emails (difficult to imagine for a secretary of state), and then is hard-pressed to explain how some 2,000 emails now contain state secrets. On her own, she also trashed another 30,000 so-called private emails from her server—for example, those dealing with Chelsea's wedding to which the procuress for pedophile Jeffrey Epstein snagged an invitation.

"My guess is that Hillary's email scandal is like Watergate— the original crime (*'a third-rate burglary'*) being insignificant compared to the convoluted cover-up.

"Listening to Hillary justify her basement server (*'Every government official. . .gets to choose what is personal and what is official. . .'*) is like listening to Nixon and Bob Haldeman talking about a 'modified limited hang out' over Watergate. Nixon also said, 'When the president does it, that means that it's not illegal.' Clearly Hillary learned a lot during her time with the House judiciary committee, impeaching Nixon.

"Hillary talks about the email affair as though every secretary of state from Thomas Jefferson to Colin Powell had their own CompUSA hardware under the stairs. When that wears thin, she scoffs at the notion that the material on the emails was anything very sensitive (probably just some messages from Hill and Bill accepting that invitation to Donald's and Melania's wedding reception).

"She also says voters don't care about the email subject, and she may be right. (At the moment, they only seem eager to watch Trump's WWE goons eject hecklers from his halls.) But there is something fishy about the U.S. secretary of state working in Washington, D.C., and all her official emails are routed through, not even Yahoo! or AOL, but a server in Chappaqua, New York, where no one is home for weeks at a time—save perhaps for Russian and Chinese hackers. (*'We'll leave the light on.'*)

Trump's Disclosure Forms

"Of course, all presidential elections are played with wildcards, and what matters in March may not even get a mention in September or October.

"For the Democrats on the trail of scandal, at least they will have the 100 pages of Donald Trump's financial disclosure forms, on which he lists everything he owns or earns—from Midtown buildings to Central Park's Wollman skating rink, which Trump manages for New York City.

"And if the Democrats cannot pull out a few 30-second negative campaign spots from Trump's business career and disclosure forms, it will be said that they weren't trying very hard.

"What's interesting about Trump's disclosure forms is that they read like one of his speeches. Most people, when confronted with such forms, probably underestimate the value of their assets—fearing downturns or not being sure of market prices.

"By contrast, Trump looks at the forms as another soapbox from which to proclaim his Midas wealth. Thus when asked what positions he holds 'outside of the U.S. government,' he lists 515 posts. His title for most positions is 'president,' although in a few cases he's CEO or chairman. (I suspect many of the positions are golf club memberships.)

"As for his assets and income, the problem with the disclosure forms is that they were drawn up for mere mortals, and never contemplated that someone would run for president who would have many assets worth in excess of $50 million (the top *Jeopardy!*

category). After that, even an asset worth $1 billion is simply recorded as having a value 'in excess of $50 million.'

"For Trump's paydays, most of the reported returns are probably also inflated. For example, he reports his income from the Trump Turnberry golf club in Scotland, which he owns, as being $20,395,000. It's listed simply as 'golf related income.' Maybe, but as I have been to Turnberry, on the sleepy west coast of Scotland, I have my doubts that the club spins off $20 million net a year for Trump. Revenue perhaps, but net income?

"Trump reports another $10 million in income from a club in Ireland, and the same from Trump National in Charlotte, North Carolina. Trump Doral in Florida throws off $50 million to Donald, or so he says. His New Jersey golf club pays him $6,627,486, his Westchester (New York) club another $9,495,179, and a DC course $14,026, 420. That's more than $100 million in greens fees at a time when the Tiger-less golf industry is in severe recession.

"Without knowing for sure, I would guess that Trump, like many real estate speculators, needs always to show his banks an endless cascade of money flowing into his pockets. But not many golf courses and clubs, in my experience, even make a profit, let alone return $10 mill a year.

"But then Trump on his disclosure forms would have us believe that Wollman Rink paid out to him, in income (not revenue), $8,650,450. I can hear Garrett Morris from *Saturday Night Live* exclaiming: 'Thank you berry much. Skating has been berry, berry good to me. Thank you. God bless you. *Gracias!*'

"The only irony on the Trump look-at-me disclosure forms is that most of his oleaginous books (*Think Big and Kick Ass*, *How to Get Rich*, *The America We Deserve*, *Think Like a Billionaire*, etc.) make no money at all. Thank God he has a $110,000 pension from the Screen Actors Guild (a dollar for each time he's fired someone on air).

"By contrast, Hillary's forms (with no figures on the family foundation) list more than 75 corporate glad-handing speeches at about $225,500 a pop, given over about a year to companies on the make (many banks and brokers). Listed on the same form, Bill reports getting $500,000 a speech, at least if he travels overseas to speak. Imagine what they will charge when back in the White House.

The State of Play, March 2016

"Where does this leave us? In a New York minute, Rubio will be out of the race, followed by Kasich. Cruz, because of his money, will hang on for a while, warning of Judgement Day more than his low standing in the polls.

"Trump, meanwhile, will try (not very successfully) to act more presidential. Okay, he'll keep the conversation away from his finger (*sic*) size, but he'll still move through the primaries as if a guest host for Rush Limbaugh or Bill O'Reilly. (*'They killed Kennedy for the same reason they killed Patton. . .'*) Unlike other Fox birthers, this one will get the Republican nomination.

"On the Democratic side, Bernie will continue to run an excellent campaign, but that will not save him from Saint Hillary and the Dragon, who will have DNC Chair Debbie Wasserman Schultz return him to his collective vault and throw away the key.

"Sooner than you think, the conversations in both parties will turn toward possible running mates and the electoral map for the 2016 election. Wonks on cable TV shows will drone on endlessly about swing states (Trump in a good mood: *'They say I'm a great, great swinger'*) and balancing otherwise out-of-balance tickets.

"Trump and his people will try to 'Cosby' Bill Clinton, and Hillary's emails, in the spin cycle, will sound as if they contained the Ultra codes. In turn, her people will paint Trump the colors of the wallpaper in an AC cat house.

"Obama will get his last hurrah with a Supreme Court nominee, but stay far away from Hillary's server, perhaps fearing that he will turn up Bill's Ashley Madison account (*67Mustang?*) more than anything about the Crimean troop strength of the Russians.

"The Democrats will spend the summer taping interviews with everyone who ever lost money in a Trump casino ('*he took my children's lunch money. . .*'), and we will go into the fall despairing that the grand republic of Grant, Coolidge, Harding, and Hoover has come to this. No wonder I'm a happy man!"

Bernie Soldiers On

Wondering if the nominations would remain open until the summer political conventions, I reached out a to campaign operative who responded as follows:

New York Votes Trump and Clinton

"THANKS FOR YOUR MESSAGE. I know I should have written sooner, but I was waiting for the fallout from the voting in New York, where both Hillary and Trump won in a walk. So does that mean it's over?

"Let's start with the Republicans. Who thinks that Donald can be caught between now and the Cleveland convention? By Cruz?

"Teddy racked up 14 percent in New York (I assume that's the vote of those people on the subway muttering to themselves), and he's taking that as a mandate to steal the nomination from Trump at the convention? Dream on, smart guy.

"Same with John Kasich, who ran a distant second to Donnie all over New York State, except in Manhattan, where there are fewer Republicans than there are bull moose in Central Park.

"Meanwhile, Trump won New York City, Long Island, Westchester, and upstate, including hard-luck Buffalo (thanks to Bills Coach Rex Ryan keeping his foot out of his mouth).

"In the delegate count, Trump took home 89 and Kasich got four (at least they can rent a car for the trip out to Cleveland), while Cruz got nothing to go along with his 14 percent of the vote and his sneer about 'New York values.'

"I would say that remark was an update on Jesse Jackson's 1984 campaign aside about 'Hymietown,' except that Cruz probably wants to evoke all of lower Manhattan, in those studded motorcycle chaps, standing in line at the Ramrod, waiting for a transgender restroom.

"Not only did New Yorkers say, 'Hey, Ted Cruz, this Bud's for you,' but they voted for the Casino King with a nonchalance that implies he could well be a Rockefeller Republican, the heir to Jacob Javits, Charles Goodell, or George Pataki, if not Fiorello La Guardia.

"It's a comparison worth thinking about, as Rocky had his own divorce issues, and (with Trumpian panache) he took his curtain call on the big New York stage rolled up in the rug of his mistress (although the tabloid coverage of his *in flagrante* last stand was wall-to-wall).

"For Trump in 2016, the New York primary was better than winning the trifecta at Yonkers. He swept the delegates, making up for all those Trump defectors that Cruz has lured away among the Colorado and Louisiana delegations.

"And he managed to wedge Kasich ahead of Cruz for the leading role in 'Anybody But Trump,' which remains a struggling, Off-Broadway production. (Playbill: '*Mr. Kasich stars in this dated, if slightly amusing comedy about a midwestern governor who answers the want ad of a Grand Old Party that needs someone who isn't crazy to run for president.*')

"Not until the Republican wagon train (I know, in honor of Ronald Reagan, that should be the 20 Mule Team of Borax) finds its way to Kentucky on May 17 does Cruz or Kasich have any chance of winning a primary. I can't see either of them doing much in

Pennsylvania, New Jersey, or even California, despite their Molotov-Ribbentrop Pact to consolidate the opposition against Trump.

What Happens in Cleveland?

"Yes, it is possible that Trump may arrive in Cleveland on July 18 without sufficient delegates to win a majority on the first ballot, but those who think the Republicans will pump smoke into the convention hall and choose James Garfield on the 36th ballot (when in 1880 he pulled ahead of James G. Blaine) are indulging in Cruz-controlling fantasies.

"All Trump needs for the nomination is 1,237 delegates of which he has 845 (to Cruz's 559). Even now Kasich, with 148 delegates, lags behind Marco Rubio, who, despite dropping out of the race, is holding on to his 171 delegates.

"So even if Trump doesn't arrive in Cleveland with a majority (I think he will), once lakeside he can tape a few episodes of *The Apprentice* in which Rubio and Kasich try to trade him their delegates for a paid internship in the Trump administration. ('*Tell me about your experience with the postal service.*')

"What choice will they have other than to grovel in Trump's makeshift boardroom? Rubio will never join a Cruz alliance to deny Trump the nomination, and Kasich will realize that Trump can deliver on any deal while all Ted can do is promise to look after the Ohio governor down the road.

"The bigger question is this: Why should the Republican establishment in Cleveland take down Donald to elevate Cruz to the nomination, when most senior Republican officials hate Ted more than they do The Donald?

"Nor can anyone say that Kasich, with one primary win (in his home state of Ohio), is worthy of the Republican nomination, however brokered.

"At best that ought to get him an (off-night) speech at the convention and maybe a cabinet job in the Department of the Interior, provided he can swing Ohio to Trump in the general.

"Another reason Trump will whip the Republican convention into line is because none of the party stalwarts really want to tangle with such a gilded porcupine. House Speaker Paul Ryan, for sure, wants none of that mud wrestling. Truth be told, he doesn't even want to be speaker.

"Nor does the Republican Majority Leader Mitch McConnell want to wrangle an angry Trump into some candidate-sized Havahart trap. John Boehner? Yes, he's from Ohio, but he's out of the House and scorned for letting Obama roll him on health care, if not his crocodile tears.

"So who will lead the Cleveland coup de main? Mitt Romney? Mittens might throw a few bucks into the Dump Trump hat, but he's not going wear it backward or talk smack to GOP lieutenants in the smoke-filled rooms. Don't forget: Mitt sucked up to Trump and his billions in 2012, and Donald kept the blue dress.

Sanders Can Only Go So Far

"How, I hear you ask, did Hillary manage to run the table in New York, after Bernie won about 149 primaries in March and April?

"A large part of the reason is that, by the time he got to New York, Barefoot Bernie was tired. Don't forget, he's 74 years old, and his elections in the past only lasted a few months and took place in Vermont, where he could sleep in his own bed, in L.L. Bean flannel sheets. To win, all he had to do was hum a few union hymns and remind voters of the state's tradition of crusty independence.

"Now he's running against Clinton Incorporated (Hillary, Bill, Chelsea, Huma, and every Democratic state senator in the country). Still, he is largely beating them at their own game.

"He's flipping off Wall Street, raising campaign contributions in 'bundles' of $20, attracting millennials, and sweeping primaries in states as diverse as Nebraska, Idaho, and Michigan.

"Bernie has 1,202 delegates to Hillary's 1,446. But her lead among superdelegates (who says money doesn't buy happiness?) is 502 to 38. Case closed, unless some of them want to be paid off again, this time with $20 bills.

"My take on his New York loss is that Bernie's visit to the pope was his bridge too far. File it under hubris, fatigue, Archangel Gabriel, whatever. You followed that story, didn't you? If not, here it is:

"While Hillary was on Staten Island telling firemen that she would be 'fighting' for them in Washington (about her only applause line), Bernie decided that he would cold call on Pope Francis, and he loaded up his family and a few friends on a chartered, largely empty Delta 767 jet and flew off to Rome—yet another small-town politician petitioning for sainthood.

"Bernie may have been interested in meeting the pope, but was Frankie feeling the Bern? Apparently not so much. For starters, I am sure, Jorge Mario Bergoglio, a.k.a. Pope Francis, who grew up in Buenos Aires, probably didn't know much if anything about the independent socialist mayor of Burlington, Vermont, turned U.S. senator and presidential hopeful.

"The matchmaker for the papal visit was Monsignor Sánchez Sorondo, who booked Bernie's Delta entourage into the pope's guest house in Vatican City and leaned on his Argentine friend to say a quick hello to the Vermonter as another hero to the downtrodden.

"It must have taken quite a lot of coaxing, because instead of waving to the crowds from that balcony over St. Peter's Square, Bernie spent his first and only night in Rome cooling his heels with Professor

Jeffrey Sachs (director of The Earth Institute—how's that for a modest job description?), who was also in town to say some rosaries about climate change. I guess at the Vatican even Beltway prophets like Bernie and Jeff must look like itinerant money changers.

"Finally the monsignor prevailed with his papal pal, because Bernie was told if he was in the lobby of the guest house at 6 a.m., the pope would give him the apostolic version of a high-five on his way to the airport. (Francis was flying off to bless and rescue some Syrian refugees.)

"Bernie is not Catholic (he was born Jewish but isn't particularly religious, by his own admission). But his wife Jane is, and she went to parochial schools in Brooklyn. New Yorkers who went to Catholic schools are an important primary constituency, up there with Irish immigrants and Mets fans.

"Both Mr. and Mrs. Sanders showed up in the guesthouse lobby at 5:45 a.m. to receive the pope's blessing. (They had to dress; he could wear his robe.) In another brilliant tactical move, the Sanders campaign staff kept photographers away from the ecumenical line dance; otherwise they would have caught Francis striding toward the Popemobile and only breaking step briefly to fist bump the eager Brooklyn supplicants, who were standing near the front door like trick-or-treaters.

"Unfortunately, for Bernie, the excursion to Rome only generated cynical or bemused headlines (the *New York Post* wagged: 'Bernie Sanders invited himself to the Vatican'). Meanwhile, Hillary was kissing all the babies between Riverhead and Rochester, and she won, as they say at Aqueduct, 'going away.'

Bernie Soldiers On

"Given that Sanders is what the Bensonhurst mafia calls a 'walking corpse' (dead but he doesn't know it), why will he continue his campaign until the Democratic convention in Philadelphia at the end of July?

"I am sure much of the reason is found in the rhetorical question, 'What else does he have going on?' He has money flooding into his campaign accounts, he gets 10,000 at his rallies in Greenwich Village, and he can travel around the United States on a chartered jet, with an adoring press in attendance. Sounds better than getting back to his desk in the Senate and answering constituent complaints about Amtrak service to Brattleboro (I've taken it there; the station is literally a hole in the wall).

"Besides, Hillary isn't going to give Bernie a favor bag when he shows up at Her convention any more than she plans to hand over those transcripts of her own prayer breakfast at Goldman Sachs, when she must have said something such as:

> Bless this corporation of your poor. Uplift those proprietary traders who are cast down. For those who suffer innocently, I pray that you will sanctify their endurance of the wrongs worked on them, keeping their hearts free of bitterness and short positions. Cheer with hope and bonuses all discouraged and unhappy people, and help those who are tempted into sin by their ambition; though they be troubled on every side, suffer them not to be distressed; though they be perplexed, save them from insider trading.

"In the remaining primaries on the Democratic schedule, however, Hillary should stay even with Bernie, if not defeat him in Pennsylvania, California, Maryland, and New Jersey, which ought to ensure her nomination.

"His only hope for the nomination is if she gets sick or indicted, neither of which is impossible, give that she's 68 years old and in the past has fainted, had a blood clot, fallen, and has taken blood-thinning medication, perhaps to keep the FBI from clogging up her broadband.

"It's to her credit that she has held up as well on the campaign trail as she has. Bill, however, is starting to look like the Ghost of Elections Past (*'in my days of woe, we called them superpredators and stayed out of liquor stores with Plexiglass'*).

"Nor is it looking likely that the Obama administration will allow James Comey's FBI to run Hillary in for those 2,000 classified emails that turned up unexpectedly on her home server—as mysteriously as Hillary's missing law firm billing records resurfaced in the White House in 1996.

"Already Obama has gone on national television to say, 'I don't think it posed a national security problem,' and then to add, 'This is not a situation in which America's national security was endangered.' If that prejudicial statement, coming from the boss of the attorney general, didn't bury the case, nothing will.

"At the very least, Hillary's lawyer can subpoena the president as a character witness in case career Republican Comey doesn't get the memo about her innocence and turns Madame Secretary's aides into state's witnesses against their old boss for running the American foreign policy with the online security standards of Ashley Madison. (*'Life is short. Have a war.'*)

Ted Cruz Steps Out

"Speaking of infidelity, I trust you heard that Ted Cruz's phone number is showing up in the phone logs of a Washington, D.C. escort service and bordello. Teddy, we hardly knew ye, unless he was hooking up with angels?

"The madame in question died some years ago, and the phone numbers of her rich-and-famous clients have been available for some time. (But not the names of the callers or their *nom de nuit,* in the spirit of "Client 9," Eliot Spitzer's flag of convenience.)

"Now her lawyer has gone back to court to get permission to release the actual names on the madame's client list, which may explain why Heidi and the kids are making so many campaign appearances with Ted.

"If the press were ever to ask Trump if he had dallied in the arms of an hourly companion, he probably would say, '*Yes, and I have to tell you, I was the professional, not her.*'

"While the press had a small firestorm about Cruz's number among the brothel's phone logs (he was unmarried at the time he might have been dialing for darlings), his answer ('*I have never been unfaithful to my wife*') did not exactly match the question ('*Are you now or have you ever been affiliated with the D.C. Madam?*')

"The reason Cruz was on the hot seat was that the *National Enquirer* was at same time reporting that, while married, Preacher Ted had tarried with five other women in the political world (none of whom was the Virgin Mary).

"Leaving nothing to the imagination, the *Enquirer* ran pictures of the possible lovers (kind of like that gallery of Tiger's women) and described the lurid details of the trysts, although everything sleazy ran with the obligatory pictures of Cruz being lovey dovey with Heidi. They are the Al and Tipper of PDA in 2016, which is never a good sign.

"Cruz denied the affair reports and accused Trump of ratting him out to the *Enquirer*. Actually, their bad blood over their wives had begun earlier, when the Cruz campaign (actually a PAC called Make America Awesome) ran a picture of Melania Trump naked on fireside fur, as if posing for *Penthouse*, and included the caption: 'Meet Melania Trump, your next first lady. Or you could support Ted Cruz on Tuesday.'

"The only thing missing from the card was an 800 number, where you can 'chat live' with beautiful Russian and Ukrainian women about the Indiana primary.

"Trump then tweeted side-by-side images of Heidi Cruz and Melania. In the tweet Heidi looks caught in the act of biting the heads off kittens while Melania has the grace and poise, well, of Miss Universe. The Trump caption reads: 'The images are worth a thousand words.'

"In response, Cruz shouted and screamed, 'Leave Heidi the hell alone!' but in the exchange the pros took note that Trump is no amateur when it comes to slinging sexual mud. Bill and Hillary, take note or notes.

Television Ratings

"In general, you don't read much about the press in this election. Except for the running feud between Donald Trump and Megyn Kelly, there really aren't any storylines involving celebrated members of the fourth estate.

"There's no Hunter Thompson flying high with Wild Turkey on the press plane. Nor is there a Dan Rather stalking Richard Nixon or the Bush clan (*"No, sir, I want you to be careful, Mr. Vice president. . ."*)

"The *Morning Joe* is clearly decaf. Jon Stewart is retired (but apparently he's still chasing down wild pigs), although *Saturday Night Live* is still trying, as is Samantha Bee. I used to love Jackie Broyles and Dunlap, but they seem tired. Maybe they miss ol' Fred Thompson?

"For the rest we have the human Ambien, Wolf Blitzer, and on the other side all those chipper foxes and friends. No wonder Trump and Hillary are in a cakewalk. Who's calling them out? No one.

"Part of the reason that political reporting is a dying art is because few newspapers and magazines bother to assign full-time correspondents to the candidates.

"News coverage in this election means television, which is good at picking up an awkward soundbite or two but hopeless when it comes to deconstructing Trump's business empire or Hillary's compromises with evil.

"Most of what is written about the campaigns (especially all those political columns in places like *National Review* or *The Nation*) is based on the television coverage, which approaches the election much the way CBS lusts after the National Football League.

"Keep in mind that elections are huge sources of revenue of the large networks. When Jeb Bush blew through his $162 million war chest, most of that went into 30-second campaign spots that were posted to some network affiliate in Boston, Columbia, or Cedar Rapids. The same can be said for the $200 million that Hillary has already spent to prove her eloquence and fitness for office.

"In theory, network news divisions are separate from the advertising salesmen, but at the end of the day television broadcasters are best understood as corporate cheerleaders, not muckrakers. Think of Ron Burgundy, but without all the integrity.

"Why else did Megyn's bosses make her drop by Trump Tower and smoke a piece pipe with Donald? Because Trump is a brand, and national brands sell ad space. It's hard to imagine H.L. Mencken toadying up to Calvin Coolidge.

"Think too what it costs to hire a journalist to cover a candidate on a full-time basis. By my reckoning, you need $300,000 a year to keep a reporter on the campaign trail, which includes salary, airfare, hotels, car rentals, and all the booze that is fit to drink.

"Yes, bloggers and social mediators are important voices in the campaign, but rarely, if ever, do they see a candidate in person, except maybe at a debate or afterwards in the green room.

"Nor do the candidates feel much need to give the reporters access to their campaigns. They make it easy for camera crews to set up at staged events, but they feel no need to grant longer interviews to print reporters, who will only file 500 words on milk subsidies with the *Bangor Daily News*.

"And if you want to measure the extent to which the press has become a hostage to their own ratings, look no further than Donald's entire strategy, which is to be outrageous every single day so that the networks will clamor for interviews, and he can run his entire campaign on free airtime.

"Trump has spent almost nothing (about the same as Kasich and Scott Walker) on his campaign. Why should he? Every day he can call up Fox or some other network and answer (softball) questions from the shill host. He can do that from anywhere, and his message is out there. The others, including Bernie and Hillary, have to pay big money to be heard.

Conventional Thinking

"Speaking of the networks, the only people who think either the Republican or Democratic convention will offer more excitement than, say, the annual meeting of the United Association of Journeymen and Apprentices of the Plumbing, Pipefitting and Sprinkler Fitting Industry are the TV executives, who have to gin up enthusiasm for six of the dullest days in summer television.

"I take it you have been to one of these political Woodstocks? If not, let me explain the drill.

"Delegates arrive from all over America and are appointed to one of many local hotels where there is a hospitality buffet for the duration, plus a lot of minivans and chartered buses parked out front.

"Most delegations host a cocktail party at some point. The rest of the time, the delegates are out shopping, going to a local baseball game, visiting the botanical garden, or sampling local delicacies, which can include dishes in all shapes and sizes (and some of them even take credit cards).

"Over the three days and nights of the convention, the delegates occupy their assigned seats (Utah is in the nose-bleeders), launch balloons or wave funny hats (as directed), and cheer lustily when their chairman casts their pre-allocated votes for one candidate or another 'from the great state of. . .'

"A handful of delegates sit on the Rules or Platform committees, but most are detached from the political process. Yes, they get to hear the live speeches that never make the network feeds. Otherwise, the studio audience for *Jeopardy!* has more engagement than does your average delegate.

"Obama famously addressed the 2004 Democratic convention, which put him on the national political map. But then so, too, did Bill Clinton at the 1988 convention, when he stretched his allocated 15 minutes of fame into 48 minutes of Castro-like tedium. Delegates only cheered when he said, 'In conclusion. . .'

"Even the excitement of finding out the vice presidential candidate has largely been taken away from the convention delegates. In 1956 Adlai Stevenson II let the convention select his running mate (it went with Estes Kefauver over John F. Kennedy). In recent years, nominees select their vice presidential running mates before the convention, to give everyone ample time to vet their closet skeletons.

"In Philadelphia, Hillary will try to incorporate the Sanders wing of the Democratic Party into her supporters, while trying to move as far to the center as she can manage, without, say, being accused of selling out to Bank of America.

"The Democratic convention will show a bunch of Clinton home movies (Hillary as a Brownie, Bill shaking John Kennedy's hand, etc.); balloons will descend on the Clintons; Obama will get to drag out his long goodbye (Jeter's and Kobe's took less time); and in three days no one will remember or believe anything that has been said.

Trump: Life of the Party

"Trump's challenge at the Republican convention is less about winning the nomination than it is to come away from Cleveland with the Republican Party still a going concern and not in liquidation.

"Many party loyalists think of him as a third-party candidate who is attempting a reverse takeover of the GOP. They don't trust him to support candidates at the state and local level, and they fear an electoral disaster, of Barry Goldwater (52 electoral votes) or Alf Landon (eight) proportions, that will strip away the Republican majority in the Senate and even, God forbid, the House.

"What the Trump haters forget, however, is that he has been attending conventions his entire life, and probably enjoys them. He likes entertaining, lavish parties, wolves of Wall Street, empty platitudes, sweeping pronouncements, and golf—all of which surround the Republican summer jamboree.

"Plus, while Trump may be rude and arrogant to those he doesn't know, he's not a snob to those he meets, and in Cleveland he will happily mix with state delegations, in a way Mitt or the robotic John McCain could only dream about.

"He may well park his gold enameled plane near the convention center and let delegates tour it or he'll give them all engraved Parker pens that read: 'Make American Great Again—Best wishes, Donald J. Trump.'

"For my money, he'll turn the staid Republican convention into a live screening of *You Too Can Be a Billionaire*, and delegates will leave the shores of Lake Erie wondering why they so hated that nice man with all the gift bags.

"Only a few delegates will be reminded of Nick Carraway, Jay Gatsby's neighbor, who often looked back across the lawn at the shining lights of his friend's mansion and over-the-top parties:

> And as I sat there brooding on the old, unknown world, I thought of Gatsby's wonder when he first picked out the green light at the end of Daisy's dock. He had come a long way to this blue lawn, and his dream must have seemed so close that he could hardly fail to grasp it. He did not know that it was already behind him, somewhere back in that vast obscurity beyond the city, where the dark fields of the republic rolled on under the night.

Donald vs. Hillary

"In the general election, Trump vs. Hillary, who wins?

"That's the only question anyone on the campaign trail wants answered. They don't care about Donald having had three wives or Hillary's Whitewater condos. Nor do they care about Trump's tilted roulette wheels or Bill's so-called indiscretions. (I take it you have seen that Monica has reinvented herself as a faith healer for cyberbullying?)

"All anyone wants to know is who will win the fall election, which gets down to this question: Does America want Obama's or Bill Clinton's third term?

"Call it one or the other, but essentially Hillary is a nostalgic placeholder, as happens in countries like Peru or Argentina, when a popular president is barred from serving a third term.

"I know, she has many accomplishments in her own right—the Senate, secretary of state, etc.—but let's face it: If I gave you a week to think it over, you could not tell me anything she achieved in either position.

"Yes, you might tell me she gained experience, wisdom, or judgment, or whatever that comes from attending a human rights forum in Kazakhstan, but you won't cite something called The Clinton Doctrine, because it doesn't exist and, if it did and had some value, it might already be for sale on eBay or at Sotheby's.

"As the legal heir to either Clinton's or Obama's terms in office, however, Hillary has what the courts call 'standing,' and it could well be that the country will choose a hybrid candidate between Bill and Barack before it will go with an Atlantic City developer who is new to the political scene.

"And keep this in mind: Many are elected president only after earlier having lost a campaign for that office or something similar. Nixon lost in 1960, Reagan in 1976, Johnson in 1960, Franklin Roosevelt in 1920, and even Thomas Jefferson in 1796.

"The American electorate feels more comfortable, in general, with second-time candidates who have lost before than it does with newbie nominees. Very few candidates have come from nowhere to win a presidential election.

"Finally, the electoral map that got Bill Clinton elected in 1996 is virtually the same as that with which Obama won in 2012. Both won with a coalition that included liberal New England, the Democratic Midwest (from Ohio to Minnesota), and the liberal West Coast, plus Florida. Can Hillary duplicate this result?

"On paper, Hillary should win New England to Minnesota, at least along the Great Lakes (not Indiana), some Midwest states such as Missouri, and then California and the liberal West. She might even pick off Arizona and New Mexico, given Trump's anger at illegal immigrants. She should be strong in Florida and perhaps Ohio, especially if she picks Ohio Senator Sherrod Brown as her running mate.

"How does Hillary lose?

"She has big problems if the wildcard nature of Trump's reality show puts New York, New Jersey, and Pennsylvania into play as swing states. All of them have had Republican governors in recent years.

"Nor is Hillary lucky in having to run against an in-stater, especially one so well known. On paper, both Hillary and Trump are New Yorkers, but few in the state would tell you they consider Hillary a true New Yorker. 'Chappaqua?' I hear you ask. 'A bolt-hole,' they would respond. If anything, she's a Washingtonian. But a New Yorker? Fuhgeddaboudit.

The second big question is this: Does the novelty of Donald Trump redraw the electoral map?

"In his soundbites, Trump is a conservative, getting ready to drop the big one on ISIS or wall up the Mexican and Canadian borders. But the unpredictable Trump is also the most liberal Republican candidate to stand for President in 2016.

"Even the occasionally moderate Kasich is more doctrinaire than Trump, who on any given day can support Planned Parent-hood, gay marriage, abortion, impeaching George W. Bush, or trade tariffs.

"In the general election, the Clinton forces will play up his off-the-wall personality, but if that doesn't stick (*'Yeah, he's crazy. So what?'*) they will face a Republican candidate who is liberal on many social issues but conservative on the deficit and internation-ally. It can be a formidable combination.

"Think of Dwight Eisenhower. Admittedly, Trump is only a five-star general in his imagination, but like Eisenhower in 1952, he could just as easily have run this time as a Democrat. It was only a few weeks before the 1952 Republican convention that Eisenhower came out for the party. Similarly, Trump was registered as a Democrat from 2001 until 2009. No wonder he invited the Clintons to his third wedding.

"Trump's hybrid affiliations might be to his advantage in an era when few voters identify with party hierarchy or ideology. Forty-three percent of the electorate define themselves as independent.

"Trump's best chance to break the Democratic electoral coalition could be in Pennsylvania, which since 1988 has voted Democratic in presidential elections, but which has also elected conservative Republicans to the U.S. Senate and as governor. Pennsylvania, as James Carville said, 'is Philadelphia and Pittsburgh with Alabama in between.' For Trump, the more Alabamas the better.

"If Trump redraws the presidential map, it has to include winning in Pennsylvania, or he will lose.

Pre-convention Odds

"So what happens now?

"Both Kasich and Cruz can appear on their own cable channel (TedSic?) and speak 24/7 about how the Republican fight will 'go to the convention,' but in most of the remaining primaries neither will place better than an also-ran second.

"Kasich is audtitioning for the role of Fred MacMurray in *My Three Sons*, when what the electorate wants is a remake of *Double Indemnity*. (Film noir, about a plotting insurance salesman, also played by MacMurray.)

"Cruz would like us to believe he's 'God's other son,' but for that he might have to lay off (to use another Don Imus-ism) the hired hoes.

"Trump may try to act more presidential or not, depending on his mood. He's in the ideal position of needing neither money nor votes to catch up in the race.

"In the remaining primaries he can concentrate on two or three big races, while Cruz and Kasich, because they are so far behind in votes, delegates, and money, will have to spread themselves too thinly to get any traction.

"Hence the Cruz-Kasich (Papal?) Bull, dividing the known universe of remaining primaries into spheres of influence, for one of the either candidates. Trump also benefits from having two candidates against him, as they are dividing the Anybody But Trump vote, making the opposition look weaker than it may be.

"Finally, Trump's reality-show notoriety will feed on itself, making his events that much more popular. Even the violence that occasionally breaks out at his campaign stops helps keep him in the news.

"Why go to a Kasich event and listen to him talk about his daughters when you can catch a Trump speech (actually they are more like talk-radio ramblings) and a fight might break out. The National Hockey League operates along the same lines.

Demographically Speaking: The 2016 Election

"When the election gets down to Hillary vs. Trump, the vote will reduce to a contest between angry white males and angry white females.

"Demographically, Hillary will position her candidacy to pull in the Latino vote (*'A vote for Trump is a vote for your own deportation'*), better educated men, women of course (*'It's our time'*), and Bernie's millennials while Trump will make a play for the disaffected (men and women), those suffering from Clinton fatigue, gunners, aspirational young people, birthers writ large, 9/11 truthers, and anyone who thinks that America has lost its way, economically or internationally.

"The far right—Evangelicals and the like—and the far left (liberals who hate Obama for drones and Clinton for Wall Street pandering) may refuse to vote, leading to low turnouts in places like New York and California, although for the first time in a generation voters in each state might find themselves in a position to decide the election.

"As for the all-important swing states, I think they will be: New Hampshire, New York, Pennsylvania, New Jersey, Ohio, Iowa, Colorado, North Carolina, Virginia, and Nevada.

"Trump will win the presidency if he can carry New York and Ohio, while Hillary makes it if she wins either of those swing states, which is a lower barrier, as Democrats have often won both.

"I am assuming the Democrats will win in Florida, much of New England, and along the West Coast, although not in Nevada. I am giving the South to the Republicans, including North Carolina, but not Virginia. Missouri, I give to Hillary, but that could be a fight.

"I'm off to pick up a few credits at Trump U. As ESPN baseball analyst Tim Kurkjian likes to ask, 'Is this a great game, or what? And he only gets to cover A-Rod."

Making Trump Presidential?

Wondering if Donald Trump and Hillary Clinton will remain their party's nominees through the conventions, I reached out to an old friend on the campaign trail and got the enclosed response:

"It's a pleasure to send you my thoughts on the campaign, although just because I have spent the last 72 days eating those shrink-wrapped blueberry muffins for breakfast and talking to local anchormen doesn't make me an expert on Trumpism (the Republican Party in the early stages of a bad hair transplant) or *The Clintons!* (a political sitcom now in its 24th season but still coming up with new girlfriends for Bill).

"On paper—which, may I remind you, nobody uses anymore—Trump and Hillary have their respective nominations locked up. Donnie hasn't lost a primary since Cruz won in Wisconsin on April 5, and after Hillary won in California and New Jersey, she went the route of Napoleon and put the nomination crown on her own head, since the miserly Bernie wasn't in a ring-kissing mood. (He thinks the Clintons are Republican.)

"With both nominations settled, you would think we might get down to the short strokes of a national election. Instead all anyone feels on the campaign trail is buyer's regret. Both parties would dump their respective nominees in a heartbeat, if the rules allowed it.

"Now that Trump has pushed over the 1,237 threshold of needed delegates, the Republican hierarchs (Paul Ryan et al.) are having second thoughts about their standard bearer. Possible GOP campaign motto: 'Trump for President: Okay, Maybe We Fucked Up.'

"At the same time Democrats are spending days trying to come up with a Hillary bumper sticker that doesn't read: 'Not As Guilty As You Might Think: Clinton 2016!'

"What amazes me in this campaign is how unprepared both parties are for the general election. The Republican coffers are essentially empty—why nominate a chest-thumping billionaire and then ask your rank-and-file to pony up $200? And the Democrats still have two candidates in the race, because no one can convince Bernie that he's lost.

"But the problems go deeper for both parties. On the Republican side, Trump has offended nearly all the constituencies (women, Hispanics, African Americans, etc.) that the party has labored to cultivate in recent elections. Alas, no major party has yet to win an election based on biker gangs, birthers, gunners, and a few luxury condo associations in Florida.

"At least the Republicans are facing a Democratic Party that has yet to reassemble Franklin Roosevelt's grand coalition around Hillary, who practically ran unopposed in the primaries and still almost managed to lose.

"Both candidates should be asking: What happens if we have an election and no one shows up?

Ghosts of Presidents Past

"I have been involved with political campaigns since 1960 (I did love in 1968 the pregnant woman in a swimsuit with a sash proclaiming, 'Nixon's the One'), but I can never remember an election when both major parties nominated candidates who came with so many self-destruct buttons.

"The Republicans probably could have found stronger candidates than Barry Goldwater in 1964, Bob Dole in 1996, or John McCain in 2008, but they had their followers among the party faithful.

"Same too among the Democrats with Hubert Humphrey in 1968, Jimmy Carter in 1980, and John Kerry in 2004; all were weak, but none were reviled, at least not to the extent of Hillary and Trump.

"Fast forward, however, to 2016, and it's as if both the Republicans and Democrats have chosen third-party candidates. Trump sounds like a rerun of George Wallace (American Independent Party) while Hillary could be an odd cross between Victoria Woodhull (Equal Rights Party in 1872) and Ulysses S. Grant trying to buy the election for his cronies in 1880. (Earlier he had served two terms from 1869 to 1877, much the way Bill Clinton was in office 1993-2001. Both managed to avoid conviction, but it was a near-run thing.)

"Don't get me wrong: third-party candidates can make useful contributions. Robert La Follette Sr. and Eugene V. Debs might have lost big-time, but they did influence subsequent legislation. On the downside, so did Strom Thurmond.

"The problem with Trump and Hillary is that, sadly, one of them has to win, which will leave us, day one, with a deeply unpopular president who may serve in office with the articles of impeachment taped up menacingly to the White House fence.

"Missing from this race are nominees who actually inspire the voters. How did we get in this mess?

Head Counting Convention Votes

"Let's start with the Democrats, because it's the only race, in theory, with two candidates: Bernie Sanders and Hillary Clinton.

"If you add the super delegates (577) to those she has won in the primaries (2,203), Hillary has more than is required for the Democratic nomination (2,383). Bernie has 1,828 delegates.

"Technically, the problem with Hillary's self-proclaimed nomination is that super delegates arrive at the convention not pledged to any one candidate. They might express a preference for one or another candidate, but only when they cast ballots will we know for sure to whom they are committed.

"Alas, only 48 of the 716 super delegates who will attend the Democratic convention in Philadelphia have so far backed Bernie. But he is staying in the race (for now) on the hope that lightning might strike Hillary and that he will get many of the super delegates, if not the nomination.

"If Bernie were 52 years old, he would have quit the race after losing California and pledged to support Hillary. That he hasn't, however, says more about her vulnerable campaign than it does about Bernie's stubbornness.

"Why is he soldiering on, if only symbolically? Put simply, Bernie doesn't like the Clintons, Bill or Hillary. He doesn't like their billion-dollar slush fund, a.k.a. the Clinton Foundation, nor does he like their Wall Street pandering to companies like Goldman Sachs for about $500,000 an hour (private plane and hotel suite extra).

"Nor does Sanders like Hillary's militarism. In one debate he said, 'Let's talk about judgment. And let us talk about the worst foreign policy blunder in the modern history of this country. I led the opposition to that war. Secretary Clinton voted for it. Let's talk about judgment.'

"And he's convinced that if she ever released the transcripts of her speeches to the financial industry, she would put herself in the same big league as Joe DiMaggio when he was fronting for the Bowery Savings Bank. (On camera the Yankee Clipper as pitchman asked, '*Is there anyone who couldn't use a bundle of cash?*')

"Plus while Bernie has stated that he doesn't care about Hillary's 'damn emails,' he's enough of a Washington politician to know that the criminal investigation of Madame Secretary's stay-at-home server could possibly forward on to him the Democratic nomination. Why have such a message end up in spam?

Hillary Skirts the Law

"Hillary has scoffed at the notion that she will ever be indicted ('*That is not going to happen*'), but the chances are good that one of these days the long arm of the law may tap on the shoulder of a non-immunized Clinton underling. Initially the charges could relate to the Chappaqua self-server, but the prosecution could be after bigger game.

"Among federal prosecutors, there is a feeling that the Clintons have been playing fast and loose since Hillary cashed in a $100,000 profit trading pork bellies (on a $1,000 margin) in Arkansas in 1978-79. Add in Travelgate, Whitewater, Monica, impeachment, Vince Foster's private papers, the other Clinton women who were roughed up, etc., and in 2016 more than a few FBI agents would not mind adding their $500 haircuts to their scalp collections.

"Booking Hillary on email racketeering charges ('*you have the right to make one Twitter*'), however, is not the goal of the snooping feds. What would make their careers is to take down the Clinton Foundation as a pay-to-play pyramid operation, in which foreign governments (Saudi Arabia, Kuwait, etc.) bought influence with the secretary of state (and possibly future president) with millions of dollars in donations to a foundation that operates more like a government-in-exile than a charitable organization.

"Have a look at these numbers: In 2014, the foundation took in $177 million, presumably to be recycled into worthy deeds. Instead it spent $91 million, mostly on maintaining the vast Clinton shadow government.

"In the 1952 election, Richard Nixon had to defend himself with the so-called Checkers Speech for operating a slush fund worth about $18,000. Even if that figure is adjusted for inflation, I doubt it comes out now as $91 million, which is probably the reason Bernie is staying in the race. In-the-money options for major party nominations are as hard to find as stylish vicuna coats.

Bye-Bye, Bernie

"Knowing that she has the super delegates in her pocket, at this point Hillary could not care less whether Bernie stays in the race or drops out. Either way, when the nomination is settled, he will get a few meaningless planks in the party's platform and a not-ready-for-prime-time speech at the convention, and then he can Megabus it back to his off-the-grid lifestyle in Vermont.

"For all his success at the polls, Bernie has less influence with the Clintons right now than Senator Elizabeth Warren. He will not get consideration as a vice presidential running mate. Nor will his supporters get key appointments in the party's hierarchy. In the Clintons' view, Bernie has made them look bad. For that he'll get the bum's rush in Philadelphia, not the chance to hang around until the balloons float down on the Bill and Hill *Risorgimento*.

"Nor do I think Hillary is spending all that much time vetting possible running mates. For sure, some staffer has drawn up a serious consideration list (Julian Castro, Tim Kaine, Sherrod

Brown, Thomas Perez, yada yada yada), and when the Clintons are feeling confident they'll probably dust it off and try out the names on campaign insiders. You can believe that the list will define political correctness, so there will be no outliers such as Governor Jerry Brown or Senator Al Franken.

"In reality Bill is Hillary's running mate. She's already given him the economy, when she said: 'I told my husband he's got to come out of retirement and be in charge of this because you know he's got more ideas a minute that anybody I know.' Too bad many of those ideas involve hooking up with the Energizer.

Warren as VP: It Ain't Gonna Happen

"No, I do not believe for a minute any of the Elizabeth Warren for Vice President trial balloons that have been floated to a cable network near you. All of those leaks come from Warren's people, who screwed up her chances by not endorsing Clinton in January. Heck of a job, Liz.

"It will not be lost on Hillary that Warren waited until Clinton had a numerical majority at the convention and President Obama had pleaded with Bernie to quit the race.

"Earlier in the race Warren's support for Hillary might have slowed some of the Bernie momentum, especially in March and April when he took seven primaries in a row. Now it sounds like the endorsement of some Minnesota state senator petitioning for an interstate off-ramp in her district.

"Another reason Warren has no chance to become vice president—leaving aside that she sounds like a Clinton clone—is that the Internet is chock full of a televised 2004 interview in which an on-the-make Saint Elizabeth disses Hillary as a wholly-owned special interest of Wall Street, if not as someone who personally duped the do-gooding Massachusetts senator over a credit card bankruptcy bill. Any of these Warren interviews would save Trump the time and trouble of stitching together negative ads against Hillary.

"And finally something tells me that the Clinton campaign doesn't want to spend the fall listening to Trump's jokes on Twitter about 'Fauxcahontas,' a reference to Warren's claim of 1/32 Cherokee blood (turned out it was a stretch) when she applied for a job at Harvard Law and checked the Native American minority box.

Say Good Night, Ted

"Am I the only one who misses Ted Cruz and his painfully thin skin? I know his campaign was one entire whine—about immigration, New York values, the raptures, abortion, his fake Churchill tattoo, whatever—but without him, Trump feels like Laurel without Hardy or Abbott without Costello. It's been weeks since I have heard anyone on the campaign described as a 'serial philanderer,' 'pathological liar,' 'amoral' or a 'narcissist.' No wonder Trump is dropping in the polls. His Dr. Evil has gone missing.

"The end could not come fast enough for Ted. One moment he was vowing a fight to the finish in Cleveland and in the next instant he was quitting, although he made it sound like an overdue loan. 'From the beginning,' he said, 'I've said that I would continue on as long as there was a viable path to victory. Tonight, I'm sorry to say it appears that path has been foreclosed.'

"When we last heard from Ted, he was pushing his way onto that stage where his vice presidential designate, Carly Fiorina, was his warm up band ('*Let's welcome the next president of the United States. . .*'). Then in a flash, Carly had slipped off the platform. (It looked like she had walked off a diving board.) Cruz, however, remained oblivious to the possibility that aliens might have seized his running mate, and he continued to shake everyone's hand on stage, even those persons not paid to be up there.

"Cruz had hoped that by naming Carly early as his vice presidential running mate he might convince undecided voters that he was more sensitive to women than Trump. It could have worked, except that by this point in the campaign Carly, in her shrill attacks on Hillary, had begun sounding like the Wicked Witch of the West (*'I'll get you, my pretty, and your little dog, too!'*).

"Nor did it help Cruz that he rolled out Carly just about the time he had to deal with the Trump allegation that Ted's father, Rafael Cruz, had helped Lee Harvey Oswald, JFK's alleged assassin, pass out Fair Play for Cuba Committee literature in New Orleans in summer 1963.

"For those not dwelling in the knolls of conspiracy (*'Back and to the left'*), Oswald went to Louisiana in summer 1963 to establish street cred as a friend of Cuba. His signature moment came when he was passing out pro-Castro literature (*'Hands Off Cuba!'*) on a New Orleans sidewalk and he got into a scuffle with some anti-Castro Cubans. It was all captured on film that has been preserved and discussed ever since.

"Fifty-three years later, several tabloid newspapers, using facial recognition software, identified Ted's evangelical father, Rafael, as one of the pro-Castro Cubans who was helping Oswald leaflet in New Orleans, an allegation that became music to Trump's campaign, as he's a card-carrying birther, truther, denier, and conspiracist of the first rank. Finally, here was a campaign issue that Trump knew something about.

"Whether the New Orleans allegation is true or not—if you compare the pictures, it's not completely far-fetched and Cruz's father 'cannot remember' when he was in New Orleans in the

1960s—by this point the Cruz campaign had become a 24/7 Internet meme, with Ted having to deny not just his father's connections to Oswald, but also that his phone number was not listed with a Washington, D.C. escort service and that he had not fallen to the temptations of various campaign vixens. It was all too much. No wonder he snapped: 'Dad killed JFK, he's secretly Elvis, Jimmy Hoffa's buried in his backyard.' (The Hoffa news could have helped him in New Jersey, but by then Cruz was out of the race.)

"Ted thought he was running to purify the American soul, but instead his only associations were with the temptations of evil, and when it came time to 'suspend' his campaign he accidentally elbowed his wife in the head, yet another embrace gone wrong.

If he goes at all to the Cleveland convention, it will be to position himself to run again in 2020.

Making Trump Presidential?

"One of the hardest jobs on the campaign has been to convert Donald Trump into someone who is easily modified with the adjective 'presidential.'

"Left to his own devices Donnie thinks of politics as call-in radio or a Don Rickles TV roast, and he's at his best (this is a relative term) when he's calling in to some shock jock to rip into an opponent. He spoke of Rubio's brittle nerves at one debate: 'He wanted a full-length mirror. Maybe to make sure his pants weren't wet.'

"On these occasions Trump is 'Donnie from Queens,' and the subjects that interest him are the same as those that readers of the *New York Post* find compelling: hence, the mistresses of Bill Clinton, Hillary throwing her high heels at Secret Service agents, Chelsea's $10.5 million apartment and her ne'er-do-well money-manager husband, the saga of the Clintons' speaking fees, or whatever is floating in the gutter.

"All Trump needs to do for his campaign each morning is to skim Page Six (the gossip section) and open up the phone lines. The rest comes naturally, as he thinks and sounds like Rush Limbaugh, Sean Hannity, or Bill O'Reilly. (*Why would anybody listen to @MittRomney? He lost an election that should have easily been won against Obama. By the way, so did John McCain!*)

"After winning the majority of the delegates, however, his aides decided to buff up his image to 'presidential' status and toward that end they bought him a few Teleprompters and uploaded some speeches on foreign affairs, which Trump read with all the enthusiasm of a seventh-grader talking about climate change in the school's annual speech contest.

"To think that Trump has positions the way other candidates do is to miss entirely Trump's political appeal. Other than to build a wall on the Mexican border, Trump has no fixed ideals. At best he's a nihilist, happy to destroy things (ISIS, the EPA, etc.) but devoid of a political faith.

"In the course of a day, or even in the same speech, he can condemn George W. Bush for the war in Iraq (*We should have never been in Iraq*) and then pledge new battles against ISIS in the same country (*I would bomb the shit out of 'em. I would just bomb those suckers. That's right. I'd blow up the pipes. . . . I'd blow up every single inch. There would be nothing left*).

"On other days he equates American politics with resort development, as he writes, 'I have built an incredible company and have accumulated one of the greatest portfolios of real estate assets, many of which are considered to be among the finest and most iconic properties in the world. This is the kind of thinking the country needs.' Sounds like he would fix unemployment with room service.

"But one thing Trump does not do well is 'presidential.' He's too impatient with ceremony, and he'd rather ramble on like some Scotsman closing down a pub than read a formal speech to a chamber of commerce.

"Obama, as Reagan did, defines the presidency as a one-act play that is choreographed and produced each day for the evening news and cable feeds. (Visit Cuba, inspect a solar panel company, etc.) Trump, however, approaches the White House as a reality show with one star, endless apprentices, and audience points awarded for cutting one-liners.

"For example, despite needing Ohio to win the election, he hosed Governor John Kasich with these words: 'What people don't know about Kasich—he was a managing partner of the horrendous Lehman Brothers when it totally destroyed the economy!' Come September, Trump may be wondering why no one is meeting him at the Columbus airport.

The Boys on the Bus

"Denied the chance to write about Trump's politics (whatever they might be), the press has been reduced to analyzing peripheral issues in the campaign, such as Trump's treatment of women. I trust you saw that long *New York Times* article, "Crossing the Line: How Donald Trump Behaved With Women in Private." Would that they had written something as exhaustive about his real estate empire or how he dealt with the mob in Atlantic City?

"The point of the long exposé was to make Trump look like a star on *Playboy After Dark* (Hef with an ascot in the 1960s) or *SNL's* Leon Phelps, a.k.a. "the Ladies Man." The *Times* article cratered when several women interviewed for the story said they had been misquoted and that Trump has treated them 'with respect.' Even his ex-wives seem to like him.

"Nor was Trump brought low when a tape recording was released in which he calls a former *Penthouse* Pet of the Month 'a fucking third-rate hooker.' She said they had dated, and he denied it, but then he went on at length as if the reporter had called for his views on monetary policy or the Middle East.

"Finally speaking in sentences that his supporters could understand, Trump told the reporter: 'You think I am going out with a *Penthouse* Pet?. . . I never took her out. . . . Take a look at her picture. It's all bullshit. . . . It's just so fucking false. . . . *Penthouse*? Who the hell wants a *Penthouse* Pet? *Penthouse* is garbage, it's bankrupt, it's over. She's a 35-year-old *Penthouse* Pet? That's pretty pathetic.'

"So much for making Donald appear presidential.

Trump's Financial Disclosures

"Having established (in the interests of national security?) that he would never date a *Penthouse* Pet, Trump's bigger problem becomes his nonexistent relationship with the Republican political establishment.

"All former Republican presidents and nominees said they will not be attending the GOP convention in Cleveland, and Ronald Reagan's son Michael wrote, "This most likely would be the first time if my father was alive that he would not support the nominee of the GOP."

"For a while it looked as though Trump had found a way to work with House Speaker Paul Ryan, who has said he will 'vote for' Trump but then, on another occasion, denounced him as racist. So much for the party of accommodation.

"Does it matter that the Republican establishment hates Trump? I would say it does, because it puts Trump out there on his own, running a campaign that only has roots in the sidewalks of Trump Tower. And it denies his campaign third-party funding, if the Koch brothers and other heavy hitters are sitting on the wallets, which they are.

"Even Trump might not want to part with a billion dollars of his own money in a losing effort for the presidency. As Trump himself has said on many occasions, 'Sometimes your best investments are the ones you don't make.'

"Hillary is already $200 million ahead in fundraising while Trump is exchanging insults with the party chiefs. Strangely, Trump used the filing of his Personal Disclosure Statement to boast of his endless wealth ('in excess of $10 billion') and an annual income of $557 million, not exactly the words his fundraising team wants in the file when they go door-to-door looking for $2,000 checks.

"Without mainstream Republicans or the Bush family on his side (that cigarette boat has sailed), Trump may have an uphill battle in Florida, a must-win state for him. At one point recently, Donald posed with a Mexican dish and tweeted over it, 'I love Hispanics!,' But to carry such swing states as Florida, Arizona, and New Mexico, he will need to do more than order out from Taco Bell.

"And Trump cares so little about his potential running mate (often a sop to the party) that all he has done in that direction is to ask Dr. Ben Carson to keep his eye out for some suitable candidates.

"I see even Newt Gingrich has volunteered to become Donnie's prime minister so that he can run the government while Trump sticks to social media, but I doubt the White House has enough bandwidth to accommodate both egos.

A Few Predictions

"I know guys like you live in the forecasting world, and from me you want to know, from the inside, what will happen. But please keep in mind that insiders get this just as wrong as the newspapers:

"Trump will do better at the convention than predicted, but still leave Cleveland with the party underfunded and divided, and maybe with someone like Chris Christie or Ben Carson as his running mate. What can I say? They all like each other, and Donnie doesn't hire strangers.

"Bernie will vanish into the good night long before the Philadelphia convention, and on the second night, when the rules committee is debating time limits for the next convention, a Sanders video will run in the background (like some airplane safety announcement), but not get picked up by network television.

"Hillary will play it safe with her vice presidential candidate, and go with a centrist who can at least deliver one of the swing states. Hence Sherrod Brown of Ohio or Tim Kaine of Virginia. She will not pick another woman or someone from the Northeast, and whoever she picks will come with Bill's blessing, whose raspy voice in the campaign will increasingly start to sound like the Godfather's. (*In Sicily, women are more dangerous than shotguns.*)

"I still don't think that Hillary is out of the email woods with her server issues but most likely it will simmer (as Watergate did during 1972) and not reach a rolling boil until later. Time is running out for FBI Director James Comey to perp-walk some of her aides.

"Trump's campaign will be a ceaseless attack on the character of the Clintons: his philandering, her greed. In turn, they will attack Trump as Lyndon Johnson went after Barry Goldwater, as someone too unstable to have his finger on the bomb. Economics will be an afterthought, provided the markets don't dissolve.

"Each will use the word *cesspool* to describe the other's finances, and voters will not care. I can't tell you why, however.

"Hillary will run on the assumption that she is starting just short of a majority in the electoral college and focus all of her time on several swing states, notably Virginia, North Carolina, Iowa, Florida, and Ohio.

"Trump will ignore the advice of his professional staff (*'If they are so smart, how come they're not running for president?'*), and go after the Clintons in places where they should be most comfortable—in New Jersey, Maryland, Pennsylvania, New York, and even California. Think of Robert E. Lee marching on Gettysburg.

"His only chance to win will be to attack her in the Clinton heartland and hope that she stays focused (ever the good Democrat) on the peripheral swing states.

"Because he's a bad listener, Trump will be more prone to gaffs, not a good position to be in with the electorate in 2016. In turn, Hillary will remain teleprompter bland. (*'I want to give America a raise. . .'*)

"Hillary's risk will be if her demeanor suggests that the campaign is more a Clinton coronation than an election, and her poll numbers will remain abysmal among middle-aged men, young women, and working class voters. Hillary will stay strong among African Americans, older women, labor unions, government workers, and Latinos. She will also be the entitlement candidate, no small thing in entitled America.

"Trump will do 'better than expected' at the debates but not sufficiently well to move ahead in the polls. Overall he will win among white men, and lose among most other constituencies. By the end of the campaign voters will be 'done' with Trump and tune out his rantings. He'll start sounding like Austin Powers. (*'Behave, baby. . .yeah.'*)

"Come election day, since you asked, I predict the Democrats will win 337 electoral votes to 201 for the Republicans. She will keep New England and the Upper Midwest and do well on the West Coast. He will lose in Virginia (all those federal employees not keen on pink slips), North Carolina, and Florida. Game over. Will I see you in Cleveland?"

Who Owns the 2016 Election?

Tired of the election coverage—who isn't?—and the sound of Wolf Blitzer's voice, I reached out to someone on the inside, to get another take, and received the enclosed email, which began: "I figured between WikiLeaks, John Podesta, the Russians, Judicial Watch, the NSA, and the Clinton work-from-home server that this ought to find you. . ."

Two Clintons, No Trump

"I TAKE IT YOU WATCHED THE SECOND DEBATE? Or at least some of the beginning? Or at least the highlights? Or you read some of the press accounts that put it down as the 'ugliest debate in American history'?

"In general, these dispatches were written by those who would struggle to explain, without CliffsNotes, James Callender, Mark Hanna, or the insults hurled at the 1856 Republican presidential candidate, John C. Frémont. (A leading American newspaper summed up his platform as *'Free women, free land and Frémont. . .'*)

"And in 1864, here are some of the words that were used to describe Father Abraham Lincoln: 'Filthy story-teller; Ignoramus Abe; Despot; Old scoundrel; big secessionist; perjurer; liar; robber; thief; swindler; braggart; tyrant; buffoon; fiend; usurper;

butcher; monster; land-pirate; a long, lean, lank, lantern-jawed, high-cheeked-boned, spavined, rail-splitting stallion.'

"Actually, I found the second presidential debate refreshing in that both candidates 'hooked on' and fired broadsides at the opposing navy. Hillary went after Donald for racism, bigotry, misogyny, sexism, tax dodging, deceit, and wanting to scrap Obamacare while Donald (yes, he often looked like a professional wrestler coming over the ropes with a chair) went after her for cookie-cutter liberalism, Wall Street pandering, her email delete button, a tax-and-deficit spend mentality, talking the talk, and enabling her husband's degrading of women.

Visually, the stage, with deep blue carpeting and subdued lighting, looked like a cross between a mortuary and the set of *Let's Make a Deal*. (Monty Hall would be an improvement on the sanctimonious Anderson Cooper.) I guess everyone kept watching in the hope that behind door number three there might be a violated woman or 33,000 emails about Chelsea's wedding or her yoga class. (Huma to HRC: *'How come all we ever do is the Staff Pose?'*)

"Under the town hall format, the candidates were allowed to stroll around a conversation pit while answering the questions, most of which were filtered through the moderators.

"Both Cooper and Martha Raddatz wore the scowl of the Spanish Inquisition, at least when asking questions of Donald Trump about his sex confessional, which cast the Republican candidate in the remake of that great campaign musical, *My Fair Willie Horton*.

"When not responding or interrupting, Trump had the look of a man at an IRS audit (maybe he was?) while Clinton's handlers insisted that she smile and laugh cheerfully no matter how insulting Trump became or how biting her answers, which gave her the slightly crazed air of a Hitchcock character getting ready to do in her tormentor with scissors. *Dial T for Trump?*

Trump Updates William McKinley

"You might hate one or both candidates (most people do), but at least in the second debate the lines were correctly drawn from their historical precedents.

"If you strip away all the tweets and bluster, Republican Trump is a 'hard-money' man, a bit like William McKinley, eager to return American to the gold standard and raise tariffs to ward off foreign competition.

"At least in her scripted pronouncements, Clinton imagines herself as the spiritual heir of the Progressives, the likes of William Jennings Bryan or maybe 'Sockless' Jerry Simpson, although neither man ever pulled down $22 million by giving speeches to stock jobbers on Wall Street.

"Who won the second debate? Neither would be my answer. If you started watching the show thinking that Trump is a gutter candidate, you left the debate feeling the same way. He did not disappoint.

"And if you think the Clintons have gotten away with murder since Vince Foster's bloodless suicide, I doubt her performance will have changed your mind.

"In some ways it was one of those heavyweight fights that goes 15 rounds and ends in a draw. Trump avoided a knockdown and added some details to his policies; Hillary did well technically and with her jab, but failed to get a decision, despite mentioning Muhammad Ali by name. (I was a little surprised that Trump didn't then mimic Arsenio Hall and say: '*His momma named him Clay. I'm gonna call him Clay.*')

"In presidential debates, a tie favors the leader in the polls, so presumably Hillary left St. Louis feeling that the race is hers to win. As Mrs. Willy Loman says at the end of the play *Death of a Salesman*, 'We're free and clear.'

"Among the subjects omitted from the debate, except maybe in passing, were the Arab Spring, Israel's $38 billion in new American aid, Egypt's coup, the war in Gaza, welfare reform, Brexit, the European Union, the failures of American education, Social Security insolvency, China, Japan, infrastructure decay, youth unemployment, opioid addiction, global warming, Saudi Arabia and 9/11, banking reform, agricultural prices, high-speed rail, mental health, alcoholism, violence against children, the Keystone pipeline, pornography, and Deflategate.

So, Really, Who Was the Loser?

"Can Trump get back into the race? I don't see how. He has most Republican officials calling for his extended scalp, dropping poll numbers in such swing states as Ohio and Pennsylvania, reluctant donors of the Koch variety, and the dubious distinction (at least among presidential candidates) of caring more about the weight gains of Miss Universe than how to end the civil war in Syria.

"By contrast, Hillary can play a prevent defense for all of October, at least enough to win her the election. She need not make too many appearances (a few Oprah interviews ought to do the trick) nor take any radical positions (*I want to be president of all Americans. . .*').

"She can chant the doxology about health insurance, the war on terror, or income inequality, and as long as she 'sounds presidential,' she ought to convince enough voters that she is up to the job. Not even the traveling bevy of scorned mistresses, dressed up as *tricoteuses* beside Bill's guillotine, will sway many voters.

"Even if Hillary has another public health scare, I doubt that it would cost her the election, for the simple reason that the Clinton feel-good team has gotten too proficient at propping her up for the big games. Clinton starring in *Weekend at Hillary's* has more box office appeal than Donald's appearance in *Citizen Trump*. (*'You know, Mr. Bernstein, if I hadn't been very rich, I might have been a really great man.'*)

"Whatever the root medical cause of her dizziness and coughing, her staff has learned enough to keep both at bay, at least for 90 minutes during the prime-time debates and a few speeches. If, later in the campaign, she chucks a sickie here and there, no one will notice, especially if her staff mixes into the downtime some cable interviews and tweets from her fainting couch.

"After all, not even Hillary's cringe-worthy appearance on the faux talk show *Between Two Ferns* caused her any criticism. (Host Zach Galifianakis: *'What's the best way to reach you? Email?'*)

"Does it mean that her health can withstand the rigors of the presidency? Although I am not a doctor (nor do I play one on television), in person I can tell you that Hillary has ghostly qualities.

"Remember that weird press conference on the tarmac at Westchester County Airport, where she stood in front of humming jet engines and took unscripted questions for the first time in almost a year? To the voting public, that was a little one-act play meant to show the candidate ever on-the-go, about to board her chariot to distant coliseums.

"In fact, the runway Potemkin theater was a work of genius on the part of her staff, to keep the candidate from getting startled by the noise of cameras or press questions, and possibly putting her into one of those catatonic trances that are all over the Internet.

"The plane engines were white noise, like those waterfall tapes some people use to fall asleep, only in this case it was the voters who were sleepwalking beside Hillary.

Trump Takes a Physical

"Not that Donald Trump should get a pass on his health, as he has been no more forthcoming than Hillary in releasing his medical records. At least she came up with a form letter from her family doctor and could toss around the phrase 'seasonal allergies,' which the Clinton campaign would trot out in press releases if she were mauled by a tiger.

"For his part Trump let his doctor check him out in his limo and then went over the results with Dr. Oz on afternoon television. (A checkup on TV isn't something that comes with Obamacare.)

"Trump's borderline obesity, however, rated almost no mention in campaign coverage, just as neither candidate (Hillary is almost 69; Trump is 70) was asked during either debate about their health issues.

"That Hillary managed to dodge a public neurological exam after keeling over at the World Trade Center is testament to the savviness of her campaign staff, which by comparison makes those around Trump look as though they are auditioning for an amateur hour. In addition, Trump has gone through campaign directors as if they were Mar-a-Lago caddies.

"Neither candidate is much good at listening to their staff, but at least Hillary has a real one while those around Trump have the air of apprentices. It explains why his campaign, at best, is a traveling circus limited to the big tents that will squeeze aboard his gilded Boeing 757.

Why Trump Won the Nomination

"Trump won the Republican nomination because of his midnight tweets and off-the-cuff insults (*'Look at that face! Would anyone vote for that?'*), which played well to a primary electorate weaned on the howling of Sean Hannity, Rush Limbaugh, and Laura Ingraham. But a national campaign needs more than a few Fox & Friends.

"Part of the reason Trump's campaign came apart over the sex tape is because it's a one-man band. Since the summer, the pros in the Republican Party have been waiting for Hillary's campaign to dig up the Howard Stern interviews or to put Trump's taxes in prime time. (You have to admire them: the leaked 1040 forms were mailed to the *Times* in a Trump Organization envelope.)

"Everyone knew they were coming, just as Hillary ought to have known that somewhere a transcript of her Wall Street encomiums or deleted emails would surface. But Trump always knows more than his campaign operatives (*'If he's so smart, how come he is willing to work for $75K?'*), and he ignored the advice to develop a strategy for either disclosure.

"You can be sure that Clinton's staff has enough raunchy revelations to fill the news cycle from now until election day, for there to be a daily 'Trump outrage.' (Great moments in journalism, this from the *Huffington Post*: 'There Are Transcripts Of Trump's Unaired Moments On *The Apprentice*. . .')

"In the 1990s Donald told Howard Stern how women approach him: 'They'll walk up, and they'll flip their top, and they'll flip their panties.' This was years before he was popping Tic Tacs with Billy Bush.

Getting Down and Dirty

"The irony of Pussygate, for Trump anyway, is that it was a form of Swift boating, but in reverse, this time going from the Democrats to the Republicans.

"During much of the campaign, the great unanswered question was whether Trump could make any electoral mileage from

Bill Clinton's sexual wanderlust. Or if he might hint broadly that Hillary—to use an old Hollywood expression—is 'a gal with her own library card.'

"In his free-form interviews and speeches, Trump is always alluding to such fixtures of the road as Jennifer Flowers, Juanita Broderick, Paula Jones, and The Energizer, not to mention Bill's global joyriding (by one report, some 26 flights) on Jeffrey Epstein's plane, nicknamed the *Lolita Express* for the age and in-flight entertainment of its hostesses.

"But now Hillary's A-team of campaign pros has managed to dress Trump in the open raincoat of a sexual predator, much the way W's team made war hero John Kerry look like a deserter in the Vietnam War, although it was George W. Bush who went AWOL from his National Guard unit in Alabama.

"From now until election day, however, it will be impossible for Trump to play the sex card on either Clinton. In thinking about the fall, Donald thought he would be campaigning from Atlantic City, dealing strip poker; instead all he has is a cold hand of Go Fish.

"Why is Hillary so good at the blame game? Look at how she uses Putin's Russia as a whipping boy for whatever problem plagues her campaign. Mention the email scandal, and right away Hillary is on about the Russians hacking 'the system' to influence the election.

"On one hand she says that none of her unprotected, home-brewed emails—those with the words 'top secret' on the subject line—were ever stolen. On the other, mention anything about cyber security, and she's blaming Putin and Russia for wanting to tilt the roulette wheel of the American election.

"By extension, Hillary casts the Putin-loving Trump as a fellow-traveler—in the great McCarthyite tradition of naming names. Putin is also to blame for all of the violence in Syria and the Middle East, not to mention fluoride in the water system, Bill's account at Ashley Madison, and why Goldman Sachs paid her $675,00 to recycle some stump speeches in the corporate boardroom.

"By the way, if you read the transcripts on WikiLeaks, what stands out is how little Hillary understands finance. The $225,000-a-pop speeches, chock full of platitudes, read like Chamber of Commerce brochures or *My Weekly Reader* editorials. I am a little surprised the banks didn't ask for a refund, for what in the trade is called 'unjust enrichment.'

Whither Mike Pence

"Is there anything to the rumor that Mike Pence will abandon the ticket over Trump's *Access Hollywood* hot mic tape? (The full quote, which falls a little short of Abraham Lincoln's second inaugural address, reads, *'And when you're a star, they let you do it. . . . Grab them by the pussy. You can do anything.'*) I am sure Pence has had some discussions with his staff about jumping off the sinking ship, and leaving the rats behind.

"If he did, and were Trump to lose to the general election, Pence would become the frontrunner for 2020, when presumably the country will be tired of yet another President Clinton and an unimpeachable Congress.

"Pence on the moral high road would certainly look better than Ted Cruz, who, in a career move, finally endorsed Donald about an hour before Trump was overheard recounting his *Playboy* lust-for-life moves in the recorded bus conversation.

"The reason I don't think Pence will bolt the ticket is because he might become the lightning rod for all the GOP establishmentarians who gave up on Trump after the sex tape and withdrew their endorsements. That list is a mile long (see Ryan, Paul et al.), but it remains to be seen if they will emerge from the electoral wreckage of the Trump campaign as traitors or idealists.

"Presumably the Trump doubters have bolted to save their own skin—that is especially the case with many Republican senators up for reelection, including senators John McCain, Marco Rubio, and Kelly Ayotte. But imagine if Trump somehow wins or at least holds serve, and if he emerges as the leader of the party after the election.

"Yes, I find a Trump resurrection almost impossible to imagine, but 2016 is a strange year so don't overlook the unimaginable, and the fault line between candidate Trump and the Republican establishment could well be the line that will eventually split the party into two new parties, Conservatives and Republicans.

"For me, the interesting aspect of Trump's sex confessions isn't that he's a groper (ever since Warren Harding most presidential candidates have had something warm in their closets), but that it is the issue that highlights how the election is a watershed between mainstream media, which is effectively dead, and the populism of social media.

Who Owns the 2016 Election?

"The 2016 election belongs to Twitter and BuzzFeed, which at best are the captions to cartoons. The boys on the bus are not Timesmen so much as bloggers, and Trump's sex tape has all the ingredients of an Instagram scoop—video that could play in 30 seconds, eavesdropping, furtive sex of the Tinder kind, horny Page Six celebrities, and, in response, moral outrage that can be expressed in 140 characters. What more can a democracy want? Who has time to read de Tocqueville anyway?

"For all I know, the affair might actually swing millennials to Trump, much the way that scandal hasn't exactly done in the Kardashians. Look at the crowds flocking to Trump rallies after the debate while Hillary still has to bus in her claque.

"According to electoral orthodoxy, Trump is roadkill, hoist, so to speak, by his own petard. He will lose Ohio, North Carolina and Florida, and thus the presidency. His hope of a new coalition that would turn Pennsylvania, Wisconsin, and North Carolina into red states is dead.

"In those swing states, the moral majority will recoil at his boorish sexism and elect Hillary Clinton. On her side, presumably, are women, minorities, and college-educated voters, few of whom ever tried to grope the host of the Miss America pageant.

"Trump will only manage to carry the Second Amendment crowd and those who think that Hillary wants to deliver America to what, in the lingua franca of the right, is called 'globalism'—a loose confederation that includes the UN and Agenda 21, gun controllers, the *New York Times*, abortionists, atheists, George Soros, the EU, Iranian sympathizers, the Federal Reserve Bank, Davos, married gays, and Angela Merkel.

"In the language of *Star Wars*, this could be the Trade Federation that Darth Trump is pledged to eliminate, at least in his fervid, 3 a.m. imagination. I can't see him winning—not during this year's ratings sweep anyway—but what will happen when the standard-bearer for Trumpism isn't someone as capricious as The Donald. Then you might want to hide the china.

"That's all for now. Write me in a day or two. By then, the world will have changed."

Sex, Lies, and
Videotaped Impeachments

"Republics come to an end through luxury;
monarchies through poverty."

—Montesquieu

Sex and the Presidential City

WHY DOES EVERYONE THINK that presidential campaigns are about "issues," when anyone over the age of consent knows they are all about sex? But it says a lot about the lasting power of Viagra that this is still the case when we have a couple of 70-year-olds on the ballot. (*"For an election lasting more than four years, please call your doctor."*)

In last week's newspaper there was a report on the 10th or 11th woman (I have lost track) to come forward to say that Donald Trump had made suggestive and "inappropriate" advances to her during a golf tournament that took place about 10 years ago.

The woman in question is Jessica Drake, who during her press conference announced that at the time of the tournament, she was working in the "the adult industry" (that's what *People* magazine calls porn) for Wicked Pictures (the 20th Century Fox of gang banging) when the randy Donald kissed and hugged her in his room.

Trump was already in his pajamas when she knocked on his door, together with two friends. Normally, in the adult business, when three porn stars knock on your hotel door, it's considered foreplay.

When Trump's effusive greeting of Miss Drake did not lead to more snuggling, let alone the suggestion to preview some of her work on the hotel television, he offered her $10,000 to satisfy his suite dreams.

Drake again demurred, saying that the next morning she needed to get back to Los Angeles "for work." By that point in her career she had already notched screen credits for *Extreme Doggie* and *Fornocopia*. I would mention other titles, but as they say at the *New York Post*, "This is a family newspaper."

That rejection prompted Donald to offer Jessica an early morning ride (of shame?) on his Trump airliner back to LA, which still didn't turn the trick.

Trump Takes a Shine to a Porn Star

Then last week, in the presence of her lawyer, Gloria Allred (the Perry Mason of many cases against Bill Cosby), Miss Drake tearfully repeated in prime time her shock and dismay that Mr. Trump had tried to take liberties with her reputation, which, after all, includes the 2009 Adult Video News Award for the "Best Double Penetration Sex Scene" in her classic work, *Fallen*.

Drake said she was coming forward now to stand in "solidarity" with the other women Trump has manhandled, although there were suggestions that her outing was timed to coincide with the launch of Drake's new online store, where devoted viewers can purcase such classics as her *Guide to BDSM for Beginners*, among other titles.

Normally scenes such as the one I am describing would be consigned to John Oliver, Monty Python, or *Saturday Night Live*, but in the new normal of presidential politics, even Miss Drake gets a respectful hearing on the issues. For example, the next day the *Huffington Post* reported: "Woman Says Trump Sexually Assaulted Her, Offered Her $10,000 For Sex." The deadpan *New York Times* wrote: "Ms. Drake, who appeared Saturday with the women's rights lawyer Gloria Allred, said Mr. Trump had hugged and kissed her and the other women without permission." The headline in *New York Magazine* read: "Adult Actress Jessica Drake Details Trump Assault, Blasts Him for 'Uncontrollable Misogyny."

Look, I have no doubt that Trump is a pig who routinely gropes and propositions women, but since when does the press in a presidential election have to source its stories in the "adult" industry?

Rerunning the Clinton Reality Show

Sadly, the answer to this question dates to winter 1992 when Bill and Hillary Clinton figured out that unless a presidential candidate has a sexual storyline, few of the voters will pay much attention to their positions on nuclear disarmament or welfare reform. During the 1992 Super Bowl, the Clintons appeared on a halftime special of *60 Minutes* to deny jointly (Bill: *"That allegation is false"*) that he had ever had an affair with Gennifer Flowers, who lived in Little Rock, Arkansas when Bill was governor and often out jogging. In this vaudeville performance, Hillary played the straight man, adding: "You know, I'm not sitting here—some little woman standing by my man like Tammy Wynette." (At least she didn't reference The Eagles.)

Only in 1998, under oath in a sworn deposition, did Bill admit to having a 12-year affair with Ms. Flowers. But neither her allegations in 1992, nor his lying about it, cost him the election that year. Just the opposite: Clinton's wanderlust might have won him sympathy among the voters (no strangers to sexual boredom) who found they had more in common with a soft-shell Baptist (Bill) than an uptight Protestant (George H.W. Bush).

Nor did Clinton's impeachment in 1998 for lying about his affair with Monica Lewinsky under oath in the Paula Jones case hurt his post-presidential career (worth $200 million +) or the electoral prospects of his wife in 2016. But it did turn sexuality into a mainstream presidential campaign issue, which is one of the reasons why this year's race seems only to be about sex.

Trump Uses Bill's Hall Pass

No doubt the Clintons do find some delicious irony in Trump's groping charges, as payback for what they view as the Republican use of sexuality to impeach Bill in 1998 and, in 2016, for the GOP plan to make his many adulterous affairs fair game for their campaign soundbites. (Cut to an online image of the White House and over it a fading picture of Bill smoking a cigar, with the caption "Here we go again?")

Without the pageant-loving, casino operating Donald Trump as the Republican nominee in 2016, Hillary Clinton could well have been vulnerable on the sexual front, with Bill's mistresses steady fodder for negative ads and the many allegations from his scorned lovers that Hillary organized the slut-shaming. Instead of the 2016 election turning on Hillary's marriage to Hugh Hefner's doppelgänger, the storyline that has played best in the media is Donald's secret life as a groper.

The press actually has given Trump a pass for his adultery but zeroed in on his groping, in part because he confessed to it on an NBC videotape and also because—think of ratings—gropers belong in the same basket of deplorables as child abusers and others lurking on subways, crowed elevators, or near schoolyards.

Best of all for the Clintons, politically anyway, is that the charge of groping is impossible for Trump to refute. Even denying it sounds sleazy. And it colors all aspects of the campaign. To wit: the *New York Times* headline when at Gettysburg Trump outlined his vision for America: "Donald Trump Pledges to 'Heal Divisions' (and Sue His Accusers)."

A Campaign of Scarlet Letters

For its mudslinging, I am sure the Trump campaign has spent many long hours brainstorming how to tar Hillary as a lesbian. But even that innuendo has fallen flat, despite the rumor mongering that she's in a Boston marriage with her assistant Huma Abedin (whose husband, Anthony Weiner, is otherwise distracted in high school chat rooms).

Several of Bill's former lovers (Sally Miller, Dolly Kyle, and Flowers) have tried to play up Bill's pillow talk that Hillary prefers the nighttime company of women. But none of these allegations have gone further than Infowars or the supermarket press. (*"Hillary Hit Man Tells All!"*) Nor have out-of-wedlock children, a staple of the 1884 campaign (as was chanted to Grover Cleveland: *"Ma, Ma, Where's my pa?"*), gotten much play in this year's presidential race.

Trump and his casino gumshoes have put considerable effort into tracking down the rumor that Danney Williams is Bill Clinton's illegitimate son by a Little Rock prostitute named Bobbie Ann Williams. Trump invited Danney (a sympathetic man) to the third presidential debate, as if to press on Bill a Scarlet Letter. Despite Williams looking very much like President Bill, the story got no more traction than did the news that Malik Obama, the president's shunned half-brother, is supporting Trump. He, too, got a debate invitation, to sit in the box presumably marked "Shame."

Also in the dustbin of history are the allegations that Flowers aborted Bill's baby in 1977 and the whispering campaign (a great political standby when proof is elusive) that Chelsea is the product of an affair between Hillary and her then law firm colleague, Webb Hubbell. The Williams and Hubbell stories come with some convincing Internet similarities, at least in the photographs, although in both cases politically, this rumor milling whiplashed against

Trump, as voters have only equated such tawdry allegations with his birther past, something that has stuck as campaign mud.

Birtherism Has Twins

Technically, birtherism doesn't directly involve sex, although it lingers on its fringes, as it speaks to Barack Obama's illegitimacy, his foreign allegiances, and possibly disputed paternity, including the claim that Frank Marshall Davis was actually Obama's biological father (another subterranean creed of Trumpism). Again, the documentary proof is a series of look-alike photographs, as close as the Internet gets to DNA. That Davis was an American Communist works well in the campaign, as it suggests the origins of Obama's political genetic code.

Ironically, for all his efforts at smear, Trump came out the loser in the debates when Hillary nailed him to birtherism, which has become a convenient code word for Trump's racism, misogyny, and intolerance of immigrants, especially Muslims. Nor, in response, did Trump have any luck in linking the birther movement to Clinton's 2008 campaign, when, according to Donald, consigliere-journalist Sidney Blumenthal delighted in the suggestion that Barack was born in Kenya. Instead, the debate claim only made Trump look disingenuous. Clinton got a pass on what her campaign may or may not have insinuated in 2008. And at this point, no one cares. But voters do remember Trump as the Imperial Wizard of birtherism.

How Republicans Are Playing the Sex Card

Republicans can only blame themselves for wanting to divide the electorate in 2016 along lines of sexual preference or deviance, although this strategy was based on Hillary being the

Democratic nominee and anyone other than Trump standing for the Republicans. Had the GOP nominee been Carly Fiorina, Jeb Bush, or John Kasich, Clinton Inc. might well have been vulnerable to possible storylines about infidelity, illegitimacy, and rape. (Cue up the Paula Jones description of Bill, during a business meeting, exposing himself in a Little Rock hotel and settling her lawsuit for $850,000.)

Instead, the Republicans went with the polyamorous Trump, who, in addition to three marriages, has bragged on morning radio about his success with young women and who since 1996 has been leering at Miss Universe contestants—a bit like Austin Powers. (*"Shall we shag now, or shall we shag later?"*) With Trump's resume of creepy perversion, you might have thought that the Republicans would drop sexual misconduct from the electoral playbook. Instead, they doubled down to make the case that both Clintons, if elected, would turn the White House into a strip club.

Not only did the Clintons shrug off such innuendo, but, in response, they said (in effect), if they did, it would be to cater to the likes of players such as Donald J. Trump (leisure suit and open collar optional). For the moment—and I can't see anything changing in the last days of the campaign—the accepted wisdom of most front pages is that Donald Trump has groped as many women as Tiger Woods has watched pole dancers in Vegas. Even the gallery of "their women" looks about the same.

Conversely, few voters seem to care that Bill might have forced himself on several women or that Hillary helped to cover up his brutality. That's a narrative of the 1990s, which is perhaps the last time Austin Danger Trump read the newspaper. (*"I've been frozen for 30 years. I've got to see if my bits and pieces are still working."*) For most voters in 2016, names such as Kathleen Willey or Juanita Broaddrick are as lost in time as Nan Britton, who just before the 1920 election bore a love child with then candidate Senator Warren

Harding. Britton and the child got Republican hush money and a sad little house in Asbury Park, New Jersey. After Harding won, she was invited to the White House but their affair, so to speak, was kept in the closet.

Elections as Political Sitcoms

If you think about elections as political sitcoms, in 1960 the Kennedys had to run as Rob and Laura Petrie on *The Dick Van Dyke Show*, complete with twin beds, long flannel pajamas, and prudent kisses on the cheek to say good night, even if *The JFK Reality Show* would make Trump, Bill Clinton, and Tiger look like apprentices at adultery.

Come 2016, only something that resembles *Modern Family* and a desperate-housewives reality show can crack network prime time, and who better to put on air than The Clintons, with their *Dallas*-like money, communal sexuality, and more illicit storylines than *CSI*? By contrast, Trump might well be in a booth at a grainy peep show. For more than 20 years, Bill and Hillary have been bringing us seasons of lust, affairs, "I-did-not-have-sex-with-that-woman," Vince Foster, Travelgate, foundation slush funds, basement servers, commodity trading, Whitewater, Bosnian snipers, pay-to-play, Benghazi, lost emails, and the like, and the ratings only continue to go up. Sure, *The Apprentice* was fun for a few episodes, but the sameness of insulting young people grew tedious. How is that supposed to compete with Bill making a pass at Huma, while her husband goes to prison for airing his junk, and Chelsea finding out about her real father. Next on *The Clintons*?

Getting the Word
on Election Day

Gobsmacked about the outcome of the election on November 8, 2020, I reached out to someone in the know, and got this response:

"It comes down to this: if the election had been a week earlier or a week later, Hillary would have won both the popular vote and the electoral college. But on Election Day, November 8, 2016, she lost, and she lost because luck wasn't with her. Napoleon liked to say, 'I would rather my generals be lucky than able.'

"Sorry to say, Hillary ran out of luck exactly on Election Day, as when some undefeated powerhouse NFL team loses to the Detroit Lions or the New York Jets. Run that election 10 times, and I bet Hillary wins nine times, but this was the unlucky 10th, and Trump is now your president (and you might want to hide the silver).

"Part of the reason she lost is that she took her foot off the pedal. As they say in Washington, she was rearranging the drapes in the Oval Office, thinking about her transition team, making calls to prospective secretaries of state, getting briefed on Iran, and not paying much attention to the (concerning) polling numbers from Michigan or Pennsylvania, which normally give their electoral votes to Democratic presidential candidates, even those who are sleep walking.

"I don't think Hillary was being arrogant. I think she was being a combination of prudent and lazy. She'd had that pneumonia in September, and remember when she almost keeled over in lower Manhattan, and the press showed her with rubber legs on a few occasions, getting carried up stairs. So come the end of October she figured, 'Why do I need to drag my sorry ass to Green Bay or Ocala to speak to a bunch of people who will vote for me anyway?' Look at her campaign schedule in September and October: she was working from home.

"I am not saying that a last-minute whistle-stop tour across the heartland on Harry Truman's campaign train would have tipped the scales, but it might have shown the voters that Hillary was hungry to win, not simply inheriting something that was written into a will or trust agreement. (*And I leave to my beloved Hillary one presidency, to use as she most sees fit. . . . '*)

"Yes, she did that Election Eve rally with Barack and Michelle in Philly (not in Lewisburg, Sunbury, Tamaqua or Jim Thorpe, mind you), and she did her pointing thing at various A-listers in the skyboxes, but it felt more like an interview with Oprah or Ellen than someone giving hell to the Republicans. She didn't look outraged at all the injustices most voters have to live with, and I think they figured: 'She's cashing in chips she got from the casino.'

"Look, it didn't help that for, what, six months, a year, Hillary never could put to rest all her computer issues—the lost emails, the server in Chappaqua, WikiLeaks, or the state secrets apparently on Anthony Weiner's laptop that he was using to send pictures of his junk to high school cheerleaders. None of that made sense to voters, even those who cannot figure out how to sign up for AOL or hook up a printer.

"My own take is that Hillary is always online, but never sure how she got there, and that in her technological insecurity her response was just to keep more and more copies of everything—on her home server, on Huma's laptop, on her four cell phones—and then when that flatfoot James Comey went looking for state secrets, he kept finding them everywhere.

"Mind you, I would not trust Comey as far as I can throw him, and he's what—six foot eight? Comey's dream was to become the Indispensable G-Man, J. Edgar Hoover II, the confidant of every president, even those he was blackmailing. When he opened his investigation, he figured Hillary would win, and that he was doing her a solid, saying, 'Nothing to see here, folks, just keep moving on.'

"Then, when it turned out that the Russians, Roger Stone, Steve Bannon, Anthony Weiner—and, who knows, maybe Sacco and Vanzetti—all had copies of her emails, he figured he might as well take another look 'at the file' on the off chance that Trump won, and he would need to curry favor at Mar-a-Lago. It just so happened that he mixed his curry 10 days before the election, which voters took to mean: the top cop thinks Hillary's a Manchurian Candidate.

"It didn't help on the last weekend, when most undecided voters make up their mind, that Hillary looked more like a Soviet mole than Joan of Arc. As the pros like to say, 'she had a lot of negatives.' She had the baggage of 25 years of Clinton scandal fatigue—Vince Foster, Whitewater, those legal bills, Paula Jones, Monica, the blue dress, the Clinton Foundation, yadda, yadda, yadda, and come Tuesday morning, when you're rushing to work and it's raining, and you have to line up in some elementary school where no one can find your voter registration card, you say to yourself, 'Let's see what this Trump has to offer.'

"Look, I don't think Trump had anything to offer that cor-responded with the values of a democratic republic, the found-ing fathers, or what Abraham Lincoln called 'the better angels of our nature.' He's a con man, a film noir grifter who took over his father's operation in Queens and managed to bilk many Wall Street banks, the New York Stock Exchange, and an endless number of widows and orphans in Florida so that his Board-walk empire in Atlantic City could then go bust and so that he could find solace in the arms of various porn stars and beauty pageant queens—those he paid and those he wrestled onto the canopied beds.

"His only success was playing a board chairman on a prime time game show, which made him money and gave him the image of a savvy corporate manager—just what a republic that thinks television is real needed to 'clean up the mess in Washington.'

"In the last days before the election, he was lucky beyond luck that none of his voters, especially soccer moms in those vans, held the *Access Hollywood* pussy-grabbing tapes against him, and that in key swing states—Michigan, Pennsylvania, Florida, North Carolina, Wisconsin—an unlikely coalition of white men, non-college graduates, white women, and senior citizens decided to hand the keys of the national car to someone who makes a living selling stolen hubcaps.

"One more thing: in many elections, people vote against the incumbent just because they've had it—with something. . .their boss at work, their losing baseball team, their receding hairline, you name it. In this election, because she's been around since Cal-vin Coolidge, Hillary was the incumbent, a stalking horse for a Clinton Risorgimento or maybe an Obama shadow presidency. To the casual voter—and most voters spend more time planning a Super Bowl party than picking a president—there was something fishy about another Clinton presidency, and just enough of them said, 'I ain't buying,' so that Trump can add the White House to his list of underwater properties."

Book Two

2020
Joe Biden's
Excellent Adventure

"There is a certain satisfaction in coming down to the lowest ground of politics, for we get rid of cant and hypocrisy."

—Ralph Waldo Emerson

Live
From the Iowa Caucuses

"It is easy to settle the world on a soap box."

—David Lloyd George

Requiem for a Lightweight: Pete Buttigieg

MY FIRST SOUNDING, at least from the 2020 political echo chamber, of the South Bend mayor came a few months ago, when my wife announced over breakfast that some of her sisters liked the cut of his jib. I looked him up online, came across McKinsey and the Rhodes scholarship, and, like the rest of the country that lives without television, struggled with the pronunciation of his Maltese surname, Buttigieg, until I learned that a simple "Mayor Pete" would suffice.

In the intervening two months, I thought little more about the mayor, other than to take note that his ranking in the early polls consigned him to that great electoral no-man's-land of about 5 percent that he was sharing with the likes of Cory Booker, Kamala Harris, and Beto O'Rourke, all of whom, someday, might regret that they had only one soundbite to give for their country. As best as I could determine, Mayor Pete was stalking a constituency of the middle ground, by uttering thoughtful cliches about the Rust Belt, the deficit, sexual equality, cops on the beat in South Bend, and the wars on terror—in which he was deployed as an onward Christian soldier.

His dream is to survive long enough in the primaries so that as a last man standing he could offer himself as an alternative either to the Democratic Shining Path (Elizabeth Warren, Bernie

Sanders) or Joe Biden's Walmart he's-hopeless-but-he-can-win Amtrak centrism. To get to the late rounds of the fight, all Mayor Pete has to do is run ahead of Beto O'Rourke (D-Vaudeville) and raise enough money (think of those earnest appeals to support public radio) to keep the campaign wolves away from the door.

Pete Plays the Y

My chance to hear Mayor Pete in front of what game-show Hollywood calls a "live audience" came when I recently flew to New York City and figured out that, while I was there, he would be speaking at the 92nd Street YMHA, which is more famous for its literary round tables featuring Norman Mailer and George Plimpton than as *a place you can go. . .when you're short on your dough.*

I managed to get a ticket for the talk and showed up about 20 minutes before the opening bell. Already there was a long line of Buttigieg supporters queueing to get in and a few security types loitering near the front doors. But this wasn't one of those Trump rallies from 2016 with sniffer dogs or one of those bus drivers from the movie *Slap Shot* denting up the campaign bus with a sledge-hammer. . . "*makin' it look mean.*" This was the Whole Foods crowd lining up for some presidential latte.

I had thought that there might be a warm-up band at the 92nd Street Y—perhaps some speeches by a few state senators already on the Buttigieg train—but instead all that greeted us on the main stage were two armchairs and a coffee table, suitable either for Gestalt therapy or a campaign rally, which in 2020 adds up to the same thing.

Once the house was full and the lights were dimmed, Mayor Pete and his questioner entered from stage left, where presumably they had been idling in a green room (that inner sanctum of the celebrity class). Were Mayor Pete more a politician (and less a culturally sensitive icon), he would have chosen to enter the hall from the lobby and would have swept down one of the aisles with handshakes, high-fives, fist bumps, and some of those Hillary finger-points for his faithful. Instead he walked on stage with that look of embarrassment and surprise that comes naturally to guests picked randomly from the crowd on *Let's Make a Deal*.

Pete's schtick is that of a working mayor, so he arrived on stage wearing a dress shirt and necktie but no suit jacket, as if maybe, just before the rally, he had been chairing a sanitation meeting or manning a 24-hour crisis hotline. But for whatever reason—his thin frame, his diffidence in front of a crowd—Pete looks like a floor walker at Barney's, maybe someone assigned to men's shoes.

The moderator this evening was Jonathan Capehart of the *Washington Post* editorial board and various talking head assignments. On paper, Capehart is a winner of the Pulitzer Prize and someone who can occasionally come up with prime-time insights into the Mueller Report on *PBS NewsHour*. On this occasion, however, he was appearing less as a grand inquisitor and more in the cheerleader role of Ellen DeGeneres, and he came on stage with the intention of "grilling" Mayor Pete on the joys of his marriage to Chasten Glezman or asking "How did it feel?" to appear on the cover of *Time* magazine. Clearly Capehart comes out of the bended-knee, finishing school of journalism.

A First at Oxford

Bizarrely, at least for someone who needs to win Ohio, Florida, and North Carolina to be elected president, Mayor Pete began the evening with a long description of his Rhodes scholarship at Oxford (England, not Old Miss), where he took "a first in PPE" (philosophy, politics, and economics) at Pembroke College. (William Pitt the Younger and Monty Python's Eric Idle are among its famous graduates.)

Perhaps confusing a campaign rally with a search committee at the Kennedy School of Government, Mayor Pete painstakingly went through what was required of a Rhodes scholar to get a degree from Pembroke (he had to make up a year's worth of economics classes in 10 weeks) and what it means to be awarded "a first." (He got his degree with "first class honors." It means an A, although for a few awkward moments Capehart kept gushing about Pete's brilliance for finishing "first" in his class at Oxford.)

The son of professors at Notre Dame, Mayor Pete loves academic questions and will, with very little prompting, explain to his listeners how he was always the smartest kid in the class. And if he was running for a position on the faculty senate at Oberlin College, I might report that he was qualified. At one point, sounding as though he was at a teach-in, he said gravely, "We have to find the right kind of vocabularies to talk about progressive values."

Acting like a kindly thesis advisor during orals, Capehart carefully went through each line of Mayor Pete's curriculum vitae, just so the audience would not miss the fact that after the years at Harvard and Oxford, Pete also got his ticket punched as a 29-year-old mayor in South Bend and as an ensign in the U.S. naval reserve, in which he was deployed as an intelligence officer to NATO command in Kabul. Oh, and by the way, he also worked as a consultant for McKinsey and, more recently, found time to write his memoir, *Shortest Way Home*. It's painting/writing by the numbers, so any aspiring candidate can sound like the father-dreaming Barack Obama (*"A river is made drop by drop"*). In Pete's telling of American history, the president is the person with the highest SAT scores and the best college essay.

The Importance of Being Mayor Pete

For all of Buttigieg's resume stops—in Oxford, South Bend, Kabul, and Cambridge, Mass.—the only subject on which he can muster much passion is that of The Importance of Being Mayor Pete. (As Brooklyn advance man Walt Whitman said, "*I celebrate myself, and sing myself. . .*")

On Afghan politics, the infighting of the Democratic Party, the budget deficit, or how McKinsey pads its billing hours, Mayor Pete sounds like a shy freshman, someone who has yet to finish the required reading. But on the subject of himself, Buttigieg might well be a tenured professor. Whenever Capehart asked him why he wanted to be president or whether he was qualified, Mayor Pete's answer was usually a soliloquy about his immaculate resume, Ivy degrees, sexual evolution, language fluency, or the high tables at which he has dwelled on St. Augustine, Teilhard de Chardin, Gary Wills, or Graham Greene.

Pete's big on theologists and writers agonizing about their faith, as was Jimmy Carter. After university, Pete transitioned from his childhood Gipper Catholicism to the Anglican and Episcopal churches (Rhodes scholars on their knees). When Capehart brought up the political question of faith, Mayor Pete responded brightly, "We could talk about this for an hour."

During a conversation with Mayor Pete, you get a lot of blurbs about "changing the course of the country" and allusions to a "new generation" and the symbolism of running as the first openly gay candidate, but you get almost nothing on Israel's occupation of the West Bank, the national debt as a payday loan, the opioid crisis, or America's potholed infrastructure. But then, I suppose, if you are running on a Selfie platform, those issues are as quaint as William McKinley speaking out on the tariff question or Andrew Jackson denouncing the Second Bank of the United States (*"The bank, Mr. Van Buren, is trying to kill me, but I will kill it. . ."*).

For a presidential candidate, Mayor Pete struck me as someone who is physically awkward, the kind of man who would prefer wandering the stacks at Harvard's Widener Library more than he would revel in kissing babies at an Iowa county fair. If you met Pete at work, you might think—at least from his brown shoes and reticent demeanor—that he was yet another outside auditor lost on his way to the cafeteria. And, yes, it is difficult to imagine him taking on Vladimir Putin and the Russians. Think of Obama in Syria, but without all the backbone.

Buttigieg has the long fingers of a concert pianist and, in person, looks a bit like Mister Rogers (*"It's a beautiful day in the neighborhood. . ."*), if not former Massachusetts Governor Michael Dukakis (who would himself occasionally, during his failed presidential campaign, make jokes in Latin). Mayor Pete also speaks in the halting cadences of an old man—or at least a full professor—and for much of the evening, I found myself wondering if the youngest candidate in the Democratic field wasn't, by chance, the oldest, and one prone to the received wisdom imported from Harvard faculty lounges.

Buttigieg did warm to Capehart's cringeworthy confession that the journalist's mother likes Mayor Pete, but otherwise the only passion he brought to the event was during an Oprah-like moment, when he spoke in teary defense of Chasten, saying: "I think all of us have a lot to repent for. . .but one thing I should absolutely not be repentant for, in the context of my marriage, is that I am in love with my husband." Don't ask, don't tell, but have ready a long rambling answer that will get the crowd on its feet. Then Capehart flashed up on a big screen tweets from Chasten's Twitter account, many of which were photographs of GIF rodents and grumpy dogs with scarves. It wasn't exactly a Woodward and Bernstein moment.

Guns or Knives, Butch

Donald Trump featured in only a few applause lines, mostly when Capehart pressed Buttigieg on whether he supported a congressional resolution calling for the impeachment of the president. Such a question was way too terrestrial for the sacerdotal Mayor Pete, but after a few go-rounds on the subject, he did say, "Yeah, I am open to that," as if Capehart had suggested heading downtown after the event for some sushi at Sugarfish.

Buttigieg is not the kind of Democrat who would spend hours, say, with Representative Adam Schiff, plotting how to take on Trump (as when Harvey Logan asks Butch Cassidy, *"Guns or knives, Butch?"*). Pete might be able to quote *The Federalist* papers on the impeachment articles or recall some details of Richard Nixon's resignation, but don't vote for the mayor if you want someone who can rein in the Pentagon, talk trash to the Saudis, or increase appropriations for more corridor rail service. Why? Because Mayor Pete is a Potemkin candidate, a mayor of symbolism, and his constituency is one of ego and self-love.

Ask him about the budget deficit, and sooner rather than later his answer will allude to the fact he is neither a millennial nor Generation X, but on the cusp of the two astrological iForces shaping the future of the country. Ask him about Iran, and pretty soon he will switch the answer to his gay marriage and his faith. Ask him about the economy, and eventually you will get an earful about his deployment to Afghanistan or the English town the great Gatsby calls "Oggsford."

Exit, Stage Left

At the end of the evening, Mayor Pete exited the stage in the same direction from which he entered—from the left. By that point the house, papered with Buttigieg supporters, was on its feet, cheering for more. All they got was some dyspeptic waving from their man, who as Capehart explained, with grave import, "had to get back to Washington." Notice he didn't say South Bend.

The security guards at the front of the hall admitted a few backstage from the donor class, presumably before Mayor Pete departed on his errand of state. The rest of the crowd drifted onto Lexington Avenue or disappeared into the Uber night, no doubt a little underwhelmed that their man had not shaken any hands or signed autographs. But then the last thing Bernie Sanders wants to do is to mix with his supporters, and look at his favorable poll numbers.

Presumably the Buttigieg campaign enthusiasm will last as long as his donors can make the lease payments on his NetJet, or whatever he uses for his magic carpet, and at that point Mayor Pete and Chasten can head back to South Bend and get serious about coaching Little League, to fill in those blanks on the CV. (They already have the obligatory dogs, Truman and Buddy, and their picture on the cover of *Time*.) In the end Mayor Pete will fall victim to what so far has delivered him to the presidential jamboree—the paper chase of credentialism.

Without Harvard, Oxford, McKinsey, and Afghanistan on his resume, Mayor Pete would look more like an overly bright *Jeopardy!* contestant than a presidential candidate. (Alex Trebek: *"He's the mayor of a midwestern city and in his spare time he wants to be president. Let's give a big welcome for Pete Buttigieg. . ."*) But with so many golden tickets in his background, after a while, when voters ask about what it will take to cut the $1 trillion blown on Homeland Security or the best way to lower carbon emissions, they will want to hear more than Pete's self-directed love songs. Whitman said, "I and this mystery, here we stand," but he wasn't running for president.

A Crooning Biden
Takes the Stage

To GET TO THE IOWA CAUCUSES, I took an indirect all-American excursion and arrived in Council Bluffs on the banks of the Missouri River by way of New York, New Jersey, Pennsylvania, Chicago, and Nebraska, largely because I wanted to get over jet lag (I live in Europe) and also because I wanted to ride trains and hear those lonesome whistles at grade crossings in the night. At least in that I was not disappointed.

Council Bluffs is a railroad town on the eastern banks of the Missouri River. Across the river is Omaha, where in the close-by suburbs both President Gerald Ford and Warren Buffett have their roots. Buffett still has his house on Farnam Street, although it has been a while since he shoveled the driveway in front of the gate. Ford's childhood house has burned down, leaving only a kiosk where you can push a recording button and hear Jerry talk about "whipping inflation now!" or how to plant a WIN garden.

By the time I got to Council Bluffs in my rental car, the sun was setting, although not on the Great Plains but in the warehouse sprawl that connects the town to the river. Council Bluffs was the eastern terminus of the transcontinental railway—deemed so by the railroad lawyer in the White House, Abraham Lincoln—and it's safe to say that the Union Pacific Railroad and E.H. Harriman got the better end of the deal than did, 150 years later, the unemployed railway brakemen and porters for whom Council Bluffs is the end of the line.

I caught up with the Joe Biden campaign at the event hall called the Grass Wagon. It looked more like a roller rink or a warehouse than a political stage. Inside, while awaiting the candidate's arrival (he was about a half hour late), I stood chatting with some Iowa firefighters whose union had endorsed Biden in the primary.

When I asked one of the firemen why Biden was their man, he said, "He's been with us every step of the way," and the way he described Joe, I got the feeling that on many dark nights in Council Bluffs, there was Joe sliding down the station fire pole and into his waiting boots.

When my questions about the Iowa caucuses became a little too technical—I was asking about how the delegates are allotted after next Monday night, when everyone in Iowa stands in the corner of the candidate of choice—one of the firemen retrieved an expert from a Washington office, and he explained how Iowa goes from 1,700 precinct votes next Monday to conventions on the county, congressional, and state levels before a few Hawkeyes are sent off to the national Democratic convention (where no one cares what they say or think).

The Grass Wagon's parking lot—mostly snow banks and patches of ice—was chock full of support trucks for C-SPAN and CNN. Plus there were vans and press cars parked haphazardly, as though maybe Joe had finally caught fire inside on the small stage. My guess is that about 200 voters were present for the event, and that about a third of them were firemen, who were wearing yellow T-shirts and waving Biden placards, so that the clips on the nightly news or the longer C-SPAN feed would convey to home viewers that Joe's supporters only arrived with semi-delirious passion. In reality, they only started their wave when Biden came through the side entrance and walked to the center of the stage, in what was a theater-in-the-round.

Biden Plays the Political Sands

Biden was dressed in a blue blazer and slacks, and his air was that of a Vegas crooner at the Sands Hotel. Think of that Dean Martin look, as everything from his neck up would seem to have been rebuilt—skin, hair, teeth.

Biden's mind strikes me as slightly addled. He sounds a bit like an old man in a retirement community, making free associations (about ISIS, health care, the cost of prescription drugs, climate change, Trump, education, terrorism, and Iraq) over cocktails overlooking the 18th hole of a golf course. Although he's taller than I expected and looks in good shape, at times Joe moves around the stage set tentatively. What redeems the Biden experience, at least on a small stage in Iowa, is that he establishes a deep emotional rapport with his audience—by evoking his hard-scrabble Scranton childhood, his middle-class values (even if he's lived most of his life in a mansion), his affection for American workers, and his love of political compromise.

At times, however, in talking about his parents and the Depression, he could sound like those Monty Python Yorkshire-men remembering their struggles as children: "House? You were lucky to have a house! We used to live in one room, all hundred and 26 of us, no furniture. Half the floor was missing; we were all huddled together in one corner for fear of falling!" To which the other Yorkshiremen respond by saying: "Luxury. . .sheer luxury."

Biden isn't running for president because he wants to sit in the White House for the rest of his life, signing proclamations. He's running for the same reason that professional golfers, once they hit age 50, go on the Senior Tour. They like the game, the hours are good, you can work from home, and, as Woody Allen's Virgil Starkwell liked to say of bank robbery, "You get to travel."

Unlike other candidates that I have seen over the years, Biden seems genuinely to like the American people and, in particular, his supporters. He knew personally a number of the firemen in the audience, and he talks about the issues as though you had bumped into Biden at Home Depot and asked him how he was fixed for dental insurance. He doesn't speak in Lincoln-Douglas complete sentences. Instead he riffs in fragments from memory (something of a risk, I am sure, to his staff) about the issues of the day while strolling around the stage with a mic in his hand—the Dr. Oz of the Iowa caucuses.

Biden's Worldview

Biden's world and emotional view seems to be stuck in 1962, when steaks were cheap, America ruled the world, gas was 25 cents, and you could still give a neck rub to one of your supporters. He conceives of foreign affairs as a country club, where to be successful you have to know the membership committee and the board, and be nice to locker room attendants. His road-tested soundbite in Iowa is that "character is on the ballot this fall," and he loves to contrast his homespun Scranton-Wilmington values with Trump's gilded cages along Fifth Avenue and Palm Beach.

To pay for his wish-list (ethanol giveaways, great salaries for teachers, conservation trusts built on land purchased from struggling Iowa farmers. . .) Biden would tax capital gains the same as ordinary income and impose a minimum corporate tax of 25 percent. I am not sure he would have campaigned with those same bumper stickers when running for reelection in Delaware, a state built on corporate giveaways and tax loopholes such that Russian oligarchs prefer Wilmington over Zurich, in terms of stashing their loot. (Irony: Despite all of Biden's macho lifeguard talk about "taking on" Vladimir Putin, Joe's home state of Delaware might already have Vlad's fortune tucked away in one of its limited liability corporations.)

A typical Biden anecdote has humor, compassion, and home-spun wisdom (*"as my mother would say, God bless him. . ."*), but then after a few asides and jokes, he forgets where the sentence was going, and moves on to some other outrage (*"we're not a country that puts kids in cages. . ."*).

A bit like Trump, Biden gets a pass for his streams of con-sciousness, especially as in many soliloquies he talks about his wife and daughter dying in a 1972 road accident or his struggles with stuttering as a child (which toughened him up and will help America in dealing with Russian and caliphate schoolyard bullies).

If Biden is the nominee, the challenge will be how to showcase his engaging personality, and not let it get lost in Gerald Ford-like gaffes. A bit like Hubert Humphrey in 1968, he would also need to slip the bonds of his president hovering in the wings, in this case Barack Obama, and convince the electorate that he's not riding on training wheels.

The Ghost of Hunter Biden

Hunter Biden is Banquo's ghost of the Iowa primary, hovering off stage and hardly speaking about the machinations that go into the making of a president or a king.

In my drives to primary events around Iowa, I have lis-tened nonstop to the impeachment hearings in the Senate, and nearly half of the Republican questions, hand-carried by pages to Chief Justice John Roberts (who strikes me as Oz-like and a long way from Kansas), are about Hunter Biden, Burisma, and those million-dollar fees to attend some Monaco board meetings. And when I spin the dial on the car radio and listen to God-fearing, corn-fed shock jocks, there Hunter is out strolling with his new 33-year-old wife while at the same time paying off his stripper baby-mama from Arkansas. Elsewhere on air there are allusions to the Navy booting him out for cocaine and his affair with his dead brother's wife.

In Joe's campaign, however, Hunter isn't dodging bailiffs in Arkansas or snorting coke on his watch, but the brother of someone who served in Iraq and the small boy who firemen saved in the car accident with the jaws of life.

Is it any wonder that the Trump Republican strategy, at the moment, is to run against Hunter Biden? It's a strategy that assumes that neither Bernie Sanders nor Elizabeth Warren are mainstream enough to defeat Trump; in this thinking, only Biden occupies that center square of the political chessboard, and for that he needs the full Willie Horton treatment that George Herbert Walker Bush gave to Michael Dukakis in 1988.

To defeat Biden, so Republican thinking goes, all that is necessary is to invoke the spirit of Hunter Biden at every turn. In that sense, even the impeachment hearings, provided things don't get out of hand, serve Trump's purposes. And if Joe does get the nomination, he can answer Hunter questions much the way Hillary spent her entire campaign explaining away her basement server or searching for those 30,000 emails about Chelsea's wedding (they must have ordered a lot of flowers).

Reaching Across the Aisle

I am not sure Joe's unity vision ("*I would reach across the aisle. . .*") will play in 2020, but it sounds good at a rally in which Trump is the 800-pound gorilla awake at 3:00 a.m. with cheeseburgers, his phone, and a few porn stars. Same with Joe's plaintive calls for more teachers, and the shoutouts to the valor of first responders and those serving in the military.

In his first 90 days in office, Biden would rejoin the Paris climate accord, send an immigration bill to Congress (muted applause on that one), and tell the Chinese to stop stealing our state secrets. Fairly vanilla, and I couldn't help but think that Biden's dream job isn't to be president (too many memos on your desk) but that of prime minister of some wobbly, centrist parliamentary coalition (like those that flipped back and forth in 19th century Britain between Gladstone and Disraeli).

Biden is a creature of the Senate more than a chief executive, even though "Barack" gave him all the tough jobs (defeating ISIS, passing health insurance, helping the farmers, etc.—listening to Biden, you do wonder what Obama was doing all those years), and his local TV ads make the point that, whatever his flaws, he's the only Democrat who can actually beat Trump in a general election.

Biden's After Party

After the event ended, I hung around on the fringes of the velvet ropes to watch Biden mix with his crowd, take selfies, sign autographs, and restrain his impulse to give everyone a squeeze. Not every politician likes to spend time with his or her supporters, but Biden is a retail candidate, and everyone who comes into the store gets a game of checkers and a story about taking down the caliphate.

On my way to Iowa, I had met a friend of Biden's from the 1970s, former Senator Adlai Stevenson III, and he asked me to give Joe his phone number, in hopes that they could reconnect. I wasn't sure if Biden's Secret Service detail or campaign staff would warm to me handing the candidate a sticky note with a phone number. But such is my respect for Adlai that I decided to give the errand a try.

It took Biden a while to work his way through the crowd of followers, but he signed every placard, stood for every selfie, and even got down on his knees to greet a physically disabled woman in a wheelchair. Hey, he's been running for offices since 1972, and that was like lining up a two-foot putt, but at least he drained it, and patted her guide dog.

When Biden got to me, I explained the connection to Adlai (we're friends, not relatives) and handed him the note, to which he said, "God bless you," as though I had granted him an indulgence. (There's a lot of altar boy in Joe.) Then his staff was all over me, wanting to know what was on the folded piece of paper. It was a slightly awkward moment for everyone—me and the staff—until Joe turned around and said to the staffer, "Hey, leave him alone. He's a good guy."

Back in the parking lot, I decided to hang around and watch the Biden campaign bus depart. "Soul of the Nation" is emblazoned on the side. By this point the crowd had drifted away, and the C-SPAN truck was loading up its wires, and Biden aides, even a few in suits, were folding up chairs that had somehow been dragged out to the parking lot.

After quite a long time—I imagine he was inside meeting with local pols—Biden walked out of the Grass Wagon and boarded his bus, which turned down a side street and vanished into the frigid Iowa night, followed by a line of chase cars containing, I am sure, aides, some press, and various remittance men. It could have been any high school team bus heading home after an away game, or maybe the circus train after striking the tents.

A Des Moines Trump Rally

WHATEVER YOU MIGHT THINK OF DONALD TRUMP in the newspaper—psychotic, pathological, delusional, etc.—in person he's light-years worse. He spoke tonight in Des Moines for 105 minutes, in that stage whisper of a madman, and the MAGA crowd devoured it all, cheering on their feet about every minute or so. Even presidents Ronald Reagan and Richard Nixon, not exactly Thomas Jefferson and James Madison, would be appalled by such a spectacle—the fast food of American fascism, delivered with droning intensity.

For a while I thought I was lucky to get inside Drake University's Knapp Center, as it was sold out days before and the Secret Service had the neighborhood on lockdown, although that didn't keep the so-called deplorables (their name of pride, from Hillary) from streaming into the event, as though for pro wrestling or mixed martial arts.

Inside the arena, I found a desk and a chair in the nose-bleeders at the top of the arena, but I still had a good view below of the dictator's ballroom. For a while, to kill time, the organizers sent out various warm-up bandsmen, including a state senator and the head of the reelection campaign, all of whom denounced the Democratic Party as a nest of treasonous vipers and confidence men. Oh, and it was pointed out that Bernie had spent his honeymoon "in the Soviet Union."

The entire evening was an exercise in dog whistling, and even in the preliminaries you got a feeling of what would animate the barking: Benghazi, abortion, guns, the Wall, Hillary (apparently, no one has the word that she isn't running), Adam Schiff, socialism, AOC, socialized medicine, and Hunter Biden.

Between the greeters and the Royal Nonesuch (Vice Pence followed by Trump), the sound system piped in a rock medley, including what is clearly the theme song of the Trump-Pence reelection campaign: "Macho Man." (*Every man wants to be a macho man/ To have the kind of body always in demand. . .*") Who knew that the Village People, for their comeback tour, would be so popular with the smart set at Mar-a-Lago? There were a number of Stone's hits on the playlist, including—go figure on this one—"Brown Sugar" ("*just like a young girl should. . .*"), which must be an allusion to those 23 women Trump groped in elevators or green rooms.

Pence Warms Up the Crowd

It is hard to describe accurately Vice President Mike Pence's refinement in the art of sycophancy. You name the milestone— low unemployment, dead Iranians, walled-in Mexicans, the end of ISIS, the Dow at 28,000, the cowed Chinese government, cheered-up veterans, NAFTA's demise, the gun on your hip, or fracking wells outside elementary schools—and the responsible party for all this good news is "my friend and our great leader, Donald J. Trump. . ." although toward the end of his speech, disciple Mike seemed to be laying on hands, and he began to evoke Trump as coming out of the Obama dessert "to heal this land."

Rather than bounce on stage after Mike departed with his thumbs in the full upright position, Trump waited a while for his entrance, giving the Trump-Pence DJ a chance to play some Michael Jackson ("*Beat it. . .*"), Bob Dylan ("*Knock knock knocking on heaven's door. . .*"), and "YMCA," which had some of the red MAGA caps rocking to the "*place you can go. . .when you're short on your dough.*"

For Trump to moonwalk from the stage curtain to the lectern took about five minutes. He had to make the thumb gesture, point to the crowd (from where I was sitting, he might well have Mussolini on his balcony saluting the *fascisti*), bow repeatedly (as if a head waiter in the Oak Room), and bask in the adulation from 8,000 supporters, each of whom shared the raptures that were visited on acolyte Pence.

Why were Trump and Pence even in Iowa? Yes, in theory they are running for the Republican nomination, and the party will conduct its own caucuses next Monday night. And yes, there are two candidates out there opposing Trump in the Republican primaries, although as best I can figure only one of them is campaigning Iowa, that being Joe Walsh, a former member of Congress and conservative radio host.

I am assuming that Pence was here to get a head start on 2024. (Possible motto for his bus: *Pence 2024—Kiss ass and take names. . .*) I am also sure that Trump loved the idea of flying into Iowa (where even Biden struggles to get 300 people to his events) and filling up the Knapp Center, especially as the impeachment hearings were riveting the nation in the Senate.

Trump Takes the Stage: Aging Rocker

At his rally, despite his banker blue suit and phallic red necktie, Trump gives off the air of an aging rocker who back in the day maybe did a little too much blow. He's bald on top and combs over his drummer mane, and the back of his hair is starting to flow over his shirt collar, as if he's trying to grow a rat tail or maybe a top knot. When he speaks, he leans and rocks forward into the mic and lectern, reminding me a bit of Harvey Weinstein gripping his walker on his way into court.

I have no idea if anyone writes Trump's speeches or whether the teleprompter just has a few high notes—*Wall, Benghazi, they're coming for your guns, Fake News,* etc.—and after that Trump is on his own. If he does have speechwriters, they are either Cheech and Chong ("*Dave ain't here. . .*") or perhaps a Dubliner who placed seventh in a write-like-James-Joyce-in-*Finegan's Wake* competition.

With his out-there theories and breathless, wheezing delivery, Trump also echoes Wizard in Martin Scorsese's *Taxi Driver,* who says to cabbie Travis Bickle:

> Look at it this way. A man takes a job, you know? And that job—I mean, like that—That becomes what he is. You know, like—You do a thing and that's what you are. Like I've been a cabbie for 13 years. Ten years at night. I still don't own my own cab. You know why? Because I don't want to. That must be what I want. To be on the night shift drivin' somebody else's cab. You understand? I mean, you become— You get a job, you become the job. One guy lives in Brooklyn. One guy lives in Sutton Place. You got a lawyer. Another guy's a doctor. Another guy dies. Another guy gets well. People are born, ya know? I envy you, your youth. Go on, get laid, get drunk. Do anything. You got no choice, anyway. I mean, we're all fucked. More or less, ya know.

That's what a Trump speech sounds like. At least in response to something that Wizard said, Bickle had the good sense to say: "That's about the dumbest thing I ever heard."

Presidential Apprentice

Well into the fourth season of *The Presidential Apprentice,* most of us are used to Trump's riffs. But this was the first time I had heard him speak in person at length, and in person his patterns of speech are those of someone who spends a lot of time in serious conversations with himself.

Trump is lucky that he's the president and, as the cliche has it, "leader of the free world," because if he were homeless and spoke as he did, he would spend most of his evenings in the back of a squad car, on his way to various padded holding pens. Trump not only asks himself questions, he then modulates his voice to answer them, and he loves to refer to himself in the third person, always in glowing terms. *"Trump did this, Trump did that, the Chinese love Trump. . ."* At other times he leans forward and stage-whispers into the mic, as if confiding to the audience the kind of state secrets he normally would only divulge to his handlers in Saudi Arabia, Russia, or Israel.

To his 8,000 confidants in the Knapp Center, the president revealed, in his falsetto, that: never before in American history have relations ever been this good with China (our rival until about two weeks ago); alter ego Trump has solved both the AIDS epidemic and the opioid crises; and diplomatic genius Trump has resolved most of the outstanding issues in the Middle East by taking out the Iranian general Qasem Soleimani.

In Trump's mind it is eternally 1979: Jimmy Carter is president, demonstrators are loose in the streets of Tehran, and American diplomats are held hostage. Now, however, it's morning in America. "Thanks to Trump," he said, "Michigan is booming." He added, "This is a happy period," to which the crowd responded with a round of "U-S-A, U-S-A!"

One Trump Hand Clapping

Trump is pleased with himself on many issues, but none more so than his usage of the word "Democrat" as adjective, in the same manner that Republican hatchet man Senator Bob

Dole liked to speak of "Democrat wars." (The thesis behind the insult is that Democrats have started most of the recent wars.) Trump has cottoned on to the slur, as if he invented a new joke, completely unaware that the insult dates to the 19th century, if not earlier.

Like some Vegas comedian with only a handful of jokes, Trump cannot mention a Democratic politician without adding his insults of choice, all of which by now are wearing a little thin. Nancy Pelosi is always "Crazy Nancy," just the way Bernie Sanders is "Crazy Bernie." Of course, Biden is "Sleepy Joe," Hillary Clinton is "Crooked Hillary," and Obama comes with emphasis on his middle name, "Hussein," Michael Bloomberg is "Mini Mike," no doubt an illusion to *Austin Powers* and Dr. Evil's son. Elizabeth Warren is predictably "Pocahontas," and Trump is now mocking Pete Buttigieg as "Boot Edge Edge," while making it clear that the former mayor is, as the phrase used to have it, of foreign extraction. I was a little surprised Trump didn't call Buttigieg a wop or dago, but he did say that many immigrants from Central America are "stone-cold rapists." Violation is a familiar image in Trumpspeak, just as it's a familiar refrain in the legal complaints many women have lodged against the president.

If you're not used to it, or even if you are, the borderline call to violence at a Trump rally is jarring. Democrats aren't simply members of the political opposition, but "treasonous radicals" and "socialists," bent on spreading "sick and hateful" un-American ideology. At his command, the audience would sack the press corps.

I would credit Trump with reviving McCarthyism, but since Trump (according to a new book) had no idea what happened in the attack on Pearl Harbor, and Senator Joseph McCarthy came along nine years later, it's safe to say that the allusion would be lost on Trump, as if it were a reference to Matthew Hopkins or Roger Nowell.

From Trump's stemwinder, I have no trouble imagining him (in a slightly altered universe) ordering the arrest of representatives Adam Schiff or Alexandria Ocasio-Cortez, the mention of whom prompted cat calls for burning stakes. In Trump's worldview, Democrats stand for "crime, corruption, and chaos," not to mention late-term abortions and coming for your guns.

I have never thought for a minute that Trump is a billionaire, unless to calculate his net worth he's allowed to add in all his past-due bank loans or accounts payable that he walked away from during his periodic bankruptcies. (He stuck one public company with $1 billion in his unpaid personal debts.) But tonight's performance was the first time I realized he's an economic moron. I listened in disbelief while Trump tried to explain tariffs to his clan, which whooped and cheered every time the president explained that China "had paid over" billions after "Trump" put tariffs on various imports from the Far East. Lost on Trump and his followers is that American consumers took the hit on the tariffs, not the Chinese.

Crazy Nancy, Sleepy Joe

From his trade deal with Mexico and Canada ("the biggest trade deal signed in the history of the world. . ."), Trump went off on an Inspector Harry Callahan (*Dirty Harry*) rant about "Crazy" Nancy Pelosi and the streets of San Francisco, which, according to Trump, are filled with used syringes ("*needles all over the place*"), yet another 1979 flashback in the world according to Trump.

The more Trump spoke—he talked for well over an hour—the more I thought I was listening to a radio shock job ranting on about: socialized medicine; rapists pouring across the border; the best way to build the Wall (lots of concrete and steel. . .); China stealing our secrets; how the Green New Deal is a hoax; welfare queens driving Rolls-Royces; and how gays and lesbians are running the editorial board of the *New York Times*.

In Trump's time-warped imagination, before he became president, the country was a variation on the South Bronx during the Jimmy Carter years. The borders were open to felons, the economy was bankrupt, terrorists ran American foreign policy, and schools were only open to teach the virtues of abortion. Since Trump has become president, high-paying jobs have become abundant, the stock market has boomed, China and Iran have fallen into line, and the criminal justice system finally works (with all those 191 new federal and conservative judges, not to mention Budweiser's favorite justice, Brett Kavanaugh, Esq.).

It was interesting to gauge which lines got the most applause and brought the crowd to its feet. I presume these lines have been well tested on watchdogs in the basement of some Trump Hotel. Clearly keeping "your guns" and "right to life" played well with the crowd, but so too did rolling back the tide of red socialism (that of Sanders, Warren, and AOC).

Not since the Miracle on Ice at the 1980 Lake Placid Winter Olympics have I heard so many "U-S-A, U-S-A!" refrains, and during the Trump rally I kept waiting for Mike Eruzione to rush the Soviet net in the third period.

The bottom line is whether Trump's Know Nothing coalition (the original one was a nativist party in the 1850s that ran against European immigration and for a brief period was wildly popular) can win a general election without many votes from African Americans, Latinos, millennials, a fair number of women, and large elements of the country with professional degrees. In terms of optics, it must say something that most Democratic candidates in Iowa struggle to fill Grange halls with supporters while Trump could easily turn out 10,000 on any given night in Des Moines.

Into the general election, I would guess that Trump will remain fairly strong with working-class voters, rural women, and a fair number of older Americans for whom the price of grain, soybeans, and mutual funds indicates how they will vote. But I do wonder how Trump's racist rants will play in ethnically diverse swing states, such as Florida and Pennsylvania, especially after Democratic operatives have stitched his xenophobic insults together in a 60-second attack ad.

Trump's Gilded Fascism

When you strip away all the hysterics that come with a Trump rally, he's little more than a traveling salesman of gilded fascism—someone who believes in the triumph of his will and hates, in no particular order, the legacies of Woodrow Wilson, Franklin Roosevelt, the Progressive era, civil and equal rights, Martin Luther King, and Jimmy Carter's foreign policies based on human rights. One of his few core beliefs is in economic and political isolation; after all, if you're an hotelier, you don't want the Chinese or Japanese building competition next to a Trump National and driving down the price of a tee time. For the rest he's a character out of the Sinclair Lewis novel *It Can't Happen Here*, about American democracy submitting to the paroxysms of homegrown national socialism.

Lewis wrote prophetically in 1935 about a strongman coming to power in America:

> The Senator was vulgar, almost illiterate, a public liar easily detected, and in his 'ideas' almost idiotic, while his celebrated piety was that of a traveling salesman for church furniture, and his yet more celebrated humor the sly cynicism of a country store. Certainly, there was nothing exhilarating in the actual

words of his speeches, nor anything convincing in his philosophy. His political platforms were only wings of a windmill.

At the end of 105 minutes on what felt like a Nuremberg parade ground in downtown Des Moines (although I suspect the Nazis were not selling bumper stickers, hats, and mugs in the parking lots), such were Trump's histrionics that I almost expected him to evoke *"Ein Volk, ein Reich, ein Führer"* or summon his party with an evocation of *Volksgemeinschaft*, the belief that racial and ethnic purity would bind the German state (to Hitler).

In Trump's case, as much as he admires those strutting on the world stage in jackboots, the only thing that he really believes in is himself, a much larger and more romantic subject than any one nation or people. As F. Scott Fitzgerald wrote of an earlier American searching for self-love and quick profits in the American imagination and on the Great Plains:

> The truth was that Jay Gatsby of West Egg, Long Island, sprang from his Platonic conception of himself. He was a son of God—a phrase which, if it means anything, means just that— and he must be about His Father's business, the service of vast, vulgar, and meretricious beauty.

No wonder that as the faithful shuffled into the cold of the Iowa night while Trump and Pence flew away on their magic carpets, the playlist coming from the eaves of the Knapp Center struck up Mick Jagger's *"You can always get what you want/But if you try sometimes you just might find/You get what you need. . ."* It's the modern equivalent of "Nearer My God to Thee," which was played on the deck of *Titanic* when it went down.

Candidates "R" Us

With the three horsemen of the impeachment—Sanders, Warren, and Klobuchar—glued to their desks during last week's trial, I fanned out across Iowa in search of the second team.

One of the myths about the Iowa caucuses is that the state is rural and small, with few urban centers, enabling candidates to meet-and-greet their way through Grange halls to a primary victory. In fact, while Iowa is largely an agricultural state, it also has a population of three million and a number of small cities— Council Bluffs, Sioux City, Iowa City, Cedar Rapids, Waterloo, and Davenport—among them. From one side of the state to the other requires five hours of driving, just as winning the caucuses requires running ads (*"and I approve this message. . ."*) in a number of discrete media markets.

In 1976 Jimmy Carter won in Iowa, giving him the halo of the people's choice, but in general all that matters in the caucus is to give off the aura of having exceeded expectations—whatever they may be. Hence the winner might simply be the candidate with the best spin doctors and not necessarily the candidate who wins the most votes on caucus night. Nor does winning in Iowa guarantee a candidate his or her party's nomination. At stake are 41 delegates, out of some 4,000 that will go to the summer party nominating convention. Among those who have won in Iowa but failed to get nomination are: Rick Santorum, Ted Cruz, Mike Huckabee, and Dick Gephardt. That said, if Bernie Sanders wins the Democratic caucuses this year in Iowa—at the moment he's ahead in the polls—and wins in New Hampshire, he will be hard to beat in the remaining Democratic primaries.

Andrew's Bigger Yang for the Buck

To connect with Andrew Yang, who was on an extended bus tour in eastern Iowa, I had to drive to Grundy Center, a one-horse town not far from Waterloo. Yang was speaking in the community center that is in the same building as the town hall. When I got there, everyone was seated on plastic chairs, as though waiting to see someone about a building permit.

The room had space for about 40 people, but about one-third were media, who filled the back of the space with bulky TV cameras. In the campaign, for the most part, venues like Grundy Center are stage sets in which the candidates put on their one-act plays for the evening news. At this point, to save money, I am a little surprised no one has come up with a virtual green screen that would allow the candidates to film their small-town docudramas in a studio and spare everyone in their wake (group-ies, staffers, media types, and TV trucks) from having to drive halfway across Iowa to hear them say exactly what they said at the previous stop.

Yang's schtick is that of tech and corporate guru, for whom government, if not the presidency, is yet another startup in need of some private equity to get things running better. In many respects he's the perfect millennial candidate, seeing the government as yet another dinosaur of the fossil fuel era. By the standards of this election, he's young—45 years old—and he has the air of someone who doesn't need to watch a YouTube tutorial either to install his router or run Linux on his laptop. To my knowledge he's never held or run for elective office. His parents were immigrants from

Taiwan who, after coming to the United States, worked to get advanced academic degrees.

Part of the second generation, Yang went to elite private schools, including Phillips Exeter (George W. Bush went to Andover) and Columbia Law School, which may explain why Yang is comfortable addressing an audience. I suspect Yang would solve many problems of the American government or society with an app. Yang speaks softly and gives no evidence of wielding a big stick. At the beginning of his talk in Grundy Center, two activists decided to gate-crash the event and held up a small, hand-printed sign (*"Andrew Yang is a robot. . ."*), accusing Yang of having funded artificial intelligence that would take jobs away from Iowans. Had it been a Trump or even a Sanders rally, and had some hacktivist rushed the podium with a grievance, security guards would have dragged away the protester, in the manner that the Chicago police cleared the streets around the 1968 Democratic convention. In this case, Yang simply stood still and did nothing, until the audience booed and chided the interlopers to leave, which they did.

Yang owes his primary longevity (he's lasted longer in the race than several professional politicians) to his plan to pay every American over age 18 $1,000 a month. He calls it the "freedom dividend" and claims the idea dates to the early days of the republic, when Tom Paine (*Common Sense*) talked up the payout (he presumably wanted to pay over the money in pieces of eight). In modern times, the state of Alaska pays its residents an annual dividend based on energy production. To pay for the giveaway, Yang would tax large tech companies, such as Google and Amazon, because, he argues, they have grown rich on gathering and selling the metadata of average Americans, who should be paid for the use of their assets. People could spend their $1,000 any way they choose, although he quips, "You might even get your own Netflix password." Mostly the money would end up back in the local economy, so it's hardly different than other government grants, including Social Security, if not the bailouts of large banks.

Most of the other candidates in the primaries do not speak so much as they bark at their audiences. For example, Bernie Sanders and Elizabeth Warren often sound like truant officers lecturing runaway students. Yang's approach is calmer. His tone is that of a corporate consultant, and he speaks in the voice of a facilitator at a company offsite, explaining how employees (well, voters in this case) can live happier, more productive and efficient lives (especially if they download the Yang voter app). He has a number of stock phrases, repeated at most events, that play well with an audience that, truth be told, only half listens to the campaign talks in Iowa and spends the rest of the time skimming their iPhones.

On addressing climate change, Yang says, "I am the ideal candidate. I am an Asian man who likes math," and he doesn't blame Trump for every ill in the society, preferring to target the Big Brother qualities of large tech, who are turning citizens, especially children, into automatons ("computer dopamine" is one of his phrases). His warnings about the brave new world include vignettes about jobs disappearing when self-driving trucks replace the three million truckers on the road (and with them go waitressing jobs in truck stops and many motel clerks), and he makes the larger point that "corporate profits don't equate to our well-being."

Mostly Yang talks about the Manichean world—hey, I said he was new age—of technology, which can be your friend and also the cause of unemployment, hunger, suicide, drug dependence, gun violence, and health issues. To combat that, he wants all Americans, in effect, to be shareholders in their enterprise, and at least to earn some money while Google and Amazon are mining your data. And he would transform government (*"it's 20 years behind the times"*) into a responsive website.

If you sat next to Yang on a flight to Dayton and if he talked about "corporate change and technology" for the entire trip, you would not give him another thought after you said goodbye and "good luck at your conference." But for the moment he's a presidential candidate, complete with his own chartered bus and a road show across Iowa—in the tracks of earlier faithful healers who looked for souls to cure on the frontier.

It says something about current times that so many candidates in the current race (Tom Steyer is another) have never run for or served in any public office, before they decided—Trump like—"I think I would make a good president." And the next thing you know, if they can pay campaign bills, they have a chartered bus, front yard signs, media attention in the back of the room, and for a brief shining moment in Iowa, some name recognition in the political world.

The event lasted about 35 minutes, and when it was done Yang shook a few hands and posed for selfies—obligatory for everyone except Bernie in this campaign. Then Yang vanished out the back door to his waiting bus, to continue his 14-stop tour in the days before the Iowa voting.

The Yang getting on the bus—looking at his phone, surrounded by young men who could themselves be working for a tech company—didn't have the look of someone who lives to drink the Kool-Aid of modern political campaigns. He ignored greeting a few kids with Yang signs who were hanging around the parking lot (Biden would have given them an encouraging word), and there was no wave to the faithful, even if they were just a few crazies mumbling to themselves about Google running our lives.

I did like the Yang approach to politics, although during his talk I was reminded of something Speaker Sam Rayburn said in the JFK era about "the best and the brightest" of Ivy Leaguers then determined to engage the United States government in a Vietnam

War. Rayburn said to his friend Lyndon Johnson, "I'd feel a lot better if some of them had run for sheriff just once."

Tom Steyer Pays Himself

Tom Steyer is a billionaire in the Democratic presidential race who has never served in public office. His picture is on billboards all over the state, and usually the picture shows a humble Tom chatting up an Iowa farmer or union worker about the big issues of the day. (It's either that or he's trying to persuade the farmer to invest in Steyer's billion-dollar hedge fund.)

Under the words "TOM STEYER," the sign reads, "Democrat for President," just so that passing motorists have some clue who Steyer is and why his picture is on billboards in places like Madison County (of romantic movie fame). Otherwise, as Tom bears a slight resemblance to Clint Eastwood (Meryl Streep's love interest in the film), Iowans might think that Tom was on the lookout for their wives and that these billboards were retro Tinder ads.

I caught up with Steyer in a Des Moines restaurant where he had come to lobby for union support in the upcoming caucuses. The room was tiny, and the American Federation of State, County and Municipal Employees (AFSCME) members, about 20 or so, were seated in a semi-circle facing the front of the room, where candidates were coming to make their pitch. From the questions, I got the impression that most in the room were schoolteachers or health care professionals, all of whom had problems with their bosses (most of whom probably looked and sounded a lot like Tom Steyer).

Steyer is one of the few candidates who campaigns in a suit and necktie (Trump and Bloomberg are the others—it must be a billionaire thing). But his blue suit was rumpled and poorly cut— think of a homicide detective—and his necktie was a bright tartan plaid, as though the office he was seeking was that of Scottish highland chief.

I don't want to suggest that Steyer's eyes are rolling in his head, but he does have the look and air of a true believer—at least in the greater good of Tom Steyer. He speaks in the clipped phrases of democratic earnestness and corporate efficiency (remember Jimmy Carter and "zero-based budgeting?"), and for most of his presentation, while making it clear that he had a billion big ones stashed away in some bank (*"I can beat Trump at his own game. . ."*), Steyer suggested that what had really fueled his professional career was a love of the working class (especially those in AFSCME locals).

Steyer's entrance ticket to the Democratic primaries (leaving aside that he has a billion dollars burning a hole in his pocket) came through his advocacy of Donald Trump's impeachment. For a while, he was funding those running for office who would pledge to support impeachment. After some time, he must have figured, as Winston Churchill joked, "Why talk to the monkey when you have the organ grinder in the room?" and he declared his own candidacy for the presidency (mostly with all those billboards in the fields of dreams).

Now that Trump (for a little while longer) is under impeachment, Steyer has shifted his platform to climate change, economic redevelopment, and education for the young (he said to the unionists, "I'm an education bug" and talked their ears off about how kids need to be reading by the age of three. . .). The magic of Tom Steyer is that he can speak for two hours and few will hear anything that he is saying.

I have to assume that the Democratic candidates, including marginal ones such as Tom Steyer, tailor their pitches based on what they hear from their pollsters. For example, no one out here is beating the drum over Quemoy and Matsu, capital punishment, inflation, or the Laffer Curve. Instead, all anyone talks about is health care insurance, climate change (only the vaguest platitudes about saving the planet), and student debt, and when they need a metaphor for foreign policy, the only issue worth mentioning is Iran and the killing of General Qasem Soleimani.

Although Steyer would love to convince the electorate that he's an enlightened plutocrat and more at home in a trailer park than on his 1800-acre ranch outside San Francisco, he still speaks like a guy hustling assets under management. So, in prefacing his rap on education, he says, "So here's my deal on student debt." (At that point in the talk, I had my hand on my wallet.) His plan involves free community college and debt forgiveness for those who work in the military or to serve others (that category is a bit hazy), and like all the other Democrats in the race he will pay for his gravy trains by taxing polluters, monopolies, tech giants, and freebooters—in other words, a list of companies that, back in the day, I am sure helped to make Tom his first billion.

Steyer didn't linger too long in the union cell meeting. Even he could tell that his pitch was falling on deaf ears and that most were just killing time until Bernie turned up. He drifted back into the restaurant, where there were a bevy of television reporters and enough cameras and klieg lights to make even Steyer think that his message was being heard. (Meth must give off the same highs, and it doesn't cost $25 million or require chartering a campaign bus.) Steyer took a few desultory questions from the professional chorus (he batted away one about peace in the Middle East), and then settled into a longer, more intimate interview with network television—always in search of the perfect soundbite that would somehow propel him into fourth place. But the moment Bernie walked through the front doors of the restaurant, all the cameras around Steyer vanished, and he was left alone standing next to a large pile of pizza boxes. "So here's my deal on pepperoni. . ."

Bernie Joins the Union

Bernie had not been on the schedule of the AFSCME meeting, but I am sure he could not resist the chance to stop by and flash his union credentials. His wife came with him, and Bernie only spoke for about eight minutes, ticking off the highlights of union activism, which began when he was mayor of Burlington, Vermont, in the 1980s. But there were palpable gasps in the restaurant when he came through the door, as though maybe Jesus himself had decided to drop by a local church and teach Sunday school.

As it happened I was on my way to a full-blown Bernie event at Simpson College, in Indianola, which is south of Des Moines by about 12 miles. So I got to hear him speak twice in less than two hours, which is a touch trying as Bernie repeats the same speech, word for word, syllable for syllable, at all his events.

After the second hearing of the stump speech, I did begin to wonder how anyone could take pleasure in repeating the same words over and over again. Then I bumped into one of Bernie's political rivals, who joked, "He's been making the same speech for forty years." I guess maybe that's part of the appeal, but in person it's like listening to the loop on a call center's Muzak. In the four years since I had seen Sanders (I heard him speak several times in New Hampshire in 2016), he has turned into a saint. This time there was a little more order to his hair (I am sure the campaign staff has strategy meetings with his barber), but otherwise Bernie still dresses like an unmade bed and still has the air of a wandering hermit.

Actually, Bernie's best outfit is his hair shirt, as the message he delivers (at each stop along the wandering road) is the gospel of penitence—for how the United States deals with health insurance, student debt, climate change, minimum wages, women's rights, homelessness, big pharma, corporate greed, immigration, teacher salaries, the 1 percent, tax breaks, prescription drugs, and criminal justice system. (If I am leaving out some his outrage, you can fill in the blanks.) In front of the AFSCME members, he boiled down the speech to about eight minutes—stressing his union affiliations—but then in Indianola he gave the full pre-recorded message, which lasted about 45 minutes.

Bernie Plays Simpson

At Simpson College, a pretty liberal arts school, Sanders' staff went out of their way to humanize the candidate (which I am sure isn't the easiest task in presidential politics). On the undercard were a number of speeches from supporters, including one by Representative Ilhan Omar, best known today (at least in the popular press) for ditching her husband for a campaign consultant and for her work alongside Alexandria Ocasio-Cortez in what is called "the squad."

In person Ilhan is a dreary speaker whose voice rarely misses a monotone beat, and as she spoke everyone around me was checking their phones or chatting with a neighbor. Her job as a warmup band was to emphasize, at least to the press gaggle that was everywhere around the hall, that Bernie is "electable," which is the adjective of choice among Democratic operatives. Biden, Buttigieg, and Klobuchar all make the point, in their messages, that Bernie and Warren are "un-electable," meaning they would lose to Trump in the general election. Too much shining, not enough path. . .Hence, all the Bernie TV spots running in Iowa make the point that he's not only leading a revolution but that he can beat Trump (*"the most corrupt president in our history. . .and a pathological liar. . ."*). And that message is also delivered by his spin doctors, Representative Omar among them.

After Omar spoke, Bernie's wife, Dr. Jane Sanders, introduced her husband, again as part of the humanization process. She didn't talk about her honeymoon in the Soviet Union (a staple at Trump rallies), but made the point that Bernie at home was the same Bernie on the road—honest, caring, and always fighting for social justice.

As she spoke about her perfect husband, I imagined her asking him to take out the garbage, and Bernie responding, "What we have seen is that while the average person is working longer hours for lower wages, we have seen a huge increase in income and wealth inequality, which is now reaching obscene levels. This is a rigged economy, which works for the rich and the powerful, and is not working for ordinary Americans. . . . You know, this country just does not belong to a handful of billionaires." And then Jane saying tenderly, "I know, Bernie, and put the lid on the cans so the raccoons don't get in them. . ."

If Sanders wins the Iowa caucuses, and right now the polls are saying he will, and then he goes on to win in New Hampshire, which would make him a frontrunner for the Democratic nomination, what will have turned the tide in his favor is that his ideas, once on the fringe, are becoming more mainstream, at least among younger voters.

Twelve or even eight years ago, no one, not even the saintly Barack Obama, could have run for president on universal health care, the forgiveness of student debt, a wealth tax, and a Green New Deal that by some estimates could cost $23 trillion to implement, and to then to have gotten more than 7 percent of the vote in a few select primaries. Now, at least in a few early state primaries, Bernie's celebrity as a truth-teller (think of Savonarola preaching his bonfires of the vanities in 15th century Florence) outweighs any scrutiny of Bernie's plans, whether they would pass, and how the Congress would pay for them.

Bernie has also become a prime-time player, and that means he can campaign in an old blazer and build castles in the air by taxing climate abusers, the 1 percent, and greedy tech titans. I suspect, however, that voters in a general election would not be as reverential in their assessments as are his wife or Representative Omar.

Another advantage that Bernie enjoys in the early primaries is that in Iowa, he has been here before and has a network of activists in place, all of whom want nothing more than to knock on doors in Cedar Rapids and to drive senior citizens to caucus locations. (And he's a favorite son in New Hampshire, which is next door to his home state of Vermont.)

Supporters of Joe Biden, Amy Klobuchar, and Pete Buttigieg are thought able to get themselves to the polling places, but Bernie's campaign is a children's crusade and that should lead to heavy turnout in places such as Des Moines, Iowa City, and Ames, all of which are student cities. And as Bernie said at Simpson, "If we get a large turnout, we will win. If it's a low turnout, we will lose." And at least for a large turnout, he will have an ideal weather day—sunny and dry.

Finally, I think Bernie benefits from what might be called the Zelig vote—the inclination of voters to see in him whatever they don't like about other candidates. Purely on his record, Bernie is a windbag who, as his critic said, "has been giving the same speech for forty years." His record in Congress is that of a moral purist, with few achievements, and I suspect Hillary was speaking for more than herself when she said he had few friends in Congress and didn't play well in the sandbox of democracy. But in 2020, prickliness plays.

Look at the Republicans in the thrall of Donald Trump. Could the Democrats want some of that stridency on their side? If so, Bernie is the delivery drone of moral clarity, more so than Elizabeth Warren or Joe Biden, both of whom (less so Warren) feel somewhat tethered to terrestrial life. Bernie's home district is the cosmos, and I can well imagine voters, on both sides in 2020, wanting a spirit in the sky.

Bernie greets a few voters after his orations, but not many. He's not Elizabeth Warren with her selfie lines or Joe Biden working the velvet rope to reconnect with his firemen friends. In his persona Bernie's a professor of sociology at a left-wing university—say the New School in New York City—who is happy that you take his courses but who has no interest in drinking beer on a Thursday night after his Thorstein Veblen seminar.

In Search of Elizabeth Warren

From Indianola I had to hot-foot it to Iowa City if I was going to catch Elizabeth Warren at Iowa City West High School, which is a few miles outside the university town. Bernie finished speaking at about 1:30 p.m., and Warren was due to speak at 4:30 in the school gym. But it was more than a two-hour drive across the Iowa flatlands to get from Indianola to Iowa City.

At least the ice on the roads had melted, and I could set the rental car on cruise control to race through such towns as Marengo (named, I presume after the Napoleonic battle in Italy), Grinnell (where my good friend Stephen Beekman went to college), and What Cheer (an odd name for a decaying coal town). Along the way, I thought about how none of the Democratic candidates even makes a pretense of speaking to Iowa farmers. (Their audience is a network producer in New York City or Los Angeles.) It used to be a truism that Democratic candidates—including even urbanite JFK—had a farm policy. Now farmers are on the wrong side of the climate change barricades, and they rarely get a shoutout, except when they are enlisted (presumably against their will) to go green. Nor do the Democrats running even mention that Trump screwed over Iowa's soybean farmers with his China tariffs—when China retaliated by not buying Iowa's beans.

Warren's staff was all over the entrance of the gymnasium at West High School, and they were doing their best to get the email and phone number of every person who entered the event. (The Biden people just smile and wave you inside.) The event setup was like that of all other campaigns. The candidate speaks from a raised podium at the center of a hollow square surrounded with chairs. Behind the chairs, at least on one side but sometimes two, there are risers and platforms for television cameras; they get the box seat views.

Behind the risers are desks for print journalists, bloggers, and influencers, but those seats come with no view of the candidate. So while I have been to many events across Iowa, I have had to struggle just to see the candidate speaking. And no candidate wastes their time talking to print journalists or freelance writers, who might as well be throwing their dispatches on night trains heading for Chicago.

Warren supporters are mostly women, but they are all ages, and they are more passionate about their candidate than are the Sandernistas, who, I suspect, now communicate more through texts than by showing up at Bernie's rallies. At the Warren events I have attended, I have seen a number of supporter groups that include a mother, daughter, and grandmother all wearing Warren T-shirts or stickers.

Warren blamed her late arrival on Donald Trump and the impeachment hearings, which stuck her in the Senate until late Friday night, but she still arrived with her trademark bountiful energy, as if about to lead a Pilates class for about four hundred people. I don't think she was carrying a mat or boom box, but there was jazzercise music coming from the rafters and Elizabeth kept punching the air, especially when Aretha Franklin hit some of her high notes ("*R-E-S-P-E-C-T. . .Find out what it means to me. . .*").

I have now heard Warren speak three times (the set speech never varied, down to the attempts at humor, as in when she talks about her divorce and says: *"Well, it's never a good thing when you have to number your husbands. . ."*), and each time I felt as though I was hearing the closing argument in some pesticide lawsuit.

Elizabeth Warren is not stupid (she was a Harvard Law School professor, which must count for something). Her campaign is meticulously organized (about 20 minutes after I signed in, her press office sent me a text, inviting me to a Super Bowl party). And I imagine that she has some of the best pollsters and speechwriters in the business crafting her image (that of a struggling single mom who worked her way through law school and now wants to be president).

At each event, instead of hearing a political argument, I felt as though I were watching a Broadway production—with Aretha's music, some song and dance, and tragedy at the end of the second act (the evil 1 percent takes over America). Then in the finale, a big chorus number called "Hope Over Fear," Elizabeth is elected president and, with her 2 percent wealth tax on fortunes over $50 million, she leads the country out of the Winkie Country (it's in Oz) to a place somewhere over the rainbow.

Best of all, after the play, the lead actress comes down from the stage and poses for selfies with members of the audience. Or if she's pressed for time, she leaves behind her faithful Golden Retriever, Bailey, who, a bit like Lyle the Crocodile's friend Hector P. Valenti, has become "a star of stage and screen." Bailey did the heavy lifting for the campaign when Elizabeth was stuck in the impeachment trial, and I suspect more than a few voters wish it was Bailey Warren who could get their vote at the caucuses. (He doesn't talk as breathlessly and has fewer plans.)

The soliloquies in Warren's *I Am Woman* play tell the story of her childhood in Oklahoma (not on an Indian reservation). Her mom worked at Sears at minimum wage while her older brothers joined the military. Her childhood dream was to teach second grade in a public school (emphasis for AFSCME members on the word "public").

At age 19 Elizabeth was led into temptation, got married, and had children, until she divorced the man in the libretto called "Husband Number One," and started working her way through law school. That led to various professorships, consumer protection agencies, the U.S. Senate, and now a presidential bid, based on the premise that "Men in Suits" (it's a fairly catchy tune) are responsible for most American problems.

For someone who has spent much of her life in two of the most exclusive clubs in America—Harvard University and the U.S. Senate—Warren is, nevertheless, basing her campaign as an attack on wealth and privilege. (Harvard and the Senate don't seem to figure much in her presidential job interview.)

I don't think I need to hum all the refrains, but basically her many plans provide universal health care, free tuition and education, subsidized child care, climate change correctives, gun safety in the schools and malls, jail time for polluters and corporate embezzlers, affordable public housing and prescription drugs, write-offs of student debt, and a livable minimum wage. And if that sounds worthy if a touch expensive, she assures her audience that it's not, because to pay for everything in Oz, all that is required is to impose a wealth tax of 2 percent on American fortunes that are greater than $50 million. Who would not sign up for that?

In the song entitled, "All I Need for Christmas Is My 2 Percent," Warren hits the high notes on all of the social programs that a wealth tax will cover, and it's a bucket list of every American ill—from the opioid crisis and teen pregnancy to the gig economy and the Amazonian jungle. And all you have to do is elect Elizabeth

Warren as president and wait for the 1 percent to hand over their 2 percent.

Needless to say, for her devoted fans, Warren gets rave reviews: "*Breathtaking. . .the best play since Evita. . . . Judy Garland could not have done better. . . . When do we start marching?*" And at the beginning of the event, I was impressed with the size and energy of the crowd packed into West High's gymnasium. But then about halfway through the talk, I started to notice people streaming out of the gym, such that, at the end, I suspect about half the crowd had voted with their feet.

It is the Saturday before the caucuses, when many Iowans are window-shopping candidates, and I still think Warren's base is motivated for a good result. Plus she's been everywhere in the state, as has Bailey, and if you are from Iowa and don't have a selfie with Warren, you only have yourself to blame.

The Iowa polls have Warren finishing third, behind Bernie and Biden. I think she will do better than Biden (she has more than the firemen behind her), and her supporters are well organized and enthusiastic. I doubt that she will outpoll Bernie (although at some basic level their ideas are very similar), but at the same time I would not rule it out entirely.

On different days I heard both of them speak in the same hall at Simpson College, and if supporter energy means anything, Warren's people seemed more numerous and more committed to their candidate than were the Sandernistas, who were hard to find among all the TV reporters. Bernie may have more media cred, but I suspect Warren has a more energetic base.

A Herbert Hoover Detour

To get from the Warren musical to Mayor Pete's get-out-the-Iowa-vote rally, I took backroads. I had been to a number of rallies in the last few days and was tired of hearing the same lines in all the productions. Instead of driving directly from West High School to Cedar Rapids, I detoured through Iowa City (home to the Iowa's Writers' Workshop) and West Branch, where President Herbert Hoover was born and raised (it's about 11 miles east of Iowa City and the university).

Hoover is a cautionary tale in the election of presidents, as few men have ever brought to the presidency his sterling credentials, and few have ever failed as miserably as Hoover did in office. Before his election, Hoover had worked in business, made a modest fortune, saved millions of European refugees from starving after World War I, and worked in a senior capacity in the cabinets of Presidents Harding and Coolidge. He wrote well and had creative ideas, but as president he failed to anticipate or ameliorate the Great Depression, and Hooverville became the word to describe encampments of the homeless across the United States.

I am not sure Hoover deserves all the blame history has given him, as Franklin Roosevelt had no more success in ending the Depression than did his predecessor. But FDR understood the mythical aspects of leadership more than Hoover, whose only response to the economic collapse was to preach faith in American capitalism and individual fortitude. And the times were not on his side.

Hoover's boyhood home was closed when I got there, as was his presidential library, but I enjoyed my brisk walk in the cold around West Branch, which has saved a number of houses from Hoover's Quaker community, including the small cottage (almost a log cabin) in which he was born. The preserved village doesn't exactly have the wagons circled, but you get the picture.

It's thanks to Hoover that we now have the ritual rite of passage of post-presidential memoirs. He wrote his in two volumes, and it took him 18 years to finish them. But two volumes were not enough to change the verdict of history that Hoover was uncaring. Seen, however, in West Branch, he looks more like a frontier Quaker for whom the only program that ever worked was self-reliance, and that's not something that polls well anymore in Iowa caucuses.

Mayor Pete's Drugstore Patriotism

Mayor Pete, although he's no longer in office, had started speaking by the time I slipped into the hall. Again I was seated at a desk behind the television cameras (think of those obstructed view seats in Fenway Park), so to watch the event more closely I walked around the perimeter of the event and took up a post at the rail, closer to where Pete (in a necktie but no jacket) was speaking.

I had seen Pete in the springtime, just after he announced his candidacy, and at that event he had spent a fair amount of time speaking about his time as a Rhodes Scholar and what it meant to get "a first" at Oxford. On this occasion, for his Iowa faithful, he didn't go into his school transcript in such detail, and after a few prepared remarks, he answered questions, which is something he does better than give set speeches (in his formal remarks he sounds a bit like an awkward valedictorian).

What struck me about Pete on this occasion was the extent to which—consciously or not—his speech patterns have come to mimic those of Barack Obama. I noticed a slight southern drawl in his delivery (South Bend isn't any farther south than the South Side of Chicago), and he drops the word "folks" into his delivery on every occasion. Plus like Obama he is given over to delivering what might be called dramatic truisms, as was the case when he told the crowd that he would never cut any benefits associated with Social Security. Of course they cheered and clapped, but I don't think even Herbert Hoover would run today on cutting entitlements (a word Pete dislikes, as the "good working folks" of Iowa have earned their payouts).

I was also struck by Pete's drugstore cowboy patriotism, in all his talk about "restoring the creditability of the United States" around the world, and about how we had to have a military second to none. That said, he said as president he might re-order the priorities of military spending so that, while maintaining the capacity to make the rubble bounce, we could also in America have first-rate schools, job training centers, renewable energy, voter security, gun safety, and more efficient government.

Pete is more an heir to Jimmy Carter than Barack Obama, in that his appeal is largely that of someone new and untainted with the corruptions of Washington. Despite all of Jimmy Carter's talk about zero-based budgeting and restoring "trust" in the post-Watergate White House, essentially the Carter appeal was that he was unknown and untainted with the sins of Washington. Author and essayist Lewis Lapham wrote at the time in *Harper's Magazine* that Carter was elected "to redeem the American soul, not to govern it," and, if elected, the same might be said about Mayor Pete, who on stage in Cedar Rapids looks a bit lost and out-of-place, like some fan at a Cincinnati Reds game who is picked out of the stands and asked to play right field against the Cardinals.

Although I hardly put them in the category of daring ideas, Pete's platform includes some tepid criticism of the electoral college (*"I might get in trouble for saying this. . ."*) and adding to the number of justices on the Supreme Court (nothing in the Constitution caps the number at nine). He also speaks out in his rallies about passing as a constitutional amendment a new voting rights act for the 21st century that would put an end to voter suppression and end discrimination that amounts to a kind of poll tax.

Pete is also running as the first openly gay candidate, and he makes reference in his set speeches that in 2008, when he was knocking on doors in Iowa for Obama, he would not then have been able to marry his partner legally. To Iowans, he says of his wedding band, "You made it possible," and that's an effective applause line, as it is popular when his partner Chasten joins him on the podium and then they works the crowd for selfies.

Logic suggests that, at best, Pete is running for consideration as a vice presidential nominee, and for that he might well pair with the older Sanders or perhaps with Elizabeth Warren, although she might not want another Harvard alumnus on her ticket.

In the Iowa polls, Pete is the wildcard, as he has invested heavily in what is called out here in his "ground game" (staff on the ground in far-flung counties), and because he's a centrist who has both right and left appeal. His risk, if he doesn't get to the "viable" threshold level of 15 percent, is whether he releases his supporters to Amy Klobuchar (another centrist) or makes a deal with one of the big three, Biden, Sanders, or Warren.

Once the Iowa caucuses are over, Pete will lose whatever influence he might have as a kingmaker, as Iowa is one of the few places, on a presidential level, where there is ranked choice voting, and those behind in the polls can throw their weight to some of the leading candidates. My guess, only from event watching, is that Pete isn't comfortable with the backroom deal aspects of presidential politics, and I would think he would be most comfortable, on a personal level, dealing with another Midwesterner, Amy Klobuchar, although the risk for both of them is that they would, in military terms, be reinforcing defeat.

William Weld Takes on Trump: Is Anyone Listening?

To my surprise and pleasure, I found out that two Republican candidates were in Iowa campaigning against Donald Trump for the Republican nomination. I say pleasure because rarely, if ever, do

I hear any Republicans put the boot into Trump, and both William Weld and Joseph Walsh—the candidates out here—hate Trump with a passion. Plus they were mostly campaigning around Des Moines at coffeeshops and universities, so are easy to meet, and only a stray media person or two ever goes to their events.

I met Weld at Waveland Cafe, which is in the Des Moines suburbs but close to Drake University. He served in the Reagan justice department and then as two terms as governor of Massachusetts. He graduated from Harvard and is what was once called a "Rockefeller Republican," meaning a Republican from the Northeast with fairly liberal positions on social values. Weld was governor from 1991 to 1997, and in 2016 he ran as the Libertarian candidate for president. This time he has ruled out running as a third-party candidate (he's 74 years old) but he would like, especially in New Hampshire, to shake up the Trump campaign and pull in Republican voters who share his values and hate Trump.

Weld showed up at the Waveland with his wife and a campaign volunteer. It looked as though they arrived in a rental car; there's no charter bus in the Trump opposition. Weld is tall, with a full head of gray hair, and a pleasing, if slightly reserved, personality. He shook hands with the five people on hand to greet him, including two women who had voted for him as a Libertarian in 2016. Then a supporter with a dog showed up, and Weld tried to stoop over enough to get both him and the dog in the picture; it wasn't easy.

I asked Weld if he had ambitions beyond New Hampshire, and he said he did, adding that he hoped there were enough Republicans "out there" who wanted to reclaim the party from Donald Trump. He also pointed out that he had more executive experience than did Trump before his election, and more familiarity with foreign affairs. "I am one of the few," he said, "who has ever counted among his friends both Benjamin Netanyahu and Shimon Peres."

Weld worked his away around the Waveland Cafe, shaking hands with people eating breakfast. The customers were more accepting of the campaign intrusion than were the waitresses, who kept complaining that they had people trying to eat their meals. I still wonder if most of those who shook Weld's hand knew that he was running against Trump on the Republican ballot, but they all seemed gracious to meet him, and during the meet-and-greet some local television people showed up to tape a brief interview.

On the last Sunday before the Iowa caucuses, there are enough camera crews on hand to film games of pickup touch football in the parks. Unlike the Democrats, the Republicans do not caucus in the clusters of supporters, but vote for the candidates of their choice.

Just to be sure nothing gets out of hand, however, Trump was sending in a planeload of senior Trump officials, including his sons Don. Jr. and Eric, to speak on Trump's behalf when the Republicans gather to vote. Among those in the entourage was Mick Mulvaney, the White House chief of staff who refused to testify in the House impeachment hearings. He was on his own at an elementary school in Waukee, Iowa, a town just west of Des Moines. I thought of showing up and trying to issue a citizen's subpoena, but that might mean having to listen to Don Jr. speak on some closed-captioned hookup, and that would be more painful than a double dose of Bernie and Elizabeth Warren.

Shock Jock Joe Walsh: "I want to wake up Republicans"

The most engaging personality in the Iowa caucuses belongs to a former Republican congressman, Joe Walsh, who is also running against Trump in the caucus and who also has zero chance of winning. It's too bad, as he hates Trump as much as Adam Schiff. In fact, he sounds very similar to Adam Schiff on the subject of the sitting president.

In making the caucus rounds, I had thought about skipping the Walsh campaign and only focusing on those who might have a chance to figure in the news. But then I decided I needed to see and hear every candidate in Iowa, and that led me to track down Walsh on the campus of Simpson College, where instead of speaking at the main event hall, he was appearing in one of the classrooms.

Walsh is from the South Side of Chicago, and he was elected to Congress as a Tea Partier in 2010. He only served one term before getting "redistricted," and then he lost in the district where he tried to stand for reelection. I get the sense that, politically, he's been all over the map. Early in his career he was a social worker and history teacher. Then he was a moderate Republican before becoming a Tea Partier. After leaving office, he was a right-wing conservative radio host, but since then he has become one of the most outspoken members of the Republican Party in wanting Trump out of office—to the extent that he's now funding his own run for the presidency, just to have a platform for his Trump-hating.

He begins his talks by saying, "I am a Republican and I think Trump is unfit for office." He goes on to say, and more than once, that "Trump lies every time he opens his mouth," and to say "all Trump cares about is Donald Trump. Nothing else." Walsh says Trump is absolutely guilty as charged by the House of Representatives, and when I asked him what other Republicans in the House and Senate think about Trump he said, "They all know he's a moron. They are just scared to keep their jobs." He says everyone in Washington knows that Trump is "mean and cruel and bigoted."

Walsh believes that the Republican Party is threatened with extinction if it continues to roll over and play dead rather than take on Trump. He thinks the senators who will vote for acquittal "will pay a price" in the fall elections. He added, "They will get smoked." He does not believe that climate change is "a hoax," as Trump does, and while he is pro-life, he would love to position the Republican Party to attract more women to its traditions.

He calls the killing of Qasem Soleimani a "bad and stupid thing to do," and he's the only politician I have heard in Iowa who has said nice things about Iran as a country and as a place he would like someday to visit. "It could even be," he said, "an American ally." But whatever the subject, Walsh always comes back to Trump, "this crazy man show. . .this horrible human being in the White House." He believes Trump is driving women from the party in record numbers. He does not think the plans of Warren or Sanders make sense economically, but he said (and you don't hear this often from a Republican), "I love Bernie Sanders because he genuinely believes what he believes."

Walsh said he was getting death threats out on his campaign, and that it is personally costing him time and money to make his stand against Trump. He said he was running because, "I want to surprise him. . ..I want to get under his skin. . .and I want to wake up Republicans. . ."

In less than an hour, he was done talking. Unlike Bernie and Warren, he had engaged a roomful of students, listened to their questions, stated his views, and spoken with civility. I suspect he will get less than five hundred votes in the Republican caucuses, although I suspect anyone who has gone to his events and met him personally will vote for him.

Joe Biden at the Amen Corner

My day ended with two events—Joe Biden's preelection rally in Des Moines and Amy Klobuchar's Super Bowl party in Johnston. I had seen Biden in Council Bluffs, but I had missed Klobuchar as she had been in Washington at the Trump impeachment hearings.

Biden's get-out-the-vote rally was held at Hiatt Middle School, which is on the edge of downtown Des Moines, not far from the state capitol but in what I might call a pawn shop district. The doors for the rally opened at 3:45 p.m., and well before that there were lines of Biden supporters snaking along the school's sidewalks. Inside the school gym, literally hundreds of media types were crammed into the corners. I talked to journalists from Washington, Israel, France, and Australia, and I could see big-name anchor people squeezed up against security barriers.

At that point in the day I was more interested in the Super Bowl than in hearing another Joe Biden address, but I hoped that he might wrap things up quickly so that everyone present could get on to the greater matter of state—that of the Chiefs and 49ers. It wasn't to be.

It took forever for the state senators and members of Congress to give their speeches, and then Joe's wife Jill had to sing her husband's praises. For some of her remarks, she was speaking into a dead mic, although I don't think many in the room were there to catch Jill's encomium.

Then someone had to introduce the extended Biden clan that was seated in the bleachers, and some of the honored guests, including former presidential candidate and Secretary of State John Kerry, who was later overhead in a Des Moines hotel saying Biden was a "dead man walking" in the race and that he might have to jump in to save the republic. I am sure the Bidens were happy that they had invited him to the rally.

By the time Joe was ready to speak, the mic and the acoustics remained weak. (We were in a middle school gymnasium with concrete walls. . .) So as much as Biden wanted to sound like William Jennings Bryan, the Democratic candidate in 1896 and in two other elections (". . .*we shall answer their demands for a gold standard by saying to them, you shall not press down upon the brow of labor this crown of thorns. You shall not crucify mankind upon a cross of gold. . .*"), in the end Biden sounded like an assistant principal telling seventh-graders not to throw snowballs at recess. His voice was reedy, he sounded tired, and no one was listening. Yes, people cheered at the applause lines, but only because Biden would stop talking and wait for the clapping. In the end, with family present, it felt more like a retirement party or last hurrah than a new frontier.

Amy Klobuchar Throws a Super Bowl Party

I only went to Amy's Super Bowl party because I had yet to hear her speak and because I didn't think either Bernie or Elizabeth would have much to say about Patrick Mahomes or Deebo Samuel. One of the problems of this election is that I can't think of any candidate with whom I would want to watch the Super Bowl.

Amy's Super Bowl party wasn't in her basement wet bar but at Jethro's BBQ n' Pork Chop Grill, in Johnston, about 10 miles from Des Moines. By the time I got there, the place was packed, and the only place I could stand and watch some of the game was near the podium where Amy was supposed to speak at halftime.

The game was 3-0, and Jethro was doing a land-office business with pitchers of beers, nachos, and guacamole, but despite all the televisions around the bar I didn't sense many people were watching the game. (Good for Amy, but bad for America.)

Only 10 minutes after I got there, the front doors opened, and surrounded by a flock of television cameras, Amy walked into Jethro's. According to one of her handlers, Amy had to fly back to Washington to attend more impeachment hearings. She could not watch the game with everyone, and she would be speaking right away. (No one asked, but I wondered: What would Troy Aikman think?)

On her arrival, Amy's super fans ("*. . .real good, Bob. . .*") took up an "Amy, Amy, Amy. . ." chant. Only when she climbed onto the podium did things quiet down. Klobuchar apologized to the party for not being able to stay for the evening and mix with the crowd. She said she had work to do back in Washington, and she was sure the crowd would understand her absence and work hard to turn out voters for the caucus. She attempted to make a football joke, involving the goal line and a touchdown, but, to extend the analogy, she fumbled the ball and took the speech elsewhere—on the need to turn out voters for the caucus.

For the substance of her talk, Klobuchar spoke about her roots as a political, grassroots organizer. She even told a self-deprecating joke about an early attempt in a political campaign, when she went into a room that in theory was to have been full of Democrats, but only had six people present. She braced herself for disappointment and began to give her speech, when one of the men present said, "This is the golf club. The Democrats are next door."

If Klobuchar exceeds expectations in Iowa, it will be because she's good at grassroots politics, and because her home state of Minnesota shares a long border with Iowa. She's also vying for center space with Biden and Mayor Pete. Iowans might appreciate her Midwest accent and sensibility, but I sense she will fail to make the 15 percent cut in most precincts, and thus be left to decide whether to cut a deal with a frontrunner (say Joe Biden) or whether she would do better in the long run teaming up with someone such as Pete. (In effect, there is a second ballot in Iowa, after the results gauge who has met the 15 percent threshold.)

Her best chance is to become a vice presidential nominee, but that will only happen if, to use a Trump phrase from the impeachment hearings, she has "the deliverables." Something tells me she does not, as no Democratic candidate should need Amy to win in Minnesota. But it's a strength that she's running as someone who in Congress is very adept at getting legislation passed—to distinguish here from other senators running, Sanders and Warren, who are better at the talk end of politics than in getting bills passed through Congress.

Either Bernie Sanders or Joe Biden could pick her as a running mate, but I suspect both would lean more toward Senator Kamala Harris, if only to solidify the African American vote, which failed to turn out for Hillary in 2016 to the extent that it voted for Obama in 2012.

Soon after Klobuchar greeted her guests, she was headed toward her bus and presumably the airport for the flight to Washington. To my knowledge she didn't have any of the chicken wings being passed around or one of the 16 ounce beers that were sitting on the bar. I left at the same time, figuring I would see more of the game back in my hotel than I would sitting in a noisy bar, unable to hear Mahomes call out the MIKE (middle linebacker). As it turned out, the Klobuchar bus, "Amy For America," was parked near my car, so that as I was fumbling for my keys, I could see her walking back to her bus.

It spoke well of her that she was willing to fly all the way back to Washington to hear closing arguments in the impeachment trial, even though the acquittal is a foregone conclusion. At the same time, I never heard from Klobuchar exactly why she wants to be president. I heard that she will be a careful guardian of the state and work hard and pass bills with the Congress, but as for the substance of her campaign, it felt a little like some of Jethro's wings.

Iowa's Lost Votes

WITH 1,700 PRECINCT VOTES IN IOWA on the night of the caucuses, you would have thought that I could find one of the gatherings without breaking a sweat in the sub-freezing Des Moines night air.

I had thought about driving into the heartland and finding a caucus in some four-corners small town, to watch democracy-in-action as it is imagined in an eighth-grade civics class. One of the quirks of the caucuses is that the locations of the votes can and do change, even at the last minute. Talk to a group of Iowans about their "voting experience," and the first thing they will describe is how at the last minute the location of their caucus changed—American democracy as a variation on Three-Card Monte.

Not having found a caucus site online, I set off in my rental car, in search of an elementary school or town hall surrounded with parked cars, if not a few Bernie signs driven into the frozen snow. Given the hype surrounding the caucuses—the first primary, America speaking, cradle of the democracy, etc.—around the time voting started I had expected to find few cars on the road and stores to be empty (equivalent to the reverence of the Super Bowl). At least in the malls that I passed in my caucus searching, it was business as usual, Mammon still holding more sway than the statutes of liberty.

In something of a panic, not having found any grassroots in the snow of suburban West Des Moines, I set my sails for Drake

University, figuring that a caucus of college kids would highlight the divide between frontrunners Bernie Sanders, Elizabeth Warren, and Joe Biden.

Drake did not disappoint. Along University Avenue I found a parking lot chock-full of TV sound trucks and then got directions to the Knapp Center, where a few nights earlier I had attended a Donald Trump rally—the executive branch of government set to the strains of mixed martial arts.

The Knapp Center is Drake's basketball arena. When Trump was playing the house, it was covered in patriotic bunting and the rafters were beating to the line dances of the Village People, notably "Macho Man." (Trump and Pence had the look of a wrestling tag team.) On this evening the Knapp Center was yet again a basketball court, but this time, in addition to gathering caucusers, it was filled with TV crews in search of common man quotes from those riding the pine for their favorite candidates.

The Iowa Caucus's Chamber of Secrets

The Iowa caucuses are America's chamber of secrets—in how the votes are cast and counted—and on this particular night the Knapp Center was one of the deathly hallows.

Citizens don't vote for the candidate of their choice. They gather across the state in public spaces and then stand or sit in groups for the candidate of their choice. You get delegates to the county and state conventions if you exceed a 15 percent threshold. But that's just the start.

In the Knapp Center, after signing in and providing voter bona fides, the groups took their places in the lower stands—a bit like marching bands or booster clubs. Then there was a lull, while the caucus chairman (a local Democratic volunteer) counted the total number present in the hall. The roll call total in the Knapp Center was 849, which became the figure used to calculate what locally is called "viability," or 15 percent of the total number present.

Any candidate in the first round who did not get 15 percent of the total would be deemed "non-viable," and then, in the next round of voting, his or her supporters would be free to change their vote to one of the remaining candidates. The local term for this subsequent jockeying is "realignment," during which time spokespersons for "viable" candidates make deals with voters in search of a candidate. Before the final vote is taken, each person present at the caucus has to fill out a "presidential preference card" listing their "First Preference," which is the paper trail that was much discussed when it became clear that Iowa's caucus votes had vanished down either a rabbit or an app hole.

A Des Moines Caucus: Voter Early, Vote Often

All this at the Knapp Center took more than an hour to organize. Meanwhile, the local Democratic Party passed the hat to raise some money, and TV journalists—NBC's Katy Tur among them—frantically worked the aisles of the box seats, in search of truths that were probably self-evident. Finally, the vote totals were counted and announced over the PA system (so much for the local Democratic committee not knowing the results), and in the Knapp Center the first take looked like this:

Warren	212
Buttigieg	172
Klobuchar	140
Biden	131
Sanders	129
Yang	28

Steyer   26
Gabbard   2
Uncommitted   7

The non-viable candidates were Yang, Steyer, Gabbard, and the uncommitted, and their voters were given 15 minutes to decide on another candidate. Sometimes the voters for non-viable candidates move elsewhere as a bloc; other times they just scatter individually.

It took more than 15 minutes for realignment, after which the vote total was this:

Warren   227
Buttigieg   194
Klobuchar   149
Biden   138
Sanders   134

In the realignment Buttigieg gained the most votes (22), while Bernie gained the fewest (five). Some of the uncommitted remained uncommitted (six) and simply went home. Realignment is a public clue about the personal relations among the candidates. For example, a lot of the Yang supporters went to Warren, and not many non-viable voters went to Bernie.

The Great State of Confusion

The confusions of the Iowa caucuses don't end with realignment. All that this first round of voting determines is the election of delegates who will attend their party's county conventions, which in turn will select delegates to a state convention. In the end, the 1,700 precincts that held caucuses on February 3 will produce 41 delegates who will attend the Democratic National Convention next summer. In theory all the candidates who remain "viable" through the county and state conventions will win a proportionate number of national delegates, but sometimes the winner of the first round in the caucuses isn't the candidate who, in the end, gets the most number of delegates.

In 2012, Mitt Romney thought he had won the Republican Iowa caucuses, and on the night of the voting, he was crowned the winner on network television. Two weeks later, it became clear that Pennsylvania Senator Rick Santorum had actually won the most delegates in Iowa.

There is another quirk of the Iowa caucuses: the television networks usually report the results as a percentage of delegates won, not based on the total number of votes received. And in calculating the total number of votes a candidate receives, there are two numbers: one before and another after realignment. To put in perspective how few people actually vote in Iowa (and thus how few Americans determine the frontrunning nominees of the two major parties), consider the following statistics: Iowa has a population of roughly three million people of whom about two million are eligible to vote. Of that number about 700,000 are registered Democratic, although less than 200,000 people turn up, in presidential years, "to caucus." The so-called winner in Iowa will often receive less than 40,000 direct votes, which means that the proclaimed "winner" of the Iowa caucuses will have received the vote of 2 percent of Iowa's population. Of the 235 million eligible voters in the United States, 0.02 percent will have had a say in what is regarded as one of the most influential votes in the presidential primaries. So much for the pretensions of the democracy. (A Gallup poll of 500 Iowans would take less time and might be more accurate.)

Iowa: Not What It Used to Be

Why, you might ask, does the country, let alone the party, waste its time with an Iowa caucus, especially as an early barometer of relative strength among the presidential candidates?

Iowa is hardly representative of the nation as a whole. (It's an egg white, not an omelet.) Nor is it particularly adept at turning out voters (or, as it now turns out, counting the votes). In Chicago, they can stuff ballots faster than they can count them in Iowa.

Iowa's position as an early primary is a byproduct of its caucus system (only five states still use them). Back in the day, time was needed for Iowans to caucus at the precinct, county, and state levels, and then to send its delegates to the national convention. But those reasons to let Iowa be "the first in the nation" are no longer valid.

Another reason for Iowa's preference among presidential primaries is nostalgia and the romantic idea that almost anyone can charter a bus, raise a little money, and throw themselves at the mercy of the caucuses, which might just favor an unknown outsider, such as Jimmy Carter (1976), George H.W. Bush (1980), or Barack Obama (2008). The argument is also made, among party insiders, that Iowa "has the infrastructure" to host the early presidential vote. (It sounds a little bit like saying that Los Angeles is ideally situated to host the Rose Bowl.) In this logic, Iowa is best suited—in terms of county chairmen, chartered buses, and Grange halls—to put on the show, about which Iowans have become sentimental. Think of an apple festival in Montana.

Iowans like the quirkiness of the caucuses, which require their presence for an evening in a public space, and they like having a chance to listen in person to the candidates. They like the sociability of the night, with neighbors dragooning other neighbors to come out in the cold to support one of the candidates. But keep in mind that the crowds at a state fair are almost more representative of a state than are those who "caucus" in Iowa.

Iowans, at least those who turn up for the caucuses, have a soft spot for their idiosyncratic system. They believe that the demographics of Iowa—the mix between the larger university towns and the vast stretches of farmland—test a candidate's ability to organize a campaign and to appeal to a cross-section of Americans. Personally, I have no quibble if Iowa wants to select its delegates with a system that James Garfield might have found antiquated (he ran for president in 1880 and won the nomination at the national convention). But picking candidates in Iowa is only marginally more democratic than picking names out of a hat.

Biden's Mournful Celebration in Des Moines

Because it was close by and the night air was freezing, I decided to drop in on the Biden victory party, which was being held in another building on the Drake campus where, (most importantly) I already had a parking place.

I had thought that by the time I got there, the results of the caucus would be known and that, in the lobby around the bar, I might come across a few spin doctors, who would explain to me that Joe Biden never expected to come in better than fourth or fifth place.

The Biden party had everything except a win. It had a ballroom with bunting and TV cameras, a large press room with televisions streaming CNN, two well-stocked bars, and enough political middle men to overstaff a presidential campaign.

With no results to analyze, I took a seat in the press room. All around me were bored TV and radio crews, interviewing each other on why an app was a poor way to run an election. For two hours, I watched Wolf Blitzer tread studio water, answering his own questions. Finally, before it got too late, Joe and Jill Biden took what was scripted as a victory lap in front of the adoring crowd. Joe waved and pointed to his friends, and made a brave new world speech about how he was running a national campaign "in all 50 states. . . ," with his eyes on places such as South Carolina and Super Tuesday. I didn't get the feeling that many were buying the line. He sounded as though he was trying to convince himself.

Without any of the results in Iowa announced, here was Biden at his victory party, giving what sounded like a concession speech. Just after he stopped speaking, the party had the feel of a wake. Around the bar at the Biden after-party, the great tragedy of the Iowa vote-count debacle wasn't that the leader (in this case they were still hoping it would be Biden) was deprived of his or her 15 minutes of fame, but that the computer glitch had delayed the departure of numerous private jets that were to fly the candidates that night from Iowa to New Hampshire.

On the stump, all you ever hear from candidates such as Warren, Sanders, or Buttigieg is that climate change is threatening the planet. But to make their appointed rounds in the primaries, nearly all the candidates (I don't have an exact list) have private planes standing by, as if in a great presidential cab rank. (The term "limousine liberal" feels almost quaint.)

During the time I was in Iowa, all three senators—Warren, Sanders, and Klobuchar—made several fleeting roundtrips between Washington and Iowa, so that they could continue to campaign while attending the impeachment trial. And all the campaigns on the ground were little more than vast fleets of cars and SUVs, frantically crisscrossing Iowa as if delivering packages for FedEx. It's something to keep in mind when, for example, you review Elizabeth Warren's I-have-a-plan for reducing climate change.

The Morning After:
The Coming Democratic Wave

WHAT DOES THE IOWA CAUCUS TELL US about the general election? I didn't get many answers to that question at the Biden after-party, so the next morning, when the votes still had not been counted, I went to an early breakfast that pulled together columnists, activists, and pollsters who were making themselves available to answer insider questions.

It turned out that we were fewer than 10 at the breakfast, and nearly everyone there had voted the night before at their neighborhood caucus. (The accounts felt like those from jury duty.) Those at the breakfast told stories about caucuses that had changed their locations, and replayed the irony that all the results had been tabulated for more than 12 hours, as before adjourning for the night each precinct caucus had publicly announced the results. (A simple email to headquarters would have sufficed.)

What interested me at the breakfast was the presence of a Virginia-based political scientist, Rachel Bitecofer, who said that, prior to the 2018 election, her computer model accurately predicted that the Democrats would pick up 40 seats in the House of Representatives. I asked her a number of questions about the 2020 general election, and her answers surprised me, as the common wisdom on the ground is that Donald Trump will beat a left-wing Democratic candidate, such as Sanders or Warren. She is the first person whom I have encountered in Iowa whose data indicates a Democratic victory in 2020, no matter who the nominee is, including Sanders and Warren.

In Iowa, she was trying to gauge if turnout in the caucuses would be greater than 2012 or 2016, and if so whether it might indicate a Democratic revival in a state that otherwise has been red in recent general elections. For the moment, she was pessimistic about the possibility that Iowa would flip to the Democrats, but in broad electoral terms she described the Trump victory in 2016 as a political aberration, in which some disgruntled Democrats stayed away from Hillary Clinton while Trump energized a bloc (the MAGA crowd) that had not voted in other elections.

By her account, Democrats were not as weak nationally as anecdotal evidence might indicate. She was predicting that at least three swing seats in the Senate would flip to the Democrats—Maine, Colorado, and Arizona— although she thought the Democrats would lose in Alabama. She made the point that in 2016 Trump won in a number of swing states, but only by a plurality, and that some of those states would revert to the Democrats in 2020. In particular, she did not think Trump could win in Pennsylvania or Michigan, and she thought he was vulnerable—again, no matter who the Democrats run—in Florida, North Carolina, Arizona, and Wisconsin. (She thought Iowa stayed Republican.) She described the leadership of the Democratic Party as "strategically inept," and said that the Democrats could have won another 20 House seats in 2018 if money and time had been allocated wisely.

She emphasized that her model for 2020 was not based on any one candidate running against Trump. (She finished it in July 2019.) She said she might have to reassess her numbers if Sanders were the nominee, but said that as long as the Democratic nominee presented "an affirmative case" to the electorate he or she should win. She also emphasized that the Democratic ticket needed to "embrace diversity" to turn out a broad coalition in the general election. In 2016, a number of African Americans who had voted for Obama in 2012 did not turn out for Hillary.

Where Bitecofer thinks Trump has been strongest is in targeting and energizing his MAGA base and by having his flag-waving rallies in key swing districts around the country. In political science terms she said that he has "inflamed negative partisanship" and was very lucky with how the voting went in 2016. (*"He was a seriously flawed candidate."*) But she does not think that in 2020 Trump will carry the Democratic states that he did in 2016.

When I asked her about pivotal groups to watch in the election, she said that the bloc of 5-6 percent independent and uncommitted voters hold the key to the 2020 election. She said that in general terms this group was "motivated by change" and "never happy." In 2016, these independents stayed away from Hillary and voted for Trump (*"motivated by change"*), and that was their margin that won states such as Pennsylvania, Wisconsin, and Michigan for Trump and the Republicans. She doubts it will happen again.

I asked which potential Democratic candidate "was the biggest gamble for the Democratic Party," and she mentioned Sanders and Biden as "risks." She didn't think it was "impossible for Sanders to win," but did say that he might need to trim his socialist sails. She said Biden was a risk because of his age and his predilection to go off script. A centrist, such as Klobuchar, would probably defeat Trump easily, given her forecast of the realignment of the American electorate, and in the not-too-distant future she sees many more states in the West, including Texas, in play for the Democrats. She said Hillary was a weak candidate (those cranky independents sat on their hands) and then she became a victim to a perfect Trump storm, but Bitecofer doesn't think it will happen two elections in a row.

Iowa's Winners and Losers

The only surprise of the Iowa caucus was that Pete Buttigieg did as well as he did in precincts across the state, including in rural and suburban districts. He took the most votes from Joe Biden, who would have loved the demographics that Buttigieg won, although Pete's voters were younger than Biden could ever have expected to attract.

The Sanders vote was more regionally distinct. He did well in the university enclaves, the people's republics around Ames and Iowa City, and in pockets of Des Moines (which is more suburban than you might think). He did not do well in rural districts, which is no surprise, as in his litany of American ills Bernie never mentions the word "farmer" and he has a way of describing "the working class" that makes it sound like the *Lumpenproletariat* (a standby Karl Marx expression for those who are aggrieved but lack class consciousness). Elizabeth Warren's votes came from women of all ages, but she will need to do better among men if she wants to advance further. (Bailey didn't help there.) Nor did she win many, if any counties, placing a respectable second or third across the state.

Amy Klobuchar's spin is that she is finishing very close to Biden, in terms of total votes (the difference is less than 1 percent). She has also pointed to the fact that she started with zero name recognition in Iowa, except in counties along the Minnesota border, while Biden spent eight years as vice president under Barack Obama. She has to be a little disappointed that caucusers preferred Pete's white bread messages over her own.

Perhaps the most interesting story I picked up in the spin rooms and around Iowa is the anger that the Sanders campaign has for the Democratic National Committee and the poobahs of the party. The Sanders crowd remains angry that the DNC had its thumb on the scale for Hillary in 2016, and there were mumblings that some of the delay in announcing the caucus results was to downplay Bernie's victory and strength heading into New Hampshire, where he has a good chance of winning (and running away with the nomination). In his party, Sanders is almost as much an outsider as was Trump with the Republicans in 2016. Sanders has identified as either an independent or a socialist for most of his career. He only became a Democrat officially in 2016 to run against Hillary, and even now he looks more like William Jennings Bryan—a 19th century figure of the Progressive movement—than a president-in-waiting. Bryan ran for president three times and eventually served (very poorly) as Wilson's secretary of state. From Byran came many ideas—the income tax, child labor laws, an end to the gold standard, conservation, etc.—that later were incorporated into the liberal Democratic, New Deal canon.

Sanders is already claiming that his ideas about universal health care, a livable wage, and climate change have become mainstream Democratic principles. But whatever the pollsters say about the coming Democratic wave, I have a hard time imagining that a cranky socialist can win the general election. (Bryan lost three times, and Eugene V. Debs lost five times, running as a socialist.)

The Dark Arts of Frontrunning

The easy story in Iowa is that Joe Biden has been run over and left for dead in a cornfield near Dubuque, and that may well be the case. The Biden people that I met at the after-party and beyond all said they never expected Joe to get much traction in Iowa and that he will come alive in racially diverse South Carolina, where Buttigieg is polling at zero among African Americans, and Bernie will not have his liberal base of Sandernistas knocking on familiar doors. It's a brave face, and Biden could well be right, although three of the first four primaries (Nevada is the fourth) favor Sanders. Biden has the additional problem of Michael Bloomberg and his billions lurking around the centrist corners of the race.

In the fight for the Democratic soul of the primaries, there are those on the left wing (Sanders, Warren, Steyer, and Yang), those in the center (Biden, Klobuchar, Bloomberg), and those who wobble between several axes (Buttigieg and Gabbard), although I get the impression (without having heard her speak) that Gabbard's constituency is from Krypton. Certainly her billboards, floating above the fields in Iowa, gave her an otherworldly appearance. Biden's biggest defeat in Iowa came in the money primary. I heard that his campaign is down to $9 million and on life support from super PAC bagmen, who weren't impressed with his fourth-place finish in Iowa. (Win it, and they will come.)

Needless to say, running from the vaults of Pluto, Bloomberg has no money constraints or masters with checkbooks to appease, and he could well become the centrist survivor (along with Klobuchar) to take on Bernie and Buttigieg in the quarterfinals. That said, the last thing the Democrats want is to have two finalists for the nomination who, until recently, were never part of the Democratic Party. Ironically, despite all the network prime time devoted to the caucus returns that vanished in the night, Iowa rarely decides much of anything. It's the first game of spring training, after a four-year layoff, and for that reason the network chieftains and reporters cover Iowa as if it were the seventh game of the World Series. At this point in the counting, Sanders is ahead in the popular vote in Iowa (with about 31,000) and tied with Buttigieg with a grand total of 10 delegates pledged to him. Yet in the TV caucuses, Sanders is relegated to second place, another reason for his anger at the DNC. If Sanders does win the nomination, don't expect him to be a gracious winner. That's not how the game is played in Brooklyn.

Live from the
New Hampshire Primary

"The supply of government exceeds demand."

—Lewis H. Lapham

Retail Politics

EVEN PRESIDENTIAL PRIMARIES HAVE SNOW DAYS, and now I have had two in New Hampshire. About four inches of snow fell on the first day, and on the second day I was in the state the weather turned to sleet and freezing rain. I know that "neither snow nor rain nor heat nor gloom of night" should keep this "courier from the swift completion of [his] appointed rounds," but when the choice, on this occasion, was driving on frozen roads to hear Tulsi Gabbard address the Fireside Inn in Lebanon, New Hampshire, I didn't always summon the energy to bear witness to someone who herself might not be present.

Mr. Amy Klobuchar

Actually, for my first small steps in New Hampshire, the campaign came to me in the form of John Bessler, who is the husband of Minnesota Senator Amy Klobuchar (of 12.3 percent fame in the Iowa caucus). He was literally showing up about a mile from where I was staying, to address what used to be called "a tea" of concerned voters.

Bessler showed up right on time, despite the rain and snow. He was wearing a (slightly rumpled) blue suit, which is the exception on the trail in 2020. (Last evening in Durham, I bumped into Colorado Senator Michael Bennett, who was wearing sneakers and looked as though he was about to coach a gym class.) A tall man with a receding hairline, Bessler shook hands with everyone in the room. We were a circle of about 14 people, and then he stood near the dining room table (in what is a beautiful house, owned by an Amy for America volunteer) and spoke for close to an hour on behalf of his wife's candidacy.

By trade Bessler is a lawyer and law professor, and after he was done speaking I asked him where he was teaching and he said that he was both at Georgetown and the University of Baltimore, but that, overall, his legal and emotional base was in Minneapolis. He said that he and Amy had been married for 26 years, and that they had one daughter, who, as it turned out, was one of the reasons that Klobuchar got involved with state politics in Minnesota. Bessler told the story of how, when their daughter was born, she was not able to swallow well, and required a feeding tube to survive. After about a day in the hospital, Amy was booted out of the maternity ward while the baby remained behind for treatment (which took a long time to cure her).

At the time, Amy was a lawyer in Minneapolis, representing such clients as MCI (an upstart phone company challenging the bigger players). But her anger at being separated from her sick daughter pushed Amy to lobby the state legislature to pass a law, allowing women to remain at least 40 hours in the hospital after delivering a baby. Those were the first steps that Amy took in politics, which in time saw her elected three times to the U.S. Senate from Minneapolis and now to stand as a presidential candidate. From her first dealings with the legislature, she had an inkling, according to John, of "what an advocate can do."

In the iconography of the 2020 election, Klobuchar is the senator who can actually get something done in Congress. She's a midwestern pragmatist who can work well with moderates in both parties. Although John phrased the contrast diplomatically, what he wanted to leave behind with the tea party is that Amy "gets things done" while Senators Sanders and Warren are better at talking the talk.

Klobuchar's first elective office in Minnesota was as a county attorney, from which in 2006 she stood for the U.S. and won, by an average margin of nine votes in the precincts across Minnesota. Her reelections in 2012 and 2018 were more comfortable; those she carried by margins of 35 and 20 points.

John made the point to the crowd gathered in the living room that in 2018 Amy won 31 counties that in the 2016 presidential election had flipped from Barack Obama to Donald Trump, to indicate that, as the nominee, she would be acceptable to moderates in both parties (unlike the bomb-throwing Sanders and Warren, although he didn't say it like that).

The more I listened to Professor Bessler lecture about "Amy Klobuchar's Contract for American Renewal," the more clearly his wife and the candidate came into focus as a can-do midwestern senator, in the Progressive traditions of Senators Hubert Humphrey, Eugene McCarthy, and Walter Mondale. Like Elizabeth Warren, Klobuchar has a fair number of plans, and, as if addressing a jury, Bessler Esq. went through her ideas to invest in American infrastructure, deal with climate change (she would increase gas mileage standards and renewable energy), dedicate resources to education and job training, and even squirrel away some resources to amortize some of the $23 trillion in national debt. In all cases, John said, Amy was good (in their lives together and in the Senate) at husbanding resources. She didn't like wasting money, and she had always managed to get the most from her resources.

In the Iowa caucuses, for example, she spent the least amount of money of any of the other major candidates (Buttigieg spent about $10 million, as did Bernie Sanders and Tom Steyer while

Amy spent $3.9 million). From Bessler's remarks I got the feeling that one of the issues for which Klobuchar has the most passion is the enforcement of anti-trust legislation. It's one of her committee assignments in the Senate, and trust-busting (as it used to be called) appealed to her sense of economic level playing fields, fairness to consumers, and opposition to oligarchy. He made the point that it was two Republicans, Presidents Theodore Roosevelt and William Howard Taft, who had first enforced anti-trust legislation (first passed during the administration of Democrat Grover Cleveland but ignored by William McKinley, who was in the pocket of the bosses, notably business tycoon and fixer Mark Hanna).

If there was a consistency in the questions posed to Amy's husband, it was how, if she were the nominee, she could stand up to a lunatic such as Donald Trump who campaigns as if Mussolini on his balcony. (The questions, from the New Hampshire townspeople, were posed in a much more delicate manner.) What seemed to matter most to the people gathered (an older crowd with midday time on their hands) was beating Trump in the general election.

In that quest, as judged by questions, they were happy to hear John sing his wife's praises as a pragmatic, midwestern legislator, but really what they wanted to know is whether Amy had it in her to kick Trump in the crown jewels. (My wording, not theirs.) In response to a number of questions, Bessler said, "Trump isn't going to know how to deal with a strong willed woman such as Amy."

Over and over, he described her as task-oriented, detail-driven, and focused on the people's business. He was never entirely convincing that Amy had some of Butch Cassidy's wiliness, shown in the knife fight with Harvey Logan, which ends with Butch taking down Harvey who has challenged him for leadership of the Hole-in-the-Wall Gang. Trump is the Harvey Logan of American politics.

If there was a downside during the Q&A, it came when Bessler answered a question about how Amy would deal with Putin and Russia, and his answer, which drifted back to her Senate committee work on cross-border trade with Canada, indicated that neither Klobuchar nor her husband have much feel or experience with foreign affairs.

At one point during the reception, he had mentioned that he had grown up in a trailer park (the son of a professor) and that Amy's mother had taught second grade in a Minnesota primary school. He said that Amy's maternal grandparents (the Heubergers) had emigrated from Switzerland while his ancestors came from Germany. (Think of Willa Cather's novel *My Antonia*, about European immigrants to the Great Plains.) He evoked the Bessler-Klobuchar world as very much settled in the Midwest and now Washington, D.C. and the U.S. Senate.

The more John spoke, the more I sensed that as a political couple anyway, their world was that of Minnesota politics and its issues more than they delved too much in things such as the legacy of Brest-Litovsk and the League of Nations. A lack of experience in foreign affairs isn't at all fatal for a presidential candidate (I doubt Trump could point to Iran on a globe), but it could lead to discomfort on the campaign trail, if Amy is ever challenged, for example, about the Macedonian Question.

William Weld Shouts into the Trump Void

Deval Patrick, the former governor of Massachusetts and the close friend of Barack Obama, has gotten little respect during this Democratic political campaign. Except maybe in an early round, he has been excluded from the televised debates, and only because

CNN needed to have eight guests was he included in the Town Hall series of prime-time, hour-long interviews, although Patrick was put on in the 11:00 p.m. slot, never ideal.

To my knowledge he did not campaign in Iowa, instead deciding to husband his resources for New Hampshire, where he could hope to trade off his name recognition as the former governor of Massachusetts. Another former Massachusetts governor, William Weld on the Republican side, who is challenging Donald Trump, made the same calculation but he turned up for a whistlestop tour (okay, in a rental car) in Iowa.

I tracked down Deval Patrick at a public event held at the University of New Hampshire, which is located in Durham, not far inland from the coast. For a state university, UNH has an exceptionally pretty, red-brick campus and does not feel especially large. Overall there are some 15,000 full- and part-time students on campus. Patrick was speaking at a conference entitled College Costs & Debt in the 2020 Elections. The host was the UNH Carsey School for Public Policy, and the topic, I am sure, was chosen with the idea of luring some presidential hopefuls to campus.

As it turned out, only the second-team candidates accepted the invitation to speak at the conference. Hence, the attendees were Representative Tulsi Gabbard, Senator Michael Bennett, Weld, and Patrick, and from the list Gabbard bailed at the last minute, pleading the excuse of the weather (which remained a mixture of snow, rain, and ice). Before Patrick, Weld spoke for about 20 minutes, and he succinctly summarized the crisis in higher education, which is that many students graduate with too much debt and too few job prospects. I know he's nominally a fiscally conservative former governor, but on the stage at the UNH Carsey School he sounded like former presidential candidate George McGovern.

Weld said many college graduates had become "indentured students" to various student loan programs, and that the only way to get out from under the debt was to pay it off or die. Nor, he said, was it possible to benefit from a rate reduction as interest rates have trended lower, and if graduates missed payments on the debt, they were charged an assortment of fees and penalties, casting the student loan programs of the federal government in the guise of loan sharks. Weld did not believe that graduates should have to begin servicing their loan until they were earning enough money on the job to be comfortable in making the monthly payments. He also advocated debt forgiveness for any graduates who had served adequate time in the military or in an equivalent public-service job.

Weld's presentation was less a stump speech and more an accounting of a federal program gone awry, in that many schools (certainly many for-profit colleges) existed to recruit students who could then take out extortionate federally guaranteed loans. As he described it, much of higher education was a vicious cycle in which to get good jobs after school, students needed to attend reputable colleges and universities, and often to pay for those schools incurred crippling debt. Weld called it "the compounding problem," when graduates were forced to spend years, often at uninspiring jobs, just to service their student loans. He also warned that with the development of artificial intelligence, many workers will lose their jobs (those for which they took on high debts).

Weld isn't convinced that everyone needs to attend a four-year college or university and, like others in the presidential campaign who I have heard, spoke well of two-year community colleges and trade schools as often sufficient, and at much lower costs, for many high school graduates. As someone who has worked in both federal and state government, he recognized (painfully) that the predatory lenders did not always have the best interests of students at heart. It prompted Weld, in a slightly discursive way, to talk about his own evolution from being a conservative Republican to someone who now, he said, believes that "government has a responsibility to look after its citizens. . . ," and with that mindset he didn't like it that some aspect of public and private education has turned into a racket.

Weld himself went to Harvard, where he studied classics. When I asked him about the books that inspired him, he mentioned Friedrich Hayek's *The Constitution of Liberty*, which is a go-to treatise of libertarian political thought. In that regard, he resented that government—with its heavy-handed debt repayment schedules—had become so dominant in the lives of many graduates, who might well be pushing Sisyphean rocks up mountainous amortization schedules. By the time that Weld spoke to the conference, it was well after 6:00 p.m, and if the room had ever been full (which I doubt), by now it was largely empty. We were perhaps a group of 25, sitting in a hall that could easily accommodate a thousand people. (Even my own undergraduate classes in Greek military history drew a larger crowd.) It highlighted one of the sadnesses of the presidential primary system, which is that it is front-loaded to track polling data, gaffs, soundbites, and miscellany (Bailey Warren, Elizabeth's dog) while the good government ideas are relegated to the not-ready-for-prime-time players.

Deval Patrick Speaks Softly

Deval Patrick, another former Massachusetts governor, followed Weld to the stage, and for an applause line evoked yet another former Massachusetts governor, Mitt Romney, who had just voted to convict Donald Trump on one of the impeachment clauses. He also gave a shoutout to Weld, who after speaking had taken a seat in the audience to hear what Patrick had to say. (Not many candidates run in the listening mode.)

I had never heard Patrick speak, and he was more soft-spoken than I'd expected. His position in the race, other than running on the Largely Unknown ticket, is that of a career Democrat on the left who nonetheless would like to work with moderate Republicans (maybe that's down to Weld and Romney). Patrick is also unusual in candidate circles as he has had two distinct careers, one as a civil rights attorney in the Clinton justice department and the other in private equity, in which he was a senior officer at Bain Capital, the private equity firm that Mitt Romney helped to found. (Patrick came later to the company.) Not all hard-left Democrats appreciate Patrick's work on Wall Street, but unlike, say, Tom Steyer, who tends to gloss over his deal-making life, Patrick is clear in wanting to involve the so-called "private sector" (it sounds like a military term) in solutions to government problems.

Patrick is close to Sanders and Warren in advocating forgiveness of student debt and free tuition, but he would not make college completely free for those who can afford the tuition and fees. Patrick spoke more of getting the government student-debt loan shark off the backs of graduates, by dropping interest rates on borrowed money to zero and by making community college and trade schools free for students (and retooling workers) who need certain basic job skills to enter the economy. He made the point that in-state tuition for the University of New Hampshire is $34,000 while out-of-state costs are $54,000, which makes it beyond the reach of many middle-class students, even those with moderate savings.

Where the forum left me uneasy was in the tone stuck by many speakers and questions, in which higher education is more of a consumer good than an introduction to what Socrates called "the good life." In talking about deceptive lending practices for student loans and the for-profit colleges, Patrick (and some others) made education sound like a faulty stereo system that is being shopped online to consumers (who are often suckered into paying top dollar to enroll in a sociology seminar). In terms of the Democratic nomination, Patrick's high water mark came later that same evening, when he appeared for an hour in a one-on-one conversation on CNN's Town Hall series of candidate interviews. Patrick, however, was given the 11:00 p.m. slot, putting him in competition with QVC jewelry promos.

In the Town Hall, Patrick spoke more generally about his bipartisan credentials, record as a two-term governor, experience in business, and sense of fairness that he would bring to the White House. He spoke of "duty, decorum, respect and restraint" as the cornerstones of his candidacy, and it is a catch phrase that might have gotten more traction were he not running as a one-man band with a 2 percent standing in the polls.

Most of the questions in the forum sounded like appeals in small-claims court about shyster practices in the student-loan market, so I asked Patrick, instead, to speak about his own education at Harvard. It prompted quite a discursive answer, in which he talked about growing up poor on the South Side of Chicago, in a home with his mother and grandmother. When he was accepted at Harvard and told his grandmother of the achievement, she congratulated him and then asked, "Now where is that?" No one in his family had ever been to college.

At Harvard, which he liked for the diversity, size, and challenging intellectual life, he did say that very often, during his undergraduate life, that he lived with the unease that someone might one day tap him on the shoulder and say it had all been a mistake and that he needed to go back to his cold-water tenement on Chicago's South Side. That never happened, and he later flourished at law school. Of late, because of low poll numbers and fundraising, Patrick had not made any of the debates, so he was running on the margins of the campaign, a bit like a rock band playing in neighborhood rec rooms. My sense is that he is soldiering on, perhaps to position himself as a potential vice presidential nominee, in the event the nominee wanted a centrist African American pro-business Democrat with strong ties to the civil rights movement. It's not a bad bet in 2020, with so many older white men running for president (Patrick is 63). And the competitors for such a slot (perhaps with Kamala Harris and Cory Booker) have already withdrawn from the race.

Tulsi Gabbard Makes Contact with Earth

It took me a while to track down Representative Tulsi Gabbard, despite some of the notoriety in her wake. She had not been in Iowa when I was there (except on billboards floating above the Iowa cornfields), and in New Hampshire, for whatever reasons, her campaign felt as if it was flying by night. At most she was only appearing at one or two events each day, and then usually at some remote VFW hall in a place such as Lebanon, New Hampshire, which is an additional two-hour drive from the Boston suburbs around Nashua and Manchester. Where I found the Gabbard candidacy was in Rochester, New Hampshire, at an Elks club that was kitted out with American flags and enough chairs to seat an audience of perhaps 125 people.

Gabbard is the exception in the race for the Democratic nomination in that her campaign is focused largely on foreign affairs, notably on the issue of bringing home the troops from Afghanistan, Iraq, and northern Syria. Most of the other candidates only speak of foreign affairs in the context of the domestic budget (they want to cut military spending to devote resources to the opioid crisis or Medicare for all). Gabbard, however, speaks more openly and directly on behalf of the veterans (she is one of them) who were deployed to these savage wars of peace with no clear government objective behind them, and then largely ignored when they came home with post-traumatic stress disorders.

Gabbard is a major in the Hawaii National Guard, and at times during her candidacy she has left the campaign trail for weekend or summer duty. In many ways Gabbard speaks in the patient, direct, calming voice of a military briefing officer. At the Elks club, she didn't have a relief map of the Middle East or one of those long pointers. Nor was she in the presence of eager new National Guard recruits. Otherwise, the campaign stop was an address to military veterans, to make the point that the United States needs to stop fighting "the forever wars" in the Middle East.

If anything has defined Gabbard's candidacy in the 2020 Democratic race it is her ability to generate headlines that put her at odds with mainstream Democratic orthodoxy and its leadership. Most recently Representative Gabbard voted "present" when the articles of impeachment against Donald Trump were brought before the full House of Representatives. She was the only Democrat not to vote for impeachment. Other headline-generating events include her 2017 meeting with Syrian strongman and President, Bashar al-Assad, and her defamation lawsuit against former Secretary of State Hillary Clinton, who suggested in a tweet (without actually naming Gabbard) that the Hawaii member of Congress might well be a Russian bot or agent.

Gabbard met with Assad to make the point back home that the United States was fighting on the wrong side in Syria. To CNN she justified her meeting by saying, "Whatever you think about President Assad, the fact is that he is the president of Syria. In order for any peace agreement, in order for any possibility of a viable peace agreement to occur there has to be a conversation with him." At the Elks club she didn't mention the meeting with Assad, but she did say several times that ". . .as a veteran, I have been serving in the Army National Guard now for 16 years and continue to serve, served on two Middle East deployments. I have seen this cost of war firsthand, which is why I fight so hard for peace."

Hillary Clinton's view of Gabbard's candidacy is that she's part of an election hoax, on behalf of the Russian hacker state. She said (referring to Gabbard):

> They're also going to do third-party. I'm not making any predictions, but I think they've got their eye on somebody who's currently in the Democratic primary and are grooming her to be the third-party candidate. She's the favorite of the Russians. They have a bunch of sites and bots and other ways of supporting her so far, and that's assuming Jill Stein will give it up, which she might not, because she's also a Russian asset. Yeah, she's a Russian asset, I mean totally. They know they can't win without a third-party candidate.

Against this claim, Gabbard filed suit against Clinton, although I doubt it's more than a campaign spot, as I cannot imagine Gabbard has the appetite to sustain a civil case for five years against Clinton. For the moment, however, it's probably cheaper than running 30-second adds on Manchester television (*"and I support this lawsuit. . ."*). But Hillary could be on to something with Gabbard as at her events she loves having Republicans, Democrats, independents, and Libertarians at her rallies.

As a presidential candidate, Gabbard is an odd mix of empathy and arrogance. She speaks slowly and clearly (most candidates this year sound like carnival barkers), and in her exchanges with the audience she's listens to veterans speak about their deployments, asks appropriate questions in response, and bonds well with families and children, especially. She likes Abraham Lincoln and Martin Luther King, and likes to quote from Lincoln's House Divided speech on the impasse in Washington.

(Actually, when Lincoln gave the speech in 1858 he was still of a mind that one solution to the slavery crisis would be to deport all the slaves either back to Africa or perhaps to such a place as Guyana.)

At the same time as Gabbard is speaking for disgruntled Iraq and Afghanistan vets ("*I want to challenge the war majority coming out of Washington. . .*"), she's also given to inflated boasting, notably her claim that she has the "most experience of any candidate in the race on foreign affairs, except maybe Joe Biden." Actually she's a one-trick pony and only speaks well on the wars in the Middle East (although more with emotion than as someone who understands political intricacies). Later in her talk, Tulsi expanded the reach of her stump speech, and talked generally, as all candidates do, about health care, the opioid crisis, the Supreme Court, mental health, teacher pay, etc., and on those issues she might well be singing from the candidate hymnal. Then she ended her remarks and posed for selfies with her supporters. This wasn't Elizabeth Warren's production selfie line, as you might find in a Japanese car plant; Gabbard took time to pose and chat with each picture, and it took more than 20 minutes to go through the ritual.

I decided I had heard enough about God and country. Besides, it was well after dinnertime. But when I headed for the door, a press aide to the campaign encouraged me to stick around for "a gaggle" (a press conference, in which most of the reporters are from community college newspapers).

I agreed and waited for the gaggle to form, which it did near the American flags and eagles at the front of the room. Actually, one of the college reporters asked an insightful question, about why Gabbard only had one campaign appearance each day, and an aide tried to say that Gabbard didn't really like "to bother the voters" and that she preferred to drop in unannounced at diners or maybe a Target. It made her campaign sound like an episode of *Survivor:*

The Political Edition, in which candidates discreetly wait for voters near where you dry off your fenders at a car wash.

By this point I was done with Gabbard, but I did stick around to ask her a question about the unresolved European crisis in the Balkans. (To me the next European war, if it comes, will happen in or around Kosovo.) I figured she was fair game for the question as "the most qualified candidate in foreign affairs. . ."

Gabbard wanted nothing to do with my Balkan wars question. I even wondered if she knew where Kosovo was. Her facial expression was one of alarm and horror at the question. She cut me off and said an aide would send me an email, and as I wandered back to my car in the Elks parking lot I did think that even Hillary would have given me 10 minutes on Albanian separatism. After all, in Pristina, there's a dress shop with her name on it.

James Carville Spins Michael Bennet

The last candidate on my list was Senator Michael Bennet from Colorado, who has campaigned, without much response, across New Hampshire as if running for local office in Denver. I heard him speak at the Palace Theater in Manchester—actually the event was in a storefront next to the theater—and the only reason the event was packed was because CNN's James Carville introduced him and spoke about Bennet as the second coming in New Hampshire of Bill Clinton.

Actually, when Clinton was the "Comeback Kid" in the 1992 New Hampshire primary, he finished second behind Paul Tsongas. But it was less than a month after Gennifer Flowers had gone public with the details of their affair, and the Clintons had held their Super Bowl halftime marriage therapy session, which Carville himself had helped to orchestrate. I presume that Michael Bennet, a two-term senator, is less of duplex man than Bill Clinton.

Bennet's wife was at the rally (she pleaded his case in the prelims: "*If you will just give him a chance. . .*") as were their three daughters. The reason for the capacity crowd in the storefront wasn't to hear from Bennet or his wife (although both speak well) but from Carville, for whom politics is a blood sport.

I only had ever seen Carville on television, and then in snippets after some debate, so I wasn't quite ready for his on-stage persona, that of a ragin' Cajun. He had on an LSU jersey and a Marine Corps veteran cap, and the waist on his ratty blue jeans was too big, giving his midsection the look of a roped steer. On his feet were designer sneakers, the kind a Kardashian would wear along Rodeo Drive.

Earlier that day, loose on the campaign trail in New Hampshire, Carville had said that Sanders and Warren "were crazy" for their free-tuition plans and Medicare for all pipe dreams. At the Palace, Carville kept his remarks mostly focused on Bennet and how his Far West Democratic centrism would play well in the swing states needed to carry the election. He called Bennet "the new kid on the block" (although Bennet grew up in Washington, D.C., the son of a Democratic operative who worked with Hubert Humphrey and Chester Bowles), and praised his ecumenical appeal across the Democratic Party and beyond. On stage Carville plays up his swamp cat, southern accent and uses the kind of expressions that must fly around Bayou drinking holes just before closing time.

Carville imagined Mitch McConnell's facial expression if Republicans lost control of the Senate ("*like he'd crapped a pineapple. . .*") and put the boot into Bernie for not appealing to southern or western Democrats ("*they'll run away from Bernie Sanders like the devil running away from holy water. . .*"). According to Carville, only Bennet could win the election (he won twice in the purple state of Colorado) and save the republic from Trump ("*we're gonna change things. . .we're gonna dream*"). At times Carville, not a young man, was shouting into the mic and almost slurring his drawled words, and he used downhome phrases (about *"getting the horse out of the barn"*) to encourage those present to vote for Bennet, who of late had made 50 town hall appearances in New Hampshire and had been campaigning in the state for more than a year (*"this is a war. . ."*). And then Carville vanished from the stage, as though someone had switched off CNN.

It was hard for Bennet in person to live up to Carville's hype (*"I know this man and I know the people around him. . ."*), but Bennet's remarks were pitched well to his audience, which was that of a Saturday afternoon crowd window-shopping for a presidential candidate. Earlier that day, I had heard him speak at a candidates' forum, and there he was wearing an undertaker's blue suit and sober necktie. Here he had on jeans and a pullover sweater (plus scuffed shoes), and his main message was that he was the Democrat best able to defeat Donald Trump, as he had won several elections against Republican majorities in Colorado.

Earlier in his career, Bennet was superintendent of the Denver school system, and in many respects his political personality is that of a high school principal rallying the student body for the big game against Trump High. He speaks optimistically, and he believes that his students (in this case American voters) can always do better on their regent exams. If Bennet has a cause about which he is passionate, it is to defeat Mitch McConnell and regain Democratic control of the Senate. More than once, I heard him say, "I can't stand losing to Mitch McConnell" (another crosstown rival?), and he has a stock phrase that "no one should be as cynical or malevolent as Mitch McConnell," but he added that Democrats need to be "as strategic" as the Senate majority leader.

Bennet's problem as a candidate is that he's running as a moderate in a body politic of extremes. He speaks well and seems to have a positive and pleasing personality, not to mention the imprimatur of James Carville, who coined the phrase of electoral pragmatism, "It's the economy, stupid." But in the polls I see in New Hampshire, Bennet hardly moves the dial.

Probably the best story he told at the rally was in response to a question about his mother having escaped as a child from the Warsaw ghetto during World War II. She was born before the war and when the fighting engulfed Warsaw, her parents fled to a suburb, where they hid from the Germans and Russians, depending on the time of the war. One of her uncles in Warsaw hid in the remains of a candy factory.

After the war, her family fled to Stockholm and then Mexico City, before coming to the United States. His mother spoke only a smattering of English when they arrived but in the early 1960s she earned her undergraduate degree from Wellesley College outside Boston and married Michael's father (of *Mayflower* descendants), who was an American diplomat and political aide within the Democratic hierarchy. That Michael's mother survived the Warsaw Ghetto during World War II has no bearing on whether he would make a good president, but his telling of her ordeal suggested some compassion with European history, which otherwise is never mentioned on the campaign trail. Out here, it's America First.

The Last Weekend

On the last weekend before the vote, I crisscrossed much of southern New Hampshire and saw all of the candidates running for the Democratic nomination. Many were at a candidates' forum at New Hampshire Technical Institute, a community college, and the rest I tracked down at get-out-the-vote rallies, which have everything but a bonfire. Here are my notes of each candidate in the closing days of the campaign, in order of polling preference:

Bernie Sanders: Confident Frontrunner

Sanders is running as the confident frontrunner. His team in the field is fairly young, and what attracts most to his cause are his stances on climate change and income inequality.

What people like about Sanders in New Hampshire is that he is familiar and speaks with passion. At a women's rights forum, he drew applause lines for saying he would have a "litmus test" for judicial appointments and not appoint anyone who opposed *Roe v. Wade* and abortion rights. Where Sanders is vulnerable to a centrist challenge (Buttigieg in New Hampshire, Biden in South Carolina) is that, while many voters believe in Bernie's integrity, they don't think his Medicare-for-all, free-tuition numbers stand up. If there's a tagline that works in the campaign, it is: "How are you gonna pay for it?" Buttigieg used it repeatedly against Sanders, in his last New Hampshire rallies, and he targeted Bernie as his chief rival for the primary win.

My feeling is that momentum will carry Bernie over the line in New Hampshire, ahead of Buttigieg and Klobuchar. I don't think he will win South Carolina, but will do well in Nevada, and will be the frontrunner, perhaps against Michael Bloomberg, entering Super Tuesday.

Pete Buttigieg: All Things to All Men

The former mayor of South Bend wants to be all things to all men. He's the outsider from Indiana challenging the covey of Washington insiders. He's the antiwar Afghan war veteran (well, GI driver) who wants to "restore America's standing in the world." He's the liberal Democrat who at his rallies talks about balancing the federal budget and paying down the deficit. He's the McKinsey whizz kid who thinks it's unfair that Amazon and Chevron don't pay taxes. He's the advocate of another Peace Corps who will turn up on Fox News. He's the Leonard Zelig of the Democratic primaries.

The reason he's doing better in the polls is because many casting votes in the primaries (New Hampshire is today) are asking themselves one question: Can this candidate beat Trump? In Pete, many voters see a centrist who can bring together the left and the right, the young and the restless.

I went to one of his last rallies in New Hampshire, where he was getting out the vote, and he spoke as if he had already won the nomination. He said that Senators Harris, Warren, and Klobuchar were all "people I admire," and reached out to "future former Republicans," something Sanders would never do. In his speeches, Buttigieg lacks Bernie's (or even Warren's) fire and ice. He's more of faith healer than an old testament prophet (Bernie's calling). In short doses Pete can sound eloquent, although to me his necktie and no jacket look makes him look like a shoe salesman, although his true calling is as academic dean, not that of an American president.

On subjects such as business, the military, and politics, Pete sounds like a graduate student sitting for his oral exams. I am sure he's done the required reading and has carefully footnoted his thesis, but he's not someone who can apply well the practical experience of his life to his theories of government. Pete has worked in business and done time in the military, but he has no critical insights into the modern corporation and its powers, and his observations about Afghanistan and Iraq sound like excerpts from a *New York Times* Op-ed piece. In most of his life endeavors, he was there, as they say in the Army, to get "his ticket punched."

His undoing in this election will be among African American and young voters, who have a visceral dislike of the careerist mayor, but I can see him in the race for a while, as his vanilla messages (*"I just want to say that I will not take away your Social Security benefits. . ."*) have more reach than those of Amy Klobuchar, Michael Bennet, and Deval Patrick, other centrists in the race.

Elizabeth Warren: Turn Out the Lights

If "Dandy" Dan Meredith, former Dallas Cowboys quarterback and *Monday Night Football* color man, were covering the Warren campaign, he would be singing: "Turn out the lights, the party's over. . ." For Warren, in the big game against the Bernie Raiders, she's behind 27-7, and even though it's the second quarter and Super Tuesday comes with a big half-time show, it's still getting late early out there for Elizabeth.

Warren's views are almost identical to those of Sanders, but voters think he speaks to them with conviction while Warren tends to lecture—the American electorate as first-year law students, taking her class on the social contract. I actually think that voters' preference for Sanders over Warren is a bit unfair, as he's just as much of a carnival barker as she is, but he's considered "passionate" while she's dismissed as "strident." (To many men she sounds like a divorce lawyer, coming for their Porsche.)

Compared to Bernie, Warren has more executive experience (that consumer protection agency, etc.) and she's had fewer heart attacks. Plus she's a little younger. But voters, at least in Iowa and New Hampshire, are buying the argument.

The word most often used among insiders in these primaries is "lanes," and it refers to a candidate's chosen path through the electorate, in terms of the left, center, or right wings. Bernie's lane is on the far left wing of the Democratic Party, to the extent that he identifies with "democratic-socialism," as if lining up with some European workers' party.

In positioning her campaign, Warren chose to fight for Bernie's lane on the far left, and she ceded the center, among leading candidates, to Klobuchar and Buttigieg. Now that Sanders is "winning his lane," there's no place for Warren to go. If she shifts to the right, she will be branded a sellout for political expedience. And there's no room to the left of Sanders, except perhaps the Red Brigades or the Shining Path.

I listened to Warren at two get-out-the-vote rallies, and she hit all of her high notes: about how the economy "is working great if you're a large corporation" and about how "working moms" are getting the shaft in terms of their salaries and what it cost to pay a baby sitter. She shares the pain of her questioners about the opioid crisis and crippling student loans. Or she talks about the "gun violence" problem or making *Roe v. Wade* "the law of the land." Then she hangs around for pictures or offers up Bailey (her faithful golden retriever) to play fetch in the selfie line.

It's all well choreographed, a bit like an episode of *The Ellen DeGeneres Show* (without all the celebrity chefs and more about *"extremists controlling our courts. . ."*). But the ratings aren't there.

Amy Klobuchar: Walking the Centrist Line

Amy for America, the Klobuchar brand, has everything you might want in a presidential campaign. It has endorsements from the *New York Times* and other politically prominent newspapers. It has a 59-year-old, well-spoken woman candidate who has worked successfully in the Senate with Republicans and Democrats. It has a centrist message that ought to sell well in the mall of political America. And it has a flavor of midwestern, soccer mom sensibility (Amy is from Minneapolis) in a campaign that has far too many old white guys from the East or West Coasts. What Amy for America doesn't have is much momentum, although she did well in recent debates, and at her get-out-the-vote rallies in New Hampshire there were many enthusiasts waving her Kelly green signs.

Why hasn't Amy caught fire? I think part of the reason has to do with her tone of voice, which is that of a homeroom school teacher. It's a shame, as Klobuchar is one of the few candidates (of the 11 whom I have listened to in the last two weeks) who does not seem to believe her own press releases and who even delivered a few jokes. I think her midwestern nasal tone and slightly frumpy appearance have given voters a reason to overlook her qualities, which are many. In New Hampshire, a win for Klobuchar would be to do better than Warren and Biden, and to stay close to Buttigieg (in that lane). A fourth- or fifth-place finish, behind Warren and Biden, would kill her candidacy, as neither South Carolina nor Nevada hold much promise for Amy.

Joe Biden: Spins into Fourth

The former vice president can say he never expected to do well in Iowa and New Hampshire, but if you're leading in the national polls (although not the betting odds) and finish fourth in the first two primaries, I am not sure what's left of your candidacy. Plus losing badly in the first two primaries will kill fundraising for Super Tuesday, when he will have to face the liquid campaigns of Bernie Sanders and, I presume, Michael Bloomberg. Nor has Biden been particularly sharp in New Hampshire, after sleepwalking through Iowa. In the debates, he seemed to claim credit for every piece of social legislation that has passed since the Clinton administration. But not many in his audiences seem to connect Joe himself to the bills under review (health care, background checks for gun buyers, etc.).

It seems as if there are two Bidens running for president: one of his imagination, and the other that the voters recall, whose main job during the Obama years was to fly to state funerals. Nor do I think that the impeachment hearings did Biden any favors. I suspect more than a few voters think Trump used his office for political gain (just as they think about 24 impeachment counts could have been brought against the president and made to stick, without a stacked jury). At the same time they don't quite believe the Biden cover story that Hunter had qualities that would earn him $50,000 a month on most Ukrainian boards of directors.

I don't see how Biden can lose in Iowa and New Hampshire, and then, by virtue of winning in South Carolina, get enough momentum to win the nomination on Super Tuesday. He's dangerously low on campaign funds, and Buttigieg and Klobuchar are crowding his lanes. Joe's done, sooner than you think.

Tom Steyer: And I Approve My Message

I guess a billion dollars means less than it used to, as Steyer is going nowhere in the campaign, despite flooding the airways and highways with his paid political messages and billboards. Steyer would love to be the people's Bloomberg, and to corner the electoral market before Mike shows up with his own billions before Super Tuesday.

The problem with his campaign is that he sounds a bit like H. Ross Perot, a whiny spokesman with a bunch of great ideas to get government working—on gun safety, climate control, health care, impeachment, and free tuition, etc. I am sure at some level most Democrats support the ideas that Steyer articulates; they just don't like them coming from him.

I assume that Bloomberg doesn't get the same criticism because he was a three-term mayor of New York while Steyer has never held or run for any political office. In person at his rallies, Steyer comes across as socially awkward, with his tartan neckties and staccato delivery. In Steyer there's a little too much of *The Office* and Michael Scott (Steve Carell). You can almost hear him saying, "Make friends first, make sales second, make love third. In no particular order."

Andrew Yang: Less Than Meets the Eye

There's probably less to Yang than appears at first impression, when his irreverent humor, tech savviness, and youthful appearance make him stand out in a field of 70-year-old contenders who give the impression that they have yet to send an email. I actually think Yang's $1,000-a-month giveaway to every citizen could be grounded in serious economics, but as he presents the idea—Robin Hood soaking the tech giants—it can sound glib, at least without some of the numbers to back up the idea.

Yang's observations about the presence of technology in our lives, while on point at a seminar in Palo Alto, California or Cambridge, Massachusetts, begin to sound extraneous in a political campaign, although personally I think he makes good points about Citizens United being one of the worst judicial judgments in recent years. (He would fund campaigns by giving everyone $100 in "democracy credits" that could then be given to a candidate of choice.) Yang might be among those who are running for president for reasons that have nothing to do with holding the political office. He might see it as a way to build "his personal brand," to position himself down the road as a CEO of a hedge fund or whatever. (Apparently, even failed candidates come away with benefits.) For the moment, his new-age, app-driven campaign has been more successful than some of the traditional ones (say Biden's), and I could see Yang sticking around in the race longer than, say, Warren or Biden, if only because his message is carried further on social media and at lower cost than those delivered in TV ads.

Michael Bloomberg: The $60 Billion Invisible Man

The $60-billion-dollar man is not in New Hampshire. Nor was he in Iowa. But in both states, not to mention in Super Bowl ads, Bloomberg is the man who came to dinner. (It's a Kaufman and Hart comedy from the 1940s, about a man who comes to a house for a dinner and never leaves, turning upside down the lives of those in the house.)

Bloomberg is a bank account more than he's an idea. If he had only $1 billion and never held office, I suppose he would be Tom Steyer, trying to buy a presidential lottery ticket. But with $60 billion and as someone who has run for office as a Democrat and a Republican, Bloomberg is not just an uninvited house guest but, to many, a man in for all seasons.

Bloomberg's lane is down the center, which, if his expense budget were less, would relegate him to the worlds of Deval Patrick and Michael Bennett, both of whom can match Bloomberg for political experience but don't have his resources.

Bloomberg's strategy is to let the Democrats bloody themselves in Iowa, New Hampshire, South Carolina, and Nevada, and for the field to winnow from about nine to three or four. Ideally Bloomberg would love a Democratic field that is down to Sanders, Buttigieg, Biden, and Yang, which, in his mind, he could divide and conquer, especially as only Sanders has the rank-and-file funding for a long-term national race.

In a race against Sanders, Bloomberg would make the point that he would have a better chance of defeating Trump than someone who is a democratic-socialist. In 2016, Sanders lost the nomination on Super Tuesday, when he could not compete with Hillary's funding base to run in so many primaries on one day. A strong New Hampshire finish might line Pete's coffers for Super Tuesday, but not to the levels that Bloomberg can afford.

This year, the Super Tuesday primaries are to be held on March 3 in Alabama, Arkansas, California, Colorado, Maine, Massachusetts, Minnesota, North Carolina, Oklahoma, Tennessee, Texas, Utah, Vermont, and Virginia, and at this point only Sanders (aside from Bloomberg) has the resources to mount a media campaign in all those states.

I think Bernie would beat Bloomberg in a head-to-head campaign (Bernie's passion would do better than Mike's millions), but what will it say about the Democratic Party if the last candidates standing turn out to be three white guys (Sanders, Biden, and Bloomberg) all of whom are in their late 70s—to run against a president who will be 74 at the next election? It will say the party's over.

Trump Rallies Manchester

FOR MY LAST EVENT IN NEW HAMPSHIRE I decided to attend a Trump rally in Manchester, on the eve of the primary election. The event was taking place in the arena of Southern New Hampshire University (SNHU), not far from where I was staying, and a week after I had applied online, my credential had come through for the Trump campaign.

I didn't completely fancy spending another evening at one of Trump's red-meat rallies, but since I had seen him in Iowa, he had given his State of the Union address and been acquitted on both impeachment charges in the Senate. After a week of Democratic events, maybe a Trump rally would shed light on the possible out-come of the general election?

The SNHU Arena is located in downtown Manchester, which is more of an inner-city suburb than a city. Blocks of small, wooden-frame houses surround Manchester's downtown, which has the feel of a renovated mill city, although along the main street there are more bake shops and quirky cafés than law firms and corporate headquarters.

I parked my car several blocks from the SNHU arena and walked to the sound of the TV towers. All around the arena, at makeshift road blocks, the local police and Secret Service had parked snow plows and garbage trucks, around which police and firemen, in yellow security vests, were loitering as part of a thin blue line to protect the president inside the hall.

When I reported to the press entrance, a Secret Service agent, wearing a flak jacket, explained that I should have signed in by 4:30 p.m. (the speech started at 7:00 p.m.) and that the arena was now closed. Just before I got to the gate, he had delivered the same news to another journalist, who was weeping at her exclusion.

For my part I heard the news as a reprieve and would have clicked my heels at being spared from another Trump rally, except everyone at the gate was heavily armed. Instead of taking my seat in the press gallery, I walked around to the front of the SNHU arena, where a large crowd had gathered around an outdoor jumbotron, as if for a World Cup match.

Mixed into the crowd were numerous card tables where Trump hats, bumper stickers, T-shirts, decals, and signs were on sale. Along the barriers that lined the main street, a crowd of Trump supporters was watching the giant TV screen, on which the president's oldest son, Donald Jr., was warming up the crowd. He was dressed in a sports shirt and jacket. Otherwise, his tone was that of an attack dog.

I had never actually heard Don Jr. speak in public, and what struck me was the tone of contempt and hatred in his voice. To be sure, he was introducing his father and delivering a speech to a partisan political crowd, but he did both with a scorn unusual even in the age of Trump's bile.

Don Jr. ran down the Democrats: Bernie Sanders, Joe Biden, and Elizabeth Warren (he didn't call her Pocahantas, but analyzed her Native American DNA claim, as if an external consultant for Ancestry.com). They were socialists, terrorist enablers, and un-American, and if allowed in office would embrace open borders, late-term abortions, socialized medicine, and ruinous economic policies.

After Don Jr.'s hate speech, Mike Pence warmed up the crowd with a litany of Trump sycophancy. One can imagine Trump himself, back in the green room, watching Pence's delivery carefully, just to make sure that he parroted correctly the words that Trump had chosen for him to say. Pence repeated, almost word-for-word, what he had said at the Trump rally in Iowa although here he stuck in that the Senate had acquitted Trump of the impeachment charges "forever." And he ended by saying reverentially of Trump that "the man is in the house."

On the large screen I watched the first 20 minutes of "Trump: The Love Song," which at these rallies he sings to himself. It was a repeat performance of everything he had said in Iowa, although on this occasion he updated his paeans to include new material about the impeachment, Nancy Pelosi ("*a horrible woman*"), and the State of the Union (back from the insolvency of the Obama years).

When Trump began reading the speech from his teleprompters, I decided to leave. I had heard the canned messages of hate before, and Trump reading a speech sounds like someone, in a freshman-year language lab, trying to read aloud a text of German.

Whenever Trump mentioned someone on his enemies' list, such as Mitt Romney or Nancy Pelosi, the crowds (inside and out) would break into chants of "Lock Her Up" or "U-S-A!" While they were chanting, Trump would smirk and preen, pleased with himself for having incited his followers to hate.

Will Trump or a Democrat win in November? After only three weeks in Iowa and New Hampshire, I cannot say, but based on the turnouts in both parties, at this point the Democrats look weak and divided, while Trump, mounted on his fascist hobby horse, has the look of a supreme leader.

If the general election were held tomorrow, I could well imagine Trump winning, but that's only because in a field of nine Democratic candidates it's hard to take the measure of the opposition. Nor can much be said about the eloquence of the various Democrats, many of whom, at least in the primaries, shout catch-phrases more than they deliver speeches. Nor does it help that eloquent candidates for the nomination—such as Deval Patrick and Michael Bennet—get excluded from the debates and shut out of any publicity.

I would like to believe that the republic is capable of overcoming Trump and his henchmen (Don Jr. among them), but if you spend time listening to the Democrats' campaign and then hear the president on his gilded soapboxes, you do come away with the feeling that the United States has crossed the Rubicon, from which the return trip will not be easy.

The Super Tuesday Sting

THE FIX ON SUPER TUESDAY in the presidential election was a clubhouse deal in which the elders of the Democratic Party, led by Barack Obama, shook down the primary system to teach Bernie Sanders a civics lesson, which is that the party ideals must remain convertible into gold or silver.

I know that, at least on paper, the current Democratic Party is the heir of Thomas Jefferson and Andrew Jackson, not to mention Franklin Roosevelt and William Jennings Bryan (who in 1896 championed silver and what was called "bimetallism"), and in theory it is in the game to articulate progressive ideas for social change and betterment. Hence, all the primary blather in this cycle about addressing climate change and righting economic inequality. It sounds good at a New Hampshire town meeting, but when the SUV rubber meets the road in a candidate's motorcade, the Democratic Party is a protection racket for corporate placemen and military contractors (as is, I might add, the Republican Party).

Hence, the Biden resurrection in the days leading up to the Super Tuesday vote, in which a 77-year-old surgically enhanced, clinically dead candidate was brought back to life as Woodrow Wilson. (They would have thrown in 14 points, if any of the fix-it men thought Joe could remember more than half of them.)

Why the rage against Bernie? Granted, Sanders is a grouchy old man (Hillary: *"No one likes him. . ."*) with his own ideas on wealth and power who has rarely "self-identified" as a Democrat.

Sanders was also the socialist mayor of Burlington, Vermont, and in various runs for the House and Senate he's flown independent flags of convenience more than those of Democratic Party loyalty.

Just to run against Hillary Clinton in 2016 Bernie had to register as a Democrat, and in that election, when it looked as though he might defeat the party's preordained candidate of choice, the organization's machinery was pressed into high gear to bring him down on Super Tuesday. It's his Ides of March. In 2020, the fix was made in a series of phone calls to the likes of Pete Buttigieg and Amy Klobuchar, neither of whom (I presume) would have been delighted to hear that after campaigning for more than a year, they were 1) dropping out of the race before Super Tuesday and 2) endorsing Joe Biden.

Word has it that Obama called Buttigieg with this happy news. I cannot verify that he did, but certainly he or someone in his circle would have made the calls, with the message along the lines of "we know where you live." (Just before dropping out, Buttigieg tapped his wine cavemen for another round of campaign donations. I am sure they loved how that tasted, especially after their sommelier quit a few days later.)

Why Buttigieg and Klobuchar went along with the Democratic grifters is also easy to imagine. Vain and singing songs of himself, Buttigieg, I am sure, was told he had "run well" and had "a great future," and that if he got out now, the boys in the clubhouse would "remember him" down the road.

For Klobuchar, the deal would have gone down like this: "Get out now when your 5 percent in the polls has some value, and, while we can't promise you anything, Joe will put you on the shortlist for vice presidential consideration once he wraps up the nomination. Otherwise, don't let the door hit you on your way back to Minnesota. . ." Buttigieg and Klobuchar were both made to understand that they would have nothing to gain from an alliance with Bernie. Protection schemes operate in the same fashion.

Why would Obama orchestrate such a fix against Sanders and, at the same time, give the equally progressive Elizabeth Warren, who once worked for him, the back of his hand? I know that in the thumb-worn copies of *Dreams From My Father*, Obama is eternally the Chicago community organizer and people's tribune. But that imagery was always just another campaign bumper sticker.

Obama 2.0 is a Washington insider with a $14 million house on Martha's Vineyard and a private jet to visit the Clooneys' vacation home in Italy or Richard Branson's yacht in the Pacific, and he would have heard Bernie's soak-the-rich speeches with the same horror as would have his friends at the Columbia Country Club. For the Democratic establishment, which happily bailed out the banks in 2009 to the tune of trillions, at the very least Biden is an accommodating cog in the machine who will steady roiling markets, appoint compliant judges, fix contracts with Lockheed, and make nice to Israel (much like Obama and unlike Bernie).

In a historical context, Biden is best understood as a clubhouse-directed pol who will happily follow orders. Although he was Republican, Chester A. Arthur played this role for Roscoe Conkling, much as Democrats Martin Van Buren and James K. Polk took their instructions from the Andrew Jackson cohort. Or there's the Tammany Hall-controlled mayor of New York City who, upon his election, was asked who would be his chief of police. His answer: "I don't know. I haven't gotten the word yet."

On Super Tuesday Bernie was hung out to dry and left to run against the pumped-up Biden, a limping Bloomberg, and an isolated Warren. The rest of the field had vanished, although Tulsi Gabbard was present. I am sure the Democratic establishment made an effort to get Bloomberg out of the race before Super Tuesday but he would not budge, and probably only left afterward with the promise that he would get to be secretary of the treasury in a forthcoming Biden administration. At least they talked him out of running as an independent, and no doubt touched him up for several hundred million in campaign donations. The party would have been happy to leave Warren in place on all those Super Tuesday ballots, there to bleed Sanders all the more.

Warren was the second chump in what went down before Super Tuesday and came away with nothing, despite having done the party's bidding and taken down loose cannon Bloomberg. She quit the race without endorsing Biden or Sanders, in effect scattering her supporters to the winds. I suspect she's angry at both men: at Biden for using her to weaken Sanders on Super Tuesday; and at Sanders for their earlier unpleasant exchanges over whether he had said a woman cannot win in 2020. At least by not winning the nomination, Warren spared herself eight months on the receiving end of Trump's Twitter bile.

Will the Biden sting hold? The problem is that, even now as the frontrunner, he remains a terrible candidate, and, if required to debate Sanders, may be exposed as an empty suit prone to speaking gibberish. Biden's handlers can be happy that the next scheduled debate on March 15 is only after the vote in Michigan, which could be decisive.

Biden is what in the 19th century was called a "hurrah" candidate, for which the only requirement of his supporters was to shout "hurrah" whenever his name was mentioned. But in this election his newfound enemies will also get a chance to vote, if not to stuff their own ballot boxes.

Bernie's nuclear option is a third-party candidacy, in the tradition of his hero, Eugene V. Debs, who ran for president five times with the Socialist Party in the late 19th and early 20th century, advocating many of the same ideas that Sanders articulates today. A third-party run, or at least the threat of one, is not as far-fetched as it seems, given the screwing that the Democrats have given Bernie in 2016 and now in 2020. Certainly Sanders supporters aren't feeling much burn these days for the Democratic Party.

On the debate stages Bernie has pledged to support the eventual Democratic nominee and has championed the idea that the candidate with a plurality of delegates at the convention should be the candidate. But somewhere in Bernie's mind he must be thinking, "I didn't sign up for a tilted roulette wheel or loaded dice." For better and for worse, fielding a third-party candidate is one of the time-honored American ways to change the outcome of an election.

Running in 1912 as a "Bull Moose" (its formal name was the Progressive Party), Teddy Roosevelt denied the presidency to William Howard Taft, his successor from whom he had become estranged. Other elections in which third-party candidates influenced the outcome took place in 1824 (Henry Clay delivered the presidency to John Quincy Adams, over Andrew Jackson), 1860 (actually there were four candidates, enabling Abraham Lincoln to defeat Douglas), 1968 (George Wallace took the Democratic South away from the Democrats and gave Richard Nixon the presidency), 1992 (Ross Perot helped elect Bill Clinton), and 2000 (Ralph Nader).

Bernie might like his chances as a third-party candidate, if only to send back a message to the Obama gang. He would have no trouble raising money or volunteers, and he would begin with a solid base of support. He could make the argument that Trump and Biden (not to mention their handlers) represent a discredited establishment of wealth and privilege. Running as an independent could well speak to Bernie's political past and soul, although he might be sensitive to the charge that he would be helping to re-elect Donald Trump. Of course, standing against Bernie in a general election (as happened on Super Tuesday) would be the two parties' long experience in stealing elections. It's the great American political tradition.

In recent times the Republicans managed to fix the election in 2016 (Trump and the Russian bots), 2000 (the Supremes), and 1972 (Watergate), while the Democrats marked the cards in 1960 (the turnout from Mayor Daley's Chicago graveyards). By my counting, more than a quarter of American presidencies have been decided by factors other than the popular expression of the voters.

Maybe Biden will become the Rutherford B. Hayes of our times? He ran in the 1876 election against New York Governor Samuel J. Tilden, who won the popular vote and probably a majority in the electoral college. Republican operatives, however, threw the election to Hayes, much as George W. Bush won the presidency through a stacked Supreme Court. Of Hayes, it was later said, "He did such a good job I almost wish he had been elected."

A Couple of 70-Year-Old Guys Sitting Around Talking

"Had he never been an emperor, no one would have doubted his ability to reign."

—Tacitus

Can Biden Beat Trump?

For the Democrats to lose in 2020 to President Donald Trump, they would have to be braindead, and much evidence suggests that they are.

For this brief shining moment, Joe Biden is on his roll, winning primary states by large margins (even where he had no offices on the ground) and flooded with endorsements from Democratic stalwarts (hoping to become the vice presidential candidate?) who have finally seen the light of Joe's electoral brilliance. The Biden camp has even had the hope that Senator Bernie Sanders would quit the race prior to Sunday night's debate and spare the Democratic crown prince the indignity of a two-hour prime-time face-off (not the best place to hide your candidate if you're a Biden handler).

Now I am sure Joe's aides will plead pandemic concerns to cancel what little chance Sanders might have to pull even with the former vice president. Biden can rest assured that the fix against Sanders remains in, and that he will emerge from the Democratic primaries as the party's nominee. But does he have a chance of winning the election in the fall?

2020: Not a Normal Year

Were Biden running in a normal year, I don't think he would get anywhere against an incumbent president during a period of low unemployment and economic growth. In a general election over many months, Biden would be shown for what he is—a party hack (well past his sell-by date) who in a career of stunning, compromised mediocrity has carried the bag for credit card companies, the trashers of Anita Hill, big oil, Strom Thurmond, the right-to-life crowd, profitable prisons, and the Iraq war (to list just a few of his paymasters).

Six months before the election, and Biden is already being handled as damaged electoral goods. His staff knows not to schedule events in the afternoons (when he is probably, to use Dave Barry's phrase about Reagan, "napping toward glory"). When they do release Joe to the public, it is with a prayer that he doesn't drop too many f-bombs on those at his rallies. But that was pre-pandemic.

With the arrival of the coronavirus (yet more foreign interference in the innocent lives of the American electorate?), two things have happened, both of which favor Biden. One is that, on behalf of committees for public safely, Joe's handlers can hide him in studio blue rooms and spin fairy tales about the scrappy lad from Scranton who became President Barack Obama's point man on the great issues. Second, with the virus extending its reach into the U.S., Donald Trump may have met his Waterloo. More and more he is looking like another pathetic figure on trial, pushing a walker into a courtroom of public opinion.

Before long, I suspect, Trump will become the presidential boy in the bubble, stashed away in some mountainside retreat, enshrouded in plastic with breathing and feed tubes, maintaining his tenuous connection to reality through Twitter and a few aides brave enough to meet the press. George W. Bush on 9/11, hidden away at his underground bunker in Omaha, will look like Washington crossing the Delaware compared to Trump under siege, finally facing an opponent that his lawyers cannot buy off with hush money or that Senator Mitch McConnell cannot silence with congressional sleights of hand.

The Pandemic General Election

So what happens in a presidential race that features two incompetent men in their 70s, both of whom showing signs of intellectual impairment and physical failings at a time when the country needs political and moral leadership?

Let's start with the general election hopes of the Republicans, who have been whistling past many Trump graveyards—the president's obstructions of justice, influence peddling around his hotels, Weinstein-ish treatment of women, and obsequious compromises with Saudi and Russian strongmen, among others.

As long as Trump could fill up his MAGA rallies with the party faithful and send money down the Republican food chain to Senate and House candidates, the president was safe from censure, as witnessed by his post-impeachment high-fives to that White House gathering of his footmen. I suspect that even in decline, the president's hold on the Republican Party is sufficient to fend off a "dump Trump" movement at the national convention, but the prospect of losing the majority in the Senate is what could finally touch off a revolt in the ranks.

Nor will his media guys love it when Trump's "what we call the flu. . ." quotes come back in 30-second Biden ads. (Cut to Trump at the CDC saying: *I like this stuff. I really get it. People are surprised that I understand it. Every one of these doctors said, 'How do you know so much about this?' Maybe I have a natural ability. Maybe I should have done that instead of running for president. . ."* Cut to passengers being carried off cruise ships. *"I'm Joe Biden, and I approve this message. . ."*)

The coronavirus comes with two strains: the worldwide economic crisis, and the illness that comes with unwashed hands. Of the two, as a risk to Trump in the general election, economic decline outweighs pandemic pneumonia. Never stand between an electorate and its investment portfolios, and on this point Stock-Jobber-in-Chief Trump, who has made the Dow Jones the pulse of his administration, is vulnerable. For the Democrats' election map a recession is manna from heaven.

Even before the stock market shocks and more medical incompetence (how did that National Guard unit do against those viral particles in New Rochelle?), the Democrats were ahead in such swing states as Maine and Arizona, and could well be competitive in Colorado and North Carolina, which, if they fell to the Democrats in the Senate (even with Doug Jones losing in Alabama), would put an end (the Senate would be 50-50) to Mitch McConnell's reign of terror. In 2008, the Great Recession doomed the electoral chances of John McCain, who was running on a ticket of a Republican Continuum. If Trump is running against the same economic headwinds in 2020, there's little that all the hotelier's men can do to save him, unless of course the opposition is Joe Biden.

Trump and Biden: Shared Vulnerabilities

The Trump campaign's only hope is that Biden turns out to be the gift candidate who keeps on giving. The point about the Biden candidacy is that he shares many of the same vulnerabilities with Trump. If you're a Trump spin master worried about some aspects of your candidate, here's a checklist to brighten your day:

☑ Feeling vulnerable about your man's past treatment of women, especially as Harvey Weinstein is being sent up the river for 23 years? Not to worry, as backrub Joe will have little to say about compromising positions.

☑   Have children who are cashing in on your time in office? Again, no problem, as Hunter Biden is the antidote for any attacks on Jared's sketchy Middle East overlords or Don Jr.'s hunting in foreign fields.

☑   Wish you had not decided to run on cuts for Social Security? We've got you covered with Joe's soundbites on future reductions to entitlements.

☑   Think you're vulnerable with a candidate who is obese and lives on cheeseburgers? Here's an opposition candidate who is 77 and once had a brain aneurism.

☑   Hoping to capture some of the African American vote? Cue up Joe's Thurmond eulogy. (*"The truth and genius and virtue of Strom Thurmond is what I choose and we all choose to remember today."*)

Sometimes I get the feeling that Joe Biden has walked off a backlot from Republican central casting. No matter which way Trump turns, Biden has been there. It's what made Hillary such a weak candidate. In the 2016 election, she was time barred, as they say in court, from attacking Trump on his pussy-grabbing tape—for obvious family reasons. Nor could she go after him for economic sleaze, having served herself from the same troughs.

How can Biden attack Trump for being old and out of touch, when he's even older and more out of touch? (Yesterday on a chat show, I listened to some talking heads make the point that

Trump was "sharp," at least when compared to Biden. I guess everything is relative.)

Advantage Biden

The advantage that Biden has over Trump in 2020 is that he is, comparatively speaking, the outsider, or at least not an incumbent at a moment when the country is in crisis. In 2016, Trump won the election by less than 80,000 votes in three swing states—Wisconsin, Michigan, and Pennsylvania—all of which he carried. Trump's margin came from a larger than expected turnout among his dog-whistling base, and a lower than expected turnout for Clinton among working-class whites and African Americans, who for various reasons had other things to do on election day.

For Trump, 2016 was a perfect storm, and the chances are remote—whatever Biden's imperfections—that in 2020 the 5-6 percent bloc of undecided voters will all break again for the Republican candidate while other traditional Democratic voters stay home. (I suspect the Bernie Bros will not vote for Biden.) Even if the bloc of undecided voters were to divide evenly between Republicans and Democrats, the Democratic candidate would win the general election. Leaving aside for the moment that Biden is a dead man campaigning, I draw the electoral map as follows:

—The Democrats should win in Pennsylvania, Colorado, New Mexico, North Carolina, and Arizona, while Trump could well take Florida, Ohio, North Carolina, and Wisconsin.
—In a recession, states such as North Carolina and Florida are very much in play for the Democrats.
—Even without North Carolina, the Democrats would win.

The question then becomes: Will Biden blow it for the Democrats?

Advantage Trump

In the general election Biden is vulnerable if he becomes the poster boy for mental incapacity, and if the election media spots become one long highlight reel of Joe telling some gun guy he's "full of shit." Already it's a nightly refrain on social media, and many of these oppo tapes come from the Left.

Before the virus recession, Trump planned to run against Hunter Biden and Sleepy Joe, as placeholders for the brave old-world Democratic operatives alive and well in the swamp. In virus America, however, Hunter Biden isn't even a sideshow; he's a footnote in an academic journal article about U.S.-Ukrainian relations.

One avenue of attack open to Trump and his hate machine will be to insist that in a time of crisis (at war with a deadly virus) you don't change the commander-in-chief, even if he would seem to spend more time under his tanning lights than in meetings with medical advisors. In response, Biden's handlers—claiming the virus as a public health risk—can wall the candidate off from the public and craft a series of virtual reality videos that project Joe in the tradition of FDR, JFK, and LBJ, great liberal progressive statesmen.

It's been done before. While suffering from incipient dementia in 1984, Ronald Reagan won reelection, and many other candidates have won the presidency by hiding their vulnerabilities during the campaign. Since 1896, variations on William McKinley's front porch campaign have been the norm; crowds of supporters are stage props.

As the first AI candidate (the projection of many imaginations), Biden will run from a virtual front porch. Besides, in 2020 few will be voting for Biden or his ideas (call me when you find a few). They will just be casting a ballot against Trump or airing some other grievance. "None of the Above" would do well as the Democratic nominee. Otherwise, it's possible to imagine an election with two losers.

Wildcards in 2020

As for wildcards in the coming months, I can imagine several. If anything, 2020 has proved a year difficult to forecast.

Few predicted, for example, that the party's elders could revive Biden, given all the Do Not Resuscitate orders affixed to the body of his campaign in Iowa and New Hampshire. Nor did anyone see Pete Buttigieg, Amy Klobuchar, Tom Steyer, and Michael Bloomberg folding their hands on demand (after they collectively had anted up about $1 billion in their campaigns) and assigning the pot to Joe Biden, who was left in the game with a pair of threes.

In this year of campaigning dangerously, I could well imagine, for example, the Democratic National Committee trying to pressure a confused Biden from the ticket. For all I know, the DNC may believe that Joe has served their purpose, denying the nomination to Bernie Sanders and his anarcho-syndicalism, and now it's time move on. Maybe Michael Bloomberg and Hillary Clinton still have pretensions to the throne? Neither has ever really gone away, and their ambition knows no bounds.

I can also imagine either Biden or Trump having some kind of medical event that would force one or both from their tickets. At this point Biden looks hesitant and confused, while Trump is starting to glow in the dark. Only in presidential politics is it a country for old men, and from what I gather there is something in the air.

Will Trump Cancel the Election?

With there being no campaign left to trail, I reached out with my questions to someone on the inside, and got the following email:

"TRUMP DOESN'T CARE if three million Americans die from the virus as long as he can appear on nightly television, basking in the limelight with either immunologists or the CEO of Walmart obediently at his side.

"Trump doesn't care whether some community hospital has on hand enough masks, ventilators, aspirin, or Xeroxed copies of last rites, provided that he remains must-watch television and has better ratings than Joe Biden, who, by the way, must be the first person ever to run for president from the candidate protection program. Is Biden spending his days in a Wilmington panic room, on the phone with an aide who is explaining for the fifth time how to log into Zoom?

"I digress, and the question you asked is: Will the election be canceled?

"I have no doubt that somewhere in the depths of the White House—my suspicions are on the Stephen Miller band—there's a group of henchmen that is exploring how Trump could suspend or otherwise manipulate the 2020 election to continue governing, as if some Latin American strongman given to rambling speeches from balconies.

"Here's what they would be thinking:

"The most confusing clauses in the Constitution are those dealing with the election and succession of the president and vice president.

"Everyone talks about the 'electoral college,' as if it were Amherst or Williams, but the Constitution only speaks about electors and all it says is that they have to show up in Washington every four years and choose a president and a vice president.

"How the electors get there and how they cast their votes remain a source of endless dispute, even though the Constitution has been amended on several occasions to clean up the mess.

"In *Bush v. Gore* (yet another big-time fix, in the 2000 election), the Supreme Court made the point that the states hold the right to choose presidential electors and that they only ceded that right provisionally to the people. At any time, so the court concluded, the states are free to reclaim their right and choose whomever they want as presidential electors. In other words, the people don't own the democracy; we merely have it on a long-term rental.

"The drafters of the Constitution were leery of direct democracy and giving citizens the right to choose their president. That was why they vested more power in Congress, notably the House of Representatives. As conceived in 1789, the office of the president was more that of a sheriff or chief enforcement officer, and the occupant was there to make sure that the laws Congress passed were enacted.

"The president wasn't intended to be a king or prime minister. One of the most amusing debates in constitutional history concerned whether the members of Congress would stand up if the president ever entered the room in which they were seated. (Most thought him unworthy of such obeisance; after all, he was democracy's footman.)

"Nor did it bother the drafters of the Constitution that most presidential elections would be determined with many thumbs on the scales. In this way, slaveowners could have their say in a weak branch of government (as they did until the Civil War, if not beyond), and the rest of the country could get on with the business of making money.

"The delegation of presidential elections to electors is the opening that the Trump gang needs to keep His Rotundity (the name was first used for John Adams) in office beyond 2020.

"Technically speaking, Trump, personally, cannot cancel the November election. Various federal statutes, Congressional oversight, and state laws are the reason that the presidential vote takes place every four years (on the first Tuesday after the first Monday in November). But he can try and is not without resources to deal from the bottom of the deck.

"Amidst a Covid crisis, it is easy to imagine Trump telling the nightly press conference that he's 'looking at' delaying the election 'for the safety of all Americans' although he would have to persuade pliant governors and captive state legislatures to carry out his deferment wishes.

"For this argument, let's assume that he manages to postpone the popular vote in November 2020, at least in a number of states, including some that he needs to carry to be re-elected.

"In that event, under the Constitution, it would still be up to each state to send a slate of electors to Washington (*'on the Monday after the second Wednesday in December'*), and it would be that body (we call it the electoral college, as if it were choosing a pope) that would select the next president and vice president.

"For Trump what's important is that nearly all the key swing states, including Pennsylvania, Michigan, and Florida, have Republican control of the legislature (thanks to the munificent Koch brothers and gerrymandering).

"Throwing the presidential election into state legislatures might be Trump's only chance for victory. (Mark Twain liked to say: '*No man's life, liberty, or property are safe while the legislature is in session.*')

"Especially during a recession, Trump could well lose the popular vote in places such as Michigan or Pennsylvania, but he could well win there if the state legislatures choose their own electors.

Trump's Henchmen Work the Angles

"Here's another angle that might excite Trump's henchmen.

"If Trump has no luck in calling off the popular vote in the election (perhaps by then the country will have figured out how to vote by mail), his next best game would be somehow to deny the Democratic candidate a majority of electors and to throw the election into the House of Representatives.

"I realize that would be a long shot, but so you know, here's how that game would be played:

"In the case where there is no majority (270 electors for one candidate), the presidential election is immediately sent to the House of Representatives, which chooses the next president.

"You might think that, as the House has a Democratic majority, such a move would be against Trump's interests, but here's why you're wrong.

"In an election decided by the House (it happened in 1800, 1824, and 1876), each state delegation in the House of Representatives gets one vote. Meaning: the Montana delegation gets to cast one vote for the next president, as does the California delegation. A vote in each state's House of Representatives delegation would determine how that state's one vote would be cast for president.

"That means, while Trump would lose by huge majorities in the New York and California delegations, he would gain votes in southern and western states that have a Republican majority in their state delegations. In the current Congress, Republicans have a majority in 27 states, and those votes would re-elect Donald Trump as the next president (27-23—the District of Columbia does not get a vote if the race goes to the House).

"By the way, if, on January 20, 2021, neither the electors nor the House of Representatives has chosen a new president, the current vice president, that would be Task Rabbiter Mike Pence, would become the acting president until a new one is chosen.

"Maybe during that time he could pardon Trump? Already he takes the End of Days view that God gave us the coronavirus so that the world would finally recognize the infinite wisdom and judgment of our lord and savior, Donald J. Trump.

Is Trump Going Down?

"Is it far-fetched to think about the election in these dire terms?" Not really. In the Covid disaster and great recession to follow, Trump is going down for the count.

"I know, you think that his approval rating is up and that Americans are rallying to their president 'in a time of national crisis' and there is a lot of television palaver about how he has become a 'wartime president' with increasing public support.

"That's a sugar high of political polling, and once the out-of-work public sees Trump presiding over a daily Pearl Harbor, telling everyone who will listen how he's done a 'fantastic job' ordering up all those body bags from China, he's finished—unless, of course, he can rig the election.

"Why does Trump need to put the fix in?

"For starters, if he is turned out of office in January 2021, he will almost certainly face criminal charges as Individual-1 in the District Court for the Southern District of New York proceedings that sent Trump bagman Michael Cohen up the river for three years.

"Trump is an unindicted co-conspirator in those charges, and only by winning reelection (and serving in office for another four years) can he beat the rap by letting the statute of limitations expire in New York.

"Special Counsel Robert Mueller's great contribution to constitutional theory was to conclude that it was up to Congress alone to decide on the indictment of a sitting president. Otherwise, Trump would have been charged in New York, irrespective of what Congress decided over impeachment.

"If Trump loses the 2020 election and leaves office, he will be indicted in New York. And not many presidents win reelection when the unemployment rate is 30 percent. So he has a personal stake to remain in office.

"As I see it, Trump's only get-out-of-jail card is to steal the election. To find willing partners in such an enterprise (especially during a national emergency) should not be very difficult. Look at the phalanx of lackeys who surround his lectern each evening and nod solemnly, no matter what fantasy he is peddling. (*'We have it totally under control. . .'*)

Biden: Dead Candidate Running

"Second question: Will the Democrats cut their losses with Joe Biden and try to nominate someone else at the national convention, even if it's held on the world's largest video conference call?

"Let's get real about Biden. He's a dead candidate running, whose only role in this campaign was to deny the Democratic nomination to the bomb-throwing Bernie Sanders. Did anyone vote for Biden for his intellectual prowess, leadership qualities, or record in crisis management? I didn't think so.

"The only reason anyone voted for Biden in the primaries was because his name wasn't Sanders and because he was seen as someone who would endorse bailout checks to corporate America— whatever the crisis. The rest hardly mattered.

"Now, a month into what is called his 'presumptive' candidacy, Democrats are waking up to the fact that their nominee cannot string together three comprehensible sentences and is just as clueless as Trump and Mike Pence in dealing with a national health crisis (*"brought to you by Walmart, for all your testing needs. . ."*).

"I trust you have seen a few of the videos circulating online of Biden broadcasting from his undisclosed location. He sounds like an old man on a golf club membership committee, complaining how it's impossible to find a parking place near the men's grill on Saturdays.

"And now there's another of Joe's #MeToo moments. In case you missed it, a report has surfaced that back in the 1990s Biden mashed one of his staffers, Tara Reade, up against a congressional wall and, with his hand roaming around her skirt, asked for a little senatorial privilege.

"I don't know the woman personally, but at the very least she captured Joe's pattern of speech when she quoted him as saying (while she struggled to free herself from his grinding), "I heard you liked me, man?" For not putting out, Reade was assigned to a windowless office and then fired.

"The Reade drop came amidst the virus pandemic, and so far her allegations have largely vanished without a trace, although not before Biden apologists trashed her as a Russian plant, cultist, political wannabe, and stalker of the Squeaky Fromme variety.

"But I am sure the Trump campaign will have taken note of her complaints, and will use them should the Democrats try to trot out any of the 22 women who have come forward publicly to say that the current president groped, fondled, or otherwise forced himself on them against their wishes.

"In 2016, Hillary Clinton was unable to exploit Trump's legacy of perversion, given her own husband's touchy record on the subject. Now in 2020, the Dems seem to have gone out of their way to confront a 70-something incumbent with wandering hands and crooked kids with their own nominee who seems cloned from the same source code. Heck of a job, Brownie.

Will the Dems Cut Their Potential Losses?

"So will the Dems dump Biden before or during the national convention? I think they could, based either on the Reade allegation or his incoherent response to the Covid crisis. (*We have to take care of the cure that will make the problem worse no matter what, no matter what. . .*') Just as Republicans are good at rigging elections, Democrats are skilled at marking the cards in their primaries and caucuses.

"The reason Bernie hasn't thrown in the towel and endorsed 'my friend Joe' is because he knows how the Democratic game is played, and the party will do to Biden as it did to him—namely screw him out of the nomination. It's about all the party does well.

"Getting rid of Biden will be a lot easier than getting tested for the virus. If the remaining primaries are postponed or canceled ('*a national emergency. . .this grave crisis. . .*'), Biden would arrive at the virtual convention with 1,217 delegates (where the count stands today) while 1,991 are needed for the nomination. Nor do we know at this point what happens to the outstanding primaries. It's only the party hierarchs who will decide.

"Right now Bernie has 914, but it feels like we're done with voting. No matter how bad the health crisis becomes, the party will never turn to Sanders. No one likes a prescient loser. If no

Democratic candidate at the convention gets a majority on the first ballot, the 771 superdelegates become eligible to vote on the second and all subsequent ballots.

"That bloc should be sufficient to throw the nomination in whatever direction it chooses, especially given that superdelegates come from the ranks of senior Democratic office holders and members of the national committee.

"My guess is that, as a group, the superdelegates are tired of watching *Weekend at Biden's* (*A lively comedy about a guy who isn't. . .*') and despair that their man could lose to the criminally negligent, emoluments-rich, woman-abusing, narcissistically incompetent Trump.

"At this point, the Democrats would happily nominate some tough-talking, Covid-fighting governor on the 38th ballot so long as it was not Sanders or, now, Biden.

Democratic Self-Destruct Mode

"Standing in the way of rational behavior, of course, is the Democratic Party itself, which has been in self-destruct mode since it loaded the dice in favor of Hillary Clinton in 2016, if not long before. Remember Mike Dukakis and John Kerry?

"Note the ages of the party leadership: Biden is 77 and Nancy Pelosi is 80. (Senate Minority Leader Chuck Schumer is 69, which makes him, relatively speaking, 'the kid.') And the runner-up in this race, Bernie Sanders, is 78. Even China has done away with its gerontocracy.

"Is it any wonder that the Democratic Party has so run out of ideas that all it can think to do, during a time of national crisis, is to nominate Clueless Joe? The bungled Trump impeachment should have been an indicator that the party is over its head in national politics.

"My take is that Pelosi only went ahead with the impeachment trial (knowing it would fail) to consolidate her position as speaker in the face of opposition from the Democratic left, the Alexandria Ocasio-Cortez (AOC) wing of the party. Pelosi's fear had nothing to do with Trump's high crimes and misdemeanors in office but everything to do with not wanting her party to slide too far to the left and for AOC's squad to remove her from her beloved speakership.

"Pelosi gave Committee Chairmen Adam Schiff and Jerry Nadler the go-ahead on impeachment, knowing that the far left of the Democratic Party would be the loser. (*"You wanna impeach the guy? Here you go. . .."*) Maybe along the way some mud would stick to Trump's shoes for the 2020 election, but the goal was always to consolidate her position as speaker.

"It was a cynical power grab on Pelosi's part, as was her part in the camarilla that decided to put the boot into Sanders after New Hampshire and turn Biden into an inflatable candidate. Now she and the Democratic Party are stuck in the middle with Joe. (As he said, *'What I'm suggesting is that I know what has to be done and that in the following is that faster is better than slower. . .'*) How is that working out?

"The great irony of the 2020 Democratic primaries and the general election is that the two candidates who ran largely on medical reform, Sanders and Elizabeth Warren, stand discredited, while the last two (tired, old white) men still in the race, Trump and Biden, have nothing coherent to say about medicine (or anything else). And you wonder why the crisis is out of control."

The Great
Democratic Infomercial

"The Democrats seem to be basically nicer people, but they have demonstrated time and again that they have the management skills of celery. They're the kind of people who'd stop to help you change a flat, but would somehow manage to set your car on fire. I would be reluctant to entrust them with a Cuisinart, let alone the economy. The Republicans, on the other hand, would know how to fix your tire, but they wouldn't bother to stop because they'd want to be on time for Ugly Pants Night at the country club."

—Dave Barry, *Dave Barry Slept Here:*
A Sort of History of the United States

Conventional Thinking

I CAN'T SAY I WAS SURPRISED that the Democrats led off their four-day Zoom summer jamboree and political convention with one of the *Desperate Housewives* acting as the moderator. On the same day there appeared a newspaper picture of former President Bill Clinton getting a back rub from a young blonde while both were waiting to board pedophile Jeffrey Epstein's *Lolita Express* plane. (As early Democrat Thomas Jefferson liked to say, *"We hold these truths to be self-evident."*)

Presumably, if the Democrats had given the gavel to someone less glamorous than Eva Longoria or someone more eager to ask questions about Social Security funding or the Israel's deal with the United Arab Emirates, the ratings for the video national convention (already wobbly) would have gone in the tank. Instead, all the moderators and party frontmen pitched the 2020 election as democracy's last chance to rescue the republic from the clutches of the Trump gang, and each one (save for AOC) emphasized that no one in the country was more qualified than Joe Biden to lead the United States out of Covid's wilderness.

During the endless loop of what felt like Chevy ads (featuring mayors, senators, governors, members of Congress, schoolkids, grandchildren, wayward Republicans, vets, union members, and all sorts of common men and women), whatever the story of hardship, and there were many, the cure-all was always the presidential election of Joe Biden, who was transformed from hack politician into A Great Tribal Chief, someone who, once in office, would comfort the sick, give hope to the unemployed, bring peace to the Middle East, end terrorism, fight racism, create jobs, fight for civil rights, clean dirty air, and redeem the nation, just as he raised his sons after unimaginable loss.

Over four days, the Democrats screened what amounted to a nine-hour infomercial on the life and times of the Scranton, PA altar boy who has been chosen to carry the cross to Washington to save the American soul.

Branding the Democrats

Before all the witnessing testimony, there was a branding exercise for the Democratic Party, in which it positioned itself in the pantheon of great American consumer companies, alongside the likes of Google, Southwest Airlines, CVS, and Ford. The videos reminded me of halftime ads during the Super Bowl, only instead of happy Christmas shoppers at Walmart, Democrats were shown having social media inspiration from the likes of FDR, JFK, and Black Lives Matter.

"We are Democrats and we are ready to lead again. . ." was the outro line, said much the way that Exxon or BP ads end with the voiceover, "We stand for a renewable future" (cut to gleeful children in a playground. . .). Otherwise, the Democratic Party has the look and feel of a Johnny Carson show in the late 1970s, although Biden himself has the aura of a big band leader at the Copacabana, getting ready to break into a Charleston.

A Senate Roll Call

Doug Jones, a senator from Alabama, was beamed in from an office somewhere to make the point that "I've known Joe Biden for

40 years" and that Joe "gets things done," although I suspect one of the things Joe will not get done is to help Jones get re-elected to the Senate from Alabama. Jones is running against a retired football coach (from such SEC schools as Ole Miss and Auburn) who wants to come back as one of Trump's pulling guards, and in that game Jones is a tackling dummy.

Another Democratic Senate hopeful on the feed was Sara Gideon from Maine, who is running against incumbent Republican Senator Susan Collins, whose great contribution to the republic was to state that while she believed someone raped Christine Blasey Ford she was pretty sure it wasn't the human kegerator and future justice Brett Kavanaugh, Esquire.

It tells you something about the quality of Democratic speakers that the most eloquent speech of day one came from one of the brothers of George Floyd, the Black man who was murdered by that police officer on the streets of Minneapolis. Two of the Floyd brothers stood in what felt like their family's living room, and their calm demeanor and moving remembrance of their brother made that tragedy all the more difficult to fathom, although I am sure that at the Republican convention George will be reincarnated as Willie Horton.

Chainsaw Bernie

I have heard Bernie speak in person about half a dozen times, and while I like what he says, and the conviction of his delivery, I will say that Bernie is also a broken record who says the same thing every time he gets in front of a microphone. Here, to echo his log cabin affiliations, the DNC choreographers had him standing in front of a wall of chopped firewood, as though Bernie had come to the convention after just setting aside his chainsaw.

In a dutiful way, although without much emotion, Bernie repeated the Sanders liturgy and even spread some incense in Biden's direction, holding out the hope that it wasn't too late for "my friend Joe" to see light on the road to socialism. (Lottery tickets have better odds.) Listening to Bernie, I got the impression that he will be happier when this election is over (whoever wins), and he can go back to his rustic state of independence. Party loyalty doesn't really suit him.

Kasich Heads North by Northwest

The weirdest stage set for a convention address was given to the former Republican governor of Ohio, John Kasich, who somehow scored face time at the Democratic National Convention (presumably in exchange for a job in a Biden administration).

In case you are weak on Republican presidential candidates who flamed out in the 2016 primaries, Kasich ran on a folksy ticket of midwestern optimism, although when you dig into his core beliefs you discover a clone of Richard Nixon and other dark princes of the right.

On Day One of this convention, he was recruited to raise Biden's big tent of inclusivity, and he appeared on screen standing at a fork in the road in an Ohio cornfield (the metaphorical divide for the nation). He looked like Roger Thornhill (Cary Grant) in *North by Northwest*, about to be crop-dusted in the fields outside Chicago. As was said of the plane in the Hitchcock movie, "That fella's dusting crops where there ain't no crops."

The View of Michelle Obama

I confess I can't understand the national obsession with the greatness and goodness of Michelle Obama. I was happy, when she was first lady, that she championed the causes of kids' exercise and nutritional school lunches (I was never really convinced that Reagan's ketchup was a vegetable). But in the republic of ideas, I don't see Michelle as one of the Corinthian columns.

Here her Zoom handlers had her aggressively forward on the screen (there was no chance of a cat strolling across her desk), and she lectured the Trump presidency for what sounded like bad taste and manners. (*"He's the wrong president for our country. . . . He's just not up to the job."*) She also spoke in the tones of a dowager on *Downton Abbey*, complaining that the family manor house had been sold off to a car dealer.

Michelle got a little misty-eyed in whispering that she hates politics—leaving aside that backroom deals paid for her beach house on Martha's Vineyard and her and her husband's $60 million book advance—and implored everyone in almost biblical tones (*"we're one nation under God. . ."*) to vote. Toward the end of her soliloquy she sounded liked a weary guest on *The View* confessing that she could be ready for that glass of chardonnay.

The Dems Zoom It In

On the Waterfront with Chuck Schumer

THE EMCEE FOR HAGIOGRAPHY'S DAY TWO was TV star Tracee
Ellis Ross (*Girlfriends*, *Black-ish*), who praised Biden's "steady,
inclusive leadership" and then passed the baton to the likes of Sally
Yates, Chuck Schumer, John Kerry, Colin Powell, Bill Clinton,
Caroline Kennedy, Jimmy and Rosalyn Carter, Jill Biden, and
Alexandria Ocasio-Cortez, who stole the show just because she
wasn't collecting Social Security.

Senator Chuck Schumer, among those lionizing "my friend
Joe," spoke to the convention from the waterfront in Red Hook,
Brooklyn, so that the viewers could commune with the egalitar-
ian sentiments of the Statue of Liberty. Schumer began by saying, "Behind me is a sight I see out of my window every night,
the Statue of Liberty," although like a good New York real estate
booster (his one-time benefactor, Donald Trump, is another)
Schumer was stretching the truth of his waterfront access, as he
lives in Park Slope, some miles to the east.

Bill Clinton Kicks Back on his Sofa

When the DNC kiss cam caught up with former President Bill
Clinton at his suburban New York home, he was seated on a sofa in

his living room, although such was his cadaverous appearance that the DNC production room saw fit to add the words "Live Chappaqua, NY" to the upper right-hand corner of the TV screen, I guess so that viewers would be reassured that he was still breathing.

I cannot imagine that Clinton appreciated the lines he was asked to deliver during the national Zoom chat, as it was left to Bill—perhaps with a dollop of Shakespearean irony from some irreverent Democratic advisor?—to ridicule Trump's Animal White House. Bill said:

> At a time like this, the Oval Office should be a command center. Instead, it's a storm center. There's only chaos. Just one thing never changes—his determination to deny responsibility and shift the blame. The buck never stops there.

Imagine John Blutarsky delivering a lecture at Faber College on etiquette, although the Clintons can console themselves that while the Obamas appointed one member of the Democratic ticket (Biden) they got to select the vice presidential nominee (Kamala Harris) who several years ago had received the Clinton seal of approval. Will we ever be done with the Clintons? I suspect not. As Bluto said, "Was it over when the Germans bombed Pearl Harbor? Hell no!"

AOC: 90 Seconds of Wonder

Clearly Nancy Pelosi's parental control had a hand in limiting Alexandria Ocasio-Cortez's screen time to 90 seconds, but the member of Congress from the Bronx and Queens made the most of her spot by never mentioning Biden and using her time to second the nomination of "Bernard Sanders" for president. AOC did mention the lack of basic health care for many Americans, although in the four days of the Democratic convention no one ever bridged the gap between Obama's Affordable Care Act (once billed as "health care for all") and the some 80 million Americans (it's the figure that Sanders and Warren use in their speeches) who still lack decent or affordable health insurance.

An Express Elevator to the Nomination

I realize that there was a common-man touch in having a Black elevator operator (ironically she works at the *New York Times*) place Joe Biden's name in nomination for president. Maybe it's to Biden's credit that at the *Times* he formed a better bond with an elevator operator than he did with the editorial board (in the primaries it endorsed both Elizabeth Warren and Amy Klobuchar). At the same time Biden owes his nomination to the marked cards of Democratic power brokers (not elevator operators), who decided that Bernie, with all his talk about universal health care and cuts to military spending, was taking things "a little too far. . ."

Caroline Kennedy Collects Some More IOUs

The Democrats wheeled out two members of the Kennedy clan, Caroline Kennedy Schlossberg and her son Jack, who repeated the Biden catechism while standing in front of some Cape Cod gray shingles—the siding of choice in Hyannis Port and Camelot.

Caroline dropped in a humble brag to let us know that she had "helped to pick Joe" as Barack Obama's running mate in 2008 (in the Kennedy world, the favor bank is about the size of J.P. Morgan). It led to the slightly awkward passage when she talked about how she had "admired Joe since she was a Senate intern in 1974" (not exactly what you want on your CV these days) when he was pals with "Uncle Teddy." At that moment the Dems flashed up on the screen a flushed picture of the two womanizers-in-arms, attending to state affairs.

The Carters Speak Gravely

For a while I appreciated hearing the disembodied voices of Rosalynn and Jimmy Carter, who spoke with only place-holding photographs flipping on screen (a bit like those pictures used on cable TV to market life insurance coverage, which show sincere older couples happy with their caregivers). Yes, the Carters did sound as though they were speaking from the grave, but I admired the resonance of integrity in their voices, until Jimmy said Joe was "the right person for this moment in our nation's history," and I remembered how Jimmy's erratic judgment in crises brought down his presidency.

Good Soldiers Powell and Kerry

To make the point that Biden will be a rock of stability in foreign affairs and a beacon of light in a world of shadows, the Democrats summoned two more ghosts from the American past, former secretaries of state Colin Powell and John Kerry, perhaps on the off chance that Biden wants another crack at winning either the Vietnam or Iraq wars.

Powell was on display as a lapsed Republican, a Bush family retainer who has seen the light on Trump and his deferment bone spurs. He talked about growing up in the Bronx, his faith in the American dream, and his love of military service, and he had the good manners not to mention that he counseled Obama and Biden to stay out of Afghanistan, something they ignored.

I suspect the fix is already in for John Kerry to return as Biden's secretary of state, as Kerry was with "my friend Joe" in Iowa and in other primary fields of dreams. To hear Kerry tell the stories, the foreign policies of the "Obama-Biden administration" were the stuff of legends, with wins over Iran, ISIS, climate change, Ebola, etc. He said Joe's "moral compass has always pointed in the right direction," although I defy anyone to name three Biden foreign policy initiatives. To the DNC Zoomers Kerry said reverentially: "Only Joe Biden can make America lead like America again," although what I heard is: "Only Joe Biden will bring back John Kerry."

Un-Democratic Primaries

Between some of the canned speeches, the Democrats piped in state delegations so that the party could formally count the votes and nominate Biden to run for president. The delegation from Delaware cast its votes (remotely) for Biden from a dark platform at Amtrak's Wilmington station while other states chose culturally sensitive backdrops from which to vote "for the next president of the United States, Joe Biden."

Left out of the roll call feed was just how un-Democratic the party has become. In effect, Joe Biden wrapped up the nomination by winning 262,336 votes in the South Carolina primary (that's .08 percent of the U.S. population, for those keeping score at home). After that, and before Super Tuesday, the Democratic elders (led by Barack Obama, Nancy Pelosi, and Chuck Schumer) chased Amy Klobuchar, Michael Bloomberg, Pete Buttigieg, and Tom Steyer (among others) from the race, assuring the investiture of Joe Biden, who had been left for dead after the primaries in Iowa and New Hampshire. In a national primary of Democrats, using ranked choice voting (which assures a majority to the winning candidate), I suspect Biden would have finished third or fourth, but he was saved by divine intervention (Obama's).

Library Joe

After the presidential nomination was confirmed, the cameras cut to an obviously happy Biden, who, in the presence of a few balloons (think of a kid's birthday party), was killing time in the library of Brandywine High School while his wife was taping a speech in her old classroom. Maybe Biden used the downtime to check out a book, along the lines of *The Internet Made Easy?*

I suspect Biden is someone who has published (I didn't say written) more books than he has read in the last 50 years. He just doesn't look like a reader to me, although I could well imagine him dipping into a Tom Clancy thriller on a campaign plane. On reading, I tend to agree with Lemony Snicket who said, "Never trust anyone who has not brought a book with them."

Here's an irony of Biden's candidacy. There are only two jobs open to him in America: He can be president or he can be a greeter at The Home Depot. Not many companies are hiring 77-year-old CEOs, and Little League teams and Uber tend to shy away from those publicly accused of sexual impropriety, whatever the merits of the case.

Jill Biden Goes Back to School

I have no doubt that Jill Biden loves her classes, students, and classrooms, and that she is a good teacher, but the media reviews of her Joe Biden lesson plan (*"heartfelt. . .moving. . .compassionate. . . stirring. . ."*) strike me as grade inflation. As an English teacher, Jill surely knows the difference between bathos and pathos, although in reaching for the latter (with stories of personal and national tragedies), she delivered the former. She said, "Yes, so many classrooms are quiet right now. The playgrounds are still. But if you listen closely, you can hear the sparks of change in the air. . . . And with Joe as president, these classrooms will ring out with laughter and possibility once again."

Why in a functioning democracy does anyone need the spouse of a candidate to drone on in prime time about what a wonderful man or woman he or she is? Haven't we by now learned the lesson that, on average, political marriages are somewhat less than the average? (See Reade, Tara.)

To me Jill Biden is interesting as potentially the future Edith Galt of American politics. As you may recall, the said Mrs. Galt, a Washington jeweler, became the second Mrs. Woodrow Wilson in 1915, and when the president became ill after the U.S. rejection of the League of Nations (he collapsed after a national speaking tour undertaken to persuade the country to join the alliance), Edith Galt Wilson ran the country, as a proxy for her incapacitated husband.

There's no way of knowing, if Joe is elected president, whether he would survive a first or second term, but the chances of some medical crisis in the White House would seem to go up if and when the country were to install a 78-year-old man (with preexisting conditions) as president. Judging from her class lecture, Jill Biden would be fine as a substitute, and perhaps more capable than others on the national tickets in dealing with opposition spitballs.

I also came away from her class convinced that the most complicated relationship of a Biden presidency might well be between Jill Biden and Kamala Harris, who doesn't strike me as a teacher's aide.

Day Three of
the Great Democratic Jamboree

Warren Time

ELIZABETH WARREN WAS A WARM-UP BAND on Day Three, and, as with Jill Biden, the Democratic impresarios had her talk to an empty classroom (where before shutting down in March, the pre-K kids had the good sense to leave behind blocks spelling out "B L M"). Warren came out of the race pretty much hated by everyone, although she ran an articulate and dignified campaign, which included her golden retriever, Bailey.

The hard Democratic Left decided Warren had sold her soul to corporate moderation while the patriarchy came to the conclusion that she was coming for their BMWs. Actually, she had only two flaws in her campaign: one was that her views were identical to those of Bernie Sanders, and he was the One True Great Believer. The second was that she spoke in a breathless staccato voice, sounding more like a Pilates instructor with car problems than a Harvard law professor. Warren's best issues were economic equality and health care—both in short supply these days—but only a handful of Democrats bought into her fall line.

Here in Springfield, Massachusetts (better optics than some charter school in Cambridge?), Warren reprised the family role of schoolmarm and put Trump in the corner for his Covid-19 inaction ("*he failed miserably*"). She also hopped on the Biden peace train and tried to convince us that Joe has "some really good plans." I am sure news of those plans came as something of a surprise to Biden.

"Madame Speaker" Pelosi

During the infomercial binge broadcast, the most bizarre sequence was a video montage that I am sure the producers referred to as "Madame Speaker," in which House Speaker Nancy Pelosi morphs into an action power ranger. Nancy's MTV moment came before her formal, here-I-am-in-a-white-dress speech.

The sequence starts slowly, with Nancy as the mother of five transitioning from housewife to backroom pol. All of a sudden Nancy is striding into the camera, at the head of a rock phalanx, as if one of the Spice Girls—although in the highlight reel of "Madame Speaker" there are also touches of the Devil Wearing Prada.

Under a thumping soundtrack we are treated to a quick-cutting montage of magazine covers featuring Pelosi and reminded how the "power of the Speaker is awesome." (So awesome, in fact, that if you were menaced by someone wielding a still-legal assault rifle and asked to name one Pelosi achievement in her last six years of running the House, you would come up empty.) But wait, there is more: After film clips of Nancy finger-wagging Trump in the White House and storming out of it with Chuck Schumer (maybe they were taking his marbles and going home?), we are shown Nancy in a combat zone, wearing shades and getting off an attack helicopter surrounded by paratroops. This time Madame Speaker is off to war, perhaps after mumbling (her voice is pretty tremulous) the words of John Rambo: "Sir, do we get to win this time?"

Hillary Clinton is Served Up Some Crow

I felt a little sorry (not an easy emotion when contemplating the Clintons) for Hillary being asked to go before the camera and recite lines scripted by others about having lost in 2016 to Donald Trump. (*"Remember: Joe and Kamala can win three million more votes and still lose. Take. It. From. Me."*)

Hillary was decked out in the obligatory white suffragette dress and seated on Bill's Chappaqua (Live!) sofa, and she was asked to speak in calm, modulated tones about the greatness of Joe Biden when I am sure what she wanted to say was, "Hey, America, I gave you a blanket of virgin snow, and you pissed on it."

The signature line in Hillary's speech was: "I wish Donald Trump knew how to be a president," which suggests that he never bothered to read the instruction manual that the Clintons and Obamas worked on together and left behind in some drawer in the Oval Office. In the draft of the speech released to the press, that line was written as: "I wish Donald Trump had been a better president." Is it possible that Hillary is nervous speaking about Trump in the past tense? Or do the Clintons still feel proprietary about the Oval Office, having departed with so much of its loot?

Gabby Giffords Finds Her (Scripted) Words

It would be almost impossible for anyone not to admire the courage and fortitude of former member of Congress, and the victim of a mall shooting attack, Gabrielle Giffords in addressing the convention in her surgically reconstructed voice.

Giffords is a brave woman. I found her message compelling, especially when she said, "Words once came easily; today I struggle to speak. But I have not lost my voice. America needs all of us to speak out, even when you have to fight to find the words." Unfortunately, she was delivered up to the cameras not just as a victim of America's gun fetish, but as a party prop. She wasn't on stage to express her views about suffering or gun legislation but to recite the litany that the answer to all of the country's problems is to elect Joe Biden as president. ("*We must elect Joe Biden. He was there for me; he'll be there for you too.*")

Be great if it were true, Gabby, but Biden will duck and weave on guns (as with so many other issues) so that, depending on his audience, he will sound either like Inspector Harry Callahan ("*You've got to ask yourself one question: 'Do I feel lucky?'. . .*") or film-maker Michael Moore ("*We should be licensing everybody with a gun. . .*").

A truism of the Democratic Party (unchanged in 30 years, as this convention makes clear with its time-warp parade of Clintons, Bidens, and Obamas) is that it lost the Congress in 1994 after Bill Clinton pushed through the ban on assault rifles, which explains why Obama ran in 2008 by genuflecting to the Second Amendment and why, after the 2012 Sandy Hook shooting, we only got crocodile tears from Obama and Biden. I'm not surprised that Gabby could not find those words.

The Barack Obama Show

The press reviews of the Obama speech to the Zoom DNC convention made it sound like Lincoln at Gettysburg, or maybe Churchill on the beaches during the Battle of Britain, so when I finally roused myself to watch it, I was surprised to tune into something as banal as the soundtrack of Disney's Hall of the Presidents.

The speech was delivered in front of a display cabinet in Philadelphia's Museum of the American Revolution. Obama stood in front of the museum words "Writing the Constitution," with a portrait of James Madison looking over his shoulder. From there

Obama addressed the nation as if it were a third-grade class on a field trip to colonial Philadelphia.

Before screening his homily on democracy and the need to vote (*"You can give our democracy new meaning. . ."*), DNC videographers aired a trailer that showed Obama in the White House awarding Joe Biden the Presidential Medal of Freedom, a merit badge for the smart set. Obama made a big deal of the fact that Biden's medal came "with distinction," an honor of late only reserved for the likes of Colin Powell, Ronald Reagan, and the pope, although earlier secretaries of state and defense, Dean Rusk and Donald Rumsfeld, both got their medals "with distinction." (The medal Obama gave to Ellen DeGeneres was without.)

What is it about people in government that they feel such a need to hand each other so many awards? Aren't the helicopters, private planes, free lunches, lifetime pensions, subsequent board memberships and speaking fees, golfing vacations, ceremonial palace guards, saluting Marines, presidential libraries, and million-dollar book advances enough of an ego stroke? James Madison, for one, would despair at this transformation of ordinary government officials into an aristocratic class, with ribbons around their necks and bended knees in their politics.

Obama's 20-minute address to the convention was largely given over to platitudes (*"Our worst impulses unleashed, our proud reputation around the world badly diminished, and our democratic institutions threatened like never before. . ."*), and the hero of the tale was Obama himself, who, by inference, did everything in office that Trump had not. Hence the reason we need to install the soon-to-be octogenarian Joe Biden in office—so that we can be reminded of Obama's transcendence.

Obama also spoke in the tones of a petulant academic, as if arguing against tenure for some voluble colleague. He said of Trump, "For close to four years now, he's shown no interest in putting in the work; no interest in finding common ground; no interest in using the awesome power of his office to help anyone but himself and his friends; no interest in treating the presidency as anything but one more reality show that he can use to get the attention he craves."

Trump may be a sociopathic liar who abuses women and his oath of office, but he's free to govern in any style that he pleases (even in bed with cheeseburger wrappers on the floor), and he's not the first president who turned the presidency into a sitcom, something that goes back at least to Ronald Reagan (a genial front man for a variety show owned by the Fortune 500 and a few Vegas casinos).

If Clinton's presidency was a prequel for *Desperate Housewives*, W's was a remake of *Gunsmoke*. Even Obama himself conceived of the office as something between *The Cosby Show* (less all the necrophilia) and some daytime talk show. Why do we keep calling Obama "a brilliant politician" if his succession plan for the country's highest office consisted of Hillary Clinton and Joe Biden?

Kamala Harris Accepts with a Selfie

Before Senator Kamala Harris gave her acceptance speech, in a weirdly empty hotel ballroom (it looked like an odd cross between the starship *Enterprise* and a roller rink done over with velvet), she gave a little pep talk from a production supply room, as if she were about ready to guest-host *Saturday Night Live* ("*Hey, everybody, it's me, Kamala. . .*").

Whatever Harris said in her acceptance speech was instantly forgettable. (It's a good thing that in Trump's recent mental acuity test they didn't ask him, five minutes after it was done, what Kamala had said.) The gist of her address was this: "Because I am a success, the country will be a success." She didn't waste anyone's time talking about the Israeli annexations in the West Bank, fracking, Flint's water supply, bankrupt state budgets, virus vaccines, or soil erosion. The speech was about the immaculate conception of self.

Closing Acts

Senator Cory Booker from New Jersey led off the hit parade. I am sure he spoke in a heartfelt manner about "his friend Joe," but I remembered nothing of Cory's tribute and when I went back to my notes, all I had written down were the words "Cory Booker." The rest of the page was blank. Nor could I quite muster the enthusiasm to watch a replay of what he had said.

A grinning California Governor Gavin Newsome was patched in from a trench near a California forest fire, which I guess, from the headlines, could be almost anywhere in the state, even downtown LA. At least he made the connection between the wildfires and climate change, and Trump's climate denials, but instead of dwelling on the details of the crisis the oddly giddy Newsome switched gears to gush some over Biden. He said, breathlessly:

> I couldn't help myself on my way to one of our relief centers, one of our evacuation centers, just to jump out of the car and just express my deep reverence, my admiration to Joe Biden, to Kamala Harris, California's own. To their faith, their devotion, their constancy to their commitment, not just to the environment, but to the Commonwealth. To our kids, our kids' kids, our grandkids to our legacy. . .

Other senators, mayors, and representatives followed Newsome's Tinder ad. I liked Illinois Senator Tammy Duckworth, for her direct manner of speaking, although her words seemed to accept America having to fight permanent wars. As always, Mayor Pete Buttigieg sang a song of himself, while the upbeat Andrew Yang tried to convince himself that Biden (and his flip phone—it's in all the videos) was best placed to lead the United States into the technological brave new world.

Jon Meacham's Televangelism

Somehow the prime-time historian Jon Meacham scored about five minutes of air time during the Zoom convention. Last time we heard from Jon, he was serving as George Herbert Walker Bush's court historian. Meacham's role here turned out to be that of a hands-on-the-radio faith healer—"If we live in hope, we open our souls to the power of love. . ."—who was preaching a gospel that Biden is the spiritual heir to the likes of FDR and JFK (for the moment Jefferson and Wilson are banished from the Democratic temple for their racial indiscretions). A little weepy, Meacham said, "That's the issue of this election, the choice that goes straight to the nature of the soul of America. . . . It requires we, the people, and it requires a president of the United States with empathy, grace, a big heart, and an open mind. Joe Biden will be such a president." I thought historians only came out for the truth? Since when have they been shills?

You can be sure that this endorsement was the price that Meacham had to pay for consideration as the forthcoming Biden administration's in-house historian, the over-the-shoulder (and sycophantic) role that Arthur M. Schlesinger Jr. played for John F. Kennedy.

Failed Candidate Hollywood Squares

About the only unscripted moment of the four days was when Cory Booker convened a little prime-time game show made of up of also-ran Democratic candidates in 2020. With each candidate shown in a Zoom box, it had the feel of *Hollywood Squares*, although in place of Paul Lynde we got the equally goofy Beto O'Rourke.

Bernie emphasized Biden's only competitive advantage: He's not Trump. And for a brief moment I thought maybe the candidates might speak from the heart about running for president in 2020. Perhaps, as *Seinfeld*'s Julia Louis-Dreyfus was the evening's moderator, there might even be what during Festivus is called an airing of grievances?

Order was restored when several of the losing candidates recalled divine interventions that Saint Joe had visited upon their sinful lives. (If you have had a sadness or tragedy in your life, and Joe hasn't given you his cellphone number or called yours, you're not really trying.)

Mike Bloomberg Forecloses on Trump

Perhaps having been released from a #MeToo re-education camp, Mayor Michael Bloomberg (D-Billions) was the last speaker before Biden's (nearly endless) acceptance speech. As he should, Mike belittled Trump as a failed businessman:

> Trump says we should vote for him because he's a great businessman. Really? He drove his companies into bankruptcy, six times, always leaving behind customers and contractors who were cheated and swindled and stopped doing business with him. Well, this time, all of us are paying the price and we can't let him get away with it again.

During his brief campaign, Bloomberg came across an undertaker's assistant, and here he was a warm-up act on a slow convention night. At least he made the point that Trump had reduced the country to yet another failed Atlantic City casino.

Beau Biden Ascends on the Fourth Day

Before Biden's acceptance speech ("a path of hope and light. . ."), there was a newsreel of the candidate's formative years, the video equivalent of the *Lives of the Saints:* Joe overcoming his stutter, Joe lifeguarding at a Black public pool, Joe as a public defender, Joe surviving his father's unemployment, Joe losing his wife and daughter to tragedy, Joe honoring his sister and family, Joe finding salvation in public service, Joe as the senator from Amtrak, and Joe in Obama's Nirvana.

Biden's greatest video hits, plus an earlier tribute to his son Beau, who died in 2015, at least shows how the campaign plans to deal with the potential embarrassment that is his other son, Hunter. In case you've forgotten, in 2019 Donald Trump was impeached for digging up dirt in Ukraine over Hunter Biden's million-dollar directorship for Burisma, a dodgy Ukrainian oil and gas company, then under a corruption investigation. Burisma paid Hunter about a million dollars in exchange for doing almost nothing, as at the same time Joe was Obama's vice president and co-ordinating American policy in Ukraine, which included pushing to sack the prosecutor who was looking into Burisma.

Trump shook down Ukraine so that it would investigate Hunter's no-show directorship to reveal, he hoped, Joe Biden's influence-peddling on behalf of his son's client. In Ukraine, both Trump and the Bidens committed major improprieties, and in non-virus times they could well become election issues.

The Democrats' way out of this morass, should it come back to haunt the candidate during the campaign, is to beatify Beau and merge his identity with that of his surviving brother, Hunter.

And then, on top of all this confusion, to play up how the grieving Joe Biden dealt with the tragedy of losing his wife (and the boys' mother) in a 1972 car accident. Not even the shit-stirring Trump will want to untangle Hunter from Beau and the halo of compassion that surrounds how the story shows Joe Biden coping with his earlier family tragedy, which is at the core of his campaign identity.

Biden is now the candidate of empathy and understanding, someone capable of nurturing the grieving Covid nation much as he helped his struggling young sons, including Hunter. Even more convenient is that the Democratic vice presidential nominee, Kamala Harris, was a close friend to Beau Biden (both were their state's attorney general during the 2008 financial crisis). I am sure she can be counted on, in a prosecutorial style, to keep Trump and the Republicans away from Burisma Hunter and the taints of scandal.

Joe Biden Accepts Deification

On Day Four it took almost two hours of filler and prerecorded homilies about Father Joe before he was beamed up to the virtual Democratic cathedral and, in accepting the nomination, delivered his benediction and blessings for the lives and soul of the nation.

I know you have heard that Biden made "the speech of his life," and maybe he did, as he hit the high notes of inclusiveness (*"hope over fear. . . . It's about winning the heart, and, yes, the soul of America. . ."*) in promising, during his presidency, to end the racial divide, retool the economy, eradicate climate change, lower the cost of prescription drugs, defend Social Security, create five million new manufacturing jobs, reduce student debt, provide better health care, defeat the virus, stand tall against dictators, soak the rich, equalize pay for women, end discrimination, improve education, defend our troops, and stand tall against terrorism. In the last 50 years, I have been hearing similar speeches from the presidential candidates of both parties, but for whatever reason, after four or eight years, most presidents leave office in disgrace, as will be the case with Trump.

A large part of the problem is that to get elected, candidates have to reinvent themselves as Olympian gods, part of a race that has slipped the bonds of earthly gravity, capable of feats worthy of King Arthur or St. Francis of Assisi. In these four days of the Democratic national convention, the videographers of the Democratic Party turned Biden into yet another celluloid saint, someone who gives his cellphone number to strangers, visits emergency rooms in the dead of night to comfort the afflicted, reaches out to stuttering schoolboys, and spends his days and nights working to cure hunger, cancer, and injustice. Who wouldn't want this Biden mounted on his charger, prepared to slay the Trump dragon, or benevolently running the country from behind the curtains in Oz, despite Dorothy's exchange with the Wizard (*"I think you are a very bad man,"* said Dorothy. *"Oh, no, my dear; I'm really a very good man, but I'm a very bad Wizard. . ."*)

The problem is that American federalism wasn't designed as a prime-time monarchy to be operated from the top down; it was put together as a democracy that works best, in the hands of good men and women, from the bottom up. Perhaps Biden is a good man? I have no way of knowing. But I can tell you this: American presidents, as they are currently schemed and packaged into office, make very bad Wizards.

Trump's Republican National Convention: Casino Royale

"The dirty work at political conventions is almost always done in the grim hours between midnight and dawn. Hangmen and politicians work best when the human spirit is at its lowest ebb."

—Russell Baker, *The Sayings of Poor Russell*, 1972

God's a Republican

A Trump Roll of the Dice

I NEVER THOUGHT TRUMP RAN FOR PRESIDENT IN 2016 BECAUSE he wanted to lower the cost of prescription drugs for "our seniors," or because he wanted to start an itinerant ministry dedicated to criminal justice for ex-convicts, or institute school choice. Trump ran for the presidency to keep an array of creditors (from the Russians and Saudis to Deutsche Bank down to all those plumbers he refused to pay in Atlantic City) from foreclosing on Trump's towers of debts. Perhaps by getting into the presidential race he figured he could buy himself some time, find some new sources of cash, kite some checks or accounts receivable, or otherwise deflect the attention of those hard on his heels?

Winning the presidency was almost beside the point. It has conferred on him a form of limited immunity (the presidency as the greatest offshore trust in the world?) and has given him a place to hide that is beyond the reach of those angry investors who stumped up good money after bad to fund golf courses or (now empty) office space.

Trump's business model was never real estate development or hotel management. (If you ever want to lose a fortune, invest in a golf course.) Those were just the cover stories. Trump's profession has always been that of a grifter, and his pyramid scheme was to convince rich individuals, banks, private equity investors, sovereign funds, and countries to bankroll projects from which he could later walk, leaving behind a mountain of unpaid debts. (Which explains how it comes so easily to Trump to speak of the coronavirus in the past tense.)

Confidence is Trump's only game, so it really shouldn't be any surprise that he's now playing it on the national stage, only this time, instead of beating the Russians or the Saudis out of their billions blown on Trump Steaks, leaky condos, or failed golf clubs, Trump has managed to convince a national political party and about half of the electorate that he stands for something more than the art of dealing from the bottom of the deck.

Trump Buying Time

On what evidence do I base my suppositions that the Trump empire has long been tilting toward liquidation? Let's start with Vladimir Putin, around whom Trump acts like a squirrelly numbers runner who has failed to pay off his boss. Without so much as a peep, Trump gave Syria to Russia (at the same time, all he got from the Turks for betraying the Kurds were a few imprisoned missionaries), and during the nine hours of the RNC convention, Russia was never mentioned.

Secondly, I can't imagine why, in the first act of his presidency, he flew over to Saudi Arabia and groveled in front of its ancient king, unless it was to say, "Don't worry about that money I owe you. Where I'm working now, I'm good for billions."

Finally, I have just now sat through the nine hours of the Republican national convention, Trump's gift of himself to a grateful party and the nation. And the only language I heard, over the four days, was that of a sting.

Nearly every testament to Trump's love of America and each and every American (in on the con, Ivanka called herself *"the proud daughter of the people's president. . ."*) echoed the excuses of a bad debtor trying to convince a creditors' committee that he can work his way out of bankruptcy (*"he's done it before, and he'll do it again. . ."*).

Think of the refrain from the Republican convention, "Four More Years," which is chanted any time Trump gets near a lectern, as the eternal hymn of bad debtors everywhere. The last time we heard it, Richard Nixon was running for reelection in 1972. How did that work out?

As best I can figure, Trump has done to the American capital account what he did to that of Trump Inc.—bankrupted it about six times. In four years of Trump governance, the national debt has increased from about $20 trillion to $24 trillion, while in order to pay for the pandemic the government budget deficit has been increased by almost $3 trillion. Maybe that explains why the Republican National Convention had the feel of a cable TV ad for an extravagant Las Vegas resort hotel development that one Donald J. Trump is bringing to the market. Keep in mind: When you work in casinos, you're betting on one thing—that the people lose.

God's a Republican

Beginning with a spiritual invocation from New York's Cardinal Timothy Dolan, Day One of the Republican convention established most of the themes that would get droned into viewers over the next four days: the Democratic Party is in the clutches of the Squad, if not the Shining Path, and its nominee, Joe Biden, is the talking dummy for such ventriloquists as Bernie Sanders, AOC, and Nancy Pelosi, if not Fidel Castro, Mao Tse-tung, and the Taliban. As for its policies, as the Republicans sum them up, the Democrats come down on the side of looting, rioting, cop kill-ing, and cheerleading for ISIS and the Chinese Communist Party. And during the pandemic shutdown (emphasis on the past tense), while the Democrats were keeping you out of your churches, they were voting to make abortion clinics essential business.

Jesus Was My Roommate and an Awesome Dude

First up to lectern was the creepy campus pol Charlie Kirk, who has funding in the millions to make sure that "conserva-tive voices" are heard on university campuses. Charlie was given face time to gather in "the youth vote," although the only college students that I know who look like Kirk are those going door-to-door with brochures and ringing doorbells to ask if you have a few minutes to accept Jesus Christ (or maybe Donald Trump?) into your life. Almost in raptures, he ended by saying:

> We will be a country that makes it easier to have many children, live quiet and peaceable lives, and worship your God without a tyrant getting in the way. . . . We will build a future where America remains the greatest country ever to exist in the his-tory of the world. All of that is within our grasp if we secure four more years for the defender of Western civilization, our champion, my friend, the 45th President of the United States, President Donald J. Trump.

Clearly not a toga party.

Knowledge Is Good, But Is School Choice?

Rebecca Friedrichs delivered the next picnic at Hanging Rock. She is "a veteran California public school educator," although her mission at the convention was to string up school unions. ("*They've intentionally rewritten American history to perpetuate division, pervert the memories of our American founders, and disparage our Judeo-Christian virtues. Their lenient discipline policies morphed our schools into war zones and they back defunding police and abolishing ICE.*") Her larger point was to introduce the cause of school choice "to return control to parents, protect religious liberties, and empower kids to escape dangerous, low-performing schools."

School choice might well be called the Bankrupt Public Education Act, as it allows parents, under the false flag of "educational freedom," to draw vouchers, take their children out of the local school system, and invest the money in private education, including, and perhaps most importantly, in religious academies.

The Invasion of the Democrat Body Snatchers

Another theme hammered home early on the first day was the equation of the Democratic Party with home invasion and the specter that Joe Biden will bus large, angry Black men (think of Willie Horton, George Herbert Walker Bush's running mate in 1988) into your neighborhood, where your mothers, sisters, and daughters will never be safe. ("*At least with Republican Home Security, you'll never be alone. . .Call 1-800-DON-TRMP. . .*")

Matt Gaetz II represents Pensacola and the Florida panhandle in Congress, although he sounded more closely aligned to the *Bund deutscher Arbeiterjugend*, shouting:

We must fight to save America now or we may lose her forever. Joe Biden might not even notice. Settle for Biden, that's the hashtag promoted by AOC and the socialists. The woketopians will settle for Biden because they will make him an extra in a movie written, produced, and directed by others. It's a horror film really. They'll disarm you, empty the prisons, lock you in your home and invite MS-13 to live next door. And the police aren't coming when you call in Democrat-run cities. They're already being defunded, disbanded.

Covid-19: Not Exactly Dental Surgery

After Gaetz's jackbooted speech came a Black woman running for Congress in Baltimore (*"We want a chance to get ahead, not just get by. . ."*) and then a coalminer's daughter who served as a nurse on the virus front lines (*"I can tell you without hesitation Donald Trump's quick action and leadership saved thousands of lives during COVID-19"*). Then, Republicans marched onto the stage an oral surgeon from Louisiana to make the point that Trump is a medical genius who any day will find a cure for Covid. (*"President Trump truly moved mountains to save lives and he deserves credit. Thank you, President Trump for providing timely access to critical diagnostics and therapeutics during this pandemic."*) Perhaps now we have the name of the feel-good doctor who wrote Trump's prescription for hydroxychloroquine.

Dr. Donald J. Oz

Most Americans think that Trump is a Covid denier whose unwillingness to listen to briefings from his science and medical advisors, coupled with obsession with his reelection, will result in some 500,000 Americans dead from the virus before the pandemic is over. During the four days of the Republican convention more Americans died of the virus than were killed on 9/11, at Pearl Harbor, or on the Normandy beaches. Nevertheless, on all four nights of the RNC's utopian *Trump World* mini-series, the president was described in terms normally reserved for the likes of Florence Nightingale or Dr. Albert Schweizer.

Then there was this little reality show, in which Trump himself hosted a program in the White House where he moderated a discussion with some everyday folks who are trying to survive the pandemic ordeal. Most of the time that Trump speaks on television he looks and sounds like Herman Göring hectoring the nation about *Volksgemeinschaft*. Here, however, Trump was civil in his exchanges with this small group of ordinary Americans (there were some nurses, a postal worker, a police officer, etc.), asking them gentle questions about their experiences in the war against Covid.

Representative Jim Jordan Comes to Grief

You will remember Congressman Jim Jordan from the House impeachment hearings. He was the jacket-less attack dog for the Trump cause of innocence, and clearly earned enough street cred to speak at the virtual RNC convention and sink his teeth into Biden and the Dems. Slipping his leash, Jordan said:

> Look at what's happening in American cities, cities all run by Democrats, crime violence, and mob rule. Democrats refuse to denounce the mob, and their response to the chaos, defund the police, defund border patrol, and defund our military. While they're doing all this, they're also trying to take away your guns.

Then the Republican impresarios turned Jim into a Hallmark sympathy card. They had him tell a long story about how Trump called in person to console one of Jordan's grieving relatives. (*"For the next five minutes, family and friends sat in complete silence as the president of the United States took time to talk to a dad who was hurting. That's the president I've gotten to know the last four years. . ."*)

It had the feel of a last-minute addition, out of Republican fear that Joe Biden had cornered the grief consolation market during the Democratic convention.

Hershel Walker Runs to Darkness

Hershel Walker was a celebrated professional football player in the 1980s and '90s, when he rushed for more than 10,000 yards in the USFL and NFL. The Cowboys once traded him to the Vikings for about a dozen players and draft picks, after which he didn't do much in Minnesota.

I had not thought about Hershel since 1992, when he raced the bobsled at the Winter Olympics in Albertville, France, but here he was on screen, vouching for Trump's qualities as a friend and family man, talking up the president's fight for racial equality. (*"He shows how much he cares about social justice in the Black community through his actions. . ."*) He even tried to humanize Trump by describing a trip both families made together to Disney World, but then let slip that Don had walked around the Magic Kingdom in a suit.

Trump Straps on his Bulletproof Suit Vest

Spliced in between athletes talking about Trump and God, the RNC served up a line of cancer survivors, party officials, and Republican Black politicians, some of whom spoke about their Democratic pasts as if the broadcast were a confessional. (State representative Vernon Jones said, *"The Democratic Party does not want Black people to leave their mental plantation. We've been forced to be there for decades and generations, but I have news for Joe Biden. We are free. . ."*) Then the convention got down to the business at hand—that of making the Republican Party bulletproof on the issue of guns and the Second Amendment, a principal dog whistle during the four days.

First up was Andrew Pollock, the father of a victim of the Parkland, Florida, school shooting, who made it sound as though Biden had driven the shooter to the high school. Pollock's message was this: If you elect a Democrat, you can expect more school shootings. If you elect Trump, your kids will be safe and can play in the park. Pollock explained the decisive steps Trump had taken on the matter of guns in schools. He said, "Then the president did what he said he would do. He took action. He formed a school safety commission that issued dozens of recommendations to make school safer. . ." Case closed.

The McCloskeys Get Their Guns

Mark and Patty McCloskey are the St. Louis couple who faced down a Black Lives Matter rally passing near their front lawn by brandishing assault weapons. They took to the Republican stage to explain to the rest of America that unless you lay in a few automatic freedom dispensers, angry mobs of Black people will show up on your own front lawn. (*What you saw happened to us could just as easily happen to any of you who are watching from quiet neighborhoods around our country.*) Patty caught the spirit of the convention when she said, "America is such a great country that not only do you have the right to own a gun and use it to defend yourself, but thousands of Americans will offer you free advice on how to use it—at least that's what we experienced."

The Prime Time of Miss Kimberley Guilfoyle

Even though Trump ran for office in 2016 on a promise to drain the Swamp, he produced the entire Republican convention within several blocks of the White House and nearly all the speakers (including a number of Washington alligators) appeared on stage at the nearby Mellon Auditorium, which was illuminated with columns of light and American flags.

After the McCloskeys had pistol-whipped America ("*They want to abolish the suburbs altogether by ending single-family home zoning. . .*"), a woman in a tightly fitted red dress and flowing Kardashian hair approached the lectern. I assumed I was looking at Melania Trump, although something was just a touch off. Was it the heavy eye makeup or the extreme lip rouge? Finally, the woman said, "Good evening, America. I'm Kimberly Guilfoyle. . .," and I figured out that Donald Trump Jr. had somehow persuaded his girlfriend to transmogrify herself into a clone of his father's wife. (Dr. Freud, check your Twitter feed.)

Guilfoyle used to work for the Fox network and presumably knows something about speaking on television, but her manner (in an empty hall) was that of Evita Peron rallying the *descamisados* from a balcony in Buenos Aires. In the name of Trump, Guilfoyle wept, she pleaded, she prayed, and she exalted, so that America would let her boyfriend's father (and then maybe her big-game-hunting boyfriend?) hold the country's highest office. Nearly hysterical toward the end, Guilfoyle said:

> Rioters must not be allowed to destroy our cities. Human sex drug traffickers should not be allowed to cross our border. The same socialist policies, which destroyed places like Cuba and Venezuela, must not take root in our cities and our schools. If you want to see the socialized Biden-Harris future for our country, just take a look at California. It is a place of immense wealth, immeasurable innovation, and immaculate environment and the Democrats turned it into a land of discarded heroin needles in parks, riots in streets, and blackouts in homes. . . .

Guilfoyle ended with a Howard Dean scream, "Ladies and gentlemen, leaders and fighters for our freedom and liberty and the American dream, the best is yet to come." Had this been a Spinal Tap concert (maybe it was?), at this point Guilfoyle would have fainted. (*"Here lies David St.Hubbins...and why not?"*)

Foreign Relations: Midnight Express

Before and after some filler speakers (angry Miami Cubans, congressional candidates, etc.), the Republicans aired a short action film on foreign affairs, making the point that if the Democrats get back in power, you can expect that America will be held hostage; it will be a rerun of the Carter years.

On screen there were images of angry street scenes and captives bound and gagged. The voiceover says dramatically: "American hostages, forgotten and wasting away in far-off prisons, wrongfully detained by foreign governments. Americans were beaten, abused, starved, and left for dead until President Donald Trump stepped in." It felt like a remake of *Midnight Express.*

Cut to a White House hall, in which Trump joins a small circle of former hostages so that they can reminisce about their captivity and describe how President Donald J. Rambo rescued them from their tiger cages. I am sure the producers were hoping to feature Trump in something as gripping as *Argo* (the Ben Affleck film about American hostages in Iran), but Trump used the moment to talk up all the dictators with whom he negotiated to free the prisoners. (Trump: *"I have to say that to me, President Erdogan was very good. . ."*)

Nikki Haley Addresses Affairs of State

Nikki Haley, the former U.S. ambassador to the United Nations, endorsed President Trump's reelection, although the point of her lugubrious speech was to stake her claim to the nomination in 2024. Haley is an Asian American woman, former governor of South Carolina, and Republican, which checks a lot of boxes, but here she was just mailing it in. (*"We will build on the progress of our past and unlock the promise of our future. That future starts when the American people reelect president Donald Trump. . ."*) She got more traction back in 2018 when she called the allegations of an affair with Donald Trump "disgusting." (I take her point.)

Don Jr. Blows Away the Left

The cameras went straight to Don Trump Jr., who is a staple on the undercard at Trump rallies, feeding red meat and hats to the crowds. Here he was as amped as his girlfriend, Kimberly Guilfoyle, with a sweaty brow and dilated pupils, which the next day set the Twittersphere ablaze with suggestions that he'd fallen in line with more than just Daddy worshipping. He denied it.

I have no doubt that Don Jr. imagines himself as his father's political heir (as does his ambitious girlfriend). Despite growing up in gilded palaces, Don Jr. (sort of like George W. Bush) has taken on the persona of a gun-toting, God-fearing, pickup truck-driving, flag-waving, Chinese-hating, make-America-great-again good old boy. While Ivanka has ministered to her father in the Oval Office, Don Jr. (in no official government capacity) has been building his own base by making the rounds of state fairs, gun shows, and wrestling arenas—successfully, I might add.

Having heard Don Jr. at Trump rallies (he speaks like he's selling time shares on late-night cable TV), I have no sympathy for any of his hateful views, but listening to him drone on about casinos in the air (*"Imagine a world where the evils of communism and radical Islamic terrorism are not given a chance to spread, where heroes are celebrated and the good guys win, you can have it. That is the life, that is the country, that is the world that Donald Trump and the Republican Party are after. . .*"), I confess I did have some fleeting compassion for anyone who feels the psychological pressure to have his girlfriend look like his stepmother.

Holy Log Rolling

Day Two dawned with a religious invocation from a Las Vegas preacher, who seemed to be reciting a gambler's prayer when she said, "Lord, give us strategies from heaven." At least she didn't say, "Good girls go to Heaven, bad girls go to Vegas."

An Ex-con Bromance

The theme of the evening at the Republican convention (in theory meeting in Charlotte, North Carolina, although that venue was never seen on camera) was to celebrate America as "the land of opportunity," but very quickly it skewed into a daytime serial in which a rich man randomly bestows his grace on an astonished and grateful stranger.

This episode featured the improbable connection between President Donald Trump, an ex-con named John Ponder, and the FBI special agent, Richard Beasley, who arrested Ponder and sent him to jail. The story reminded me of television staples from my childhood, when honest cops were always finding goodness in bad men, who then went straight, either to ride with the Lone Ranger or walk with the Lord. In Ponder's case, he knocked off a series of banks and did a stretch in the big house, but by the time he got out God was driving his getaway car.

The first person to whom he spread the good word of his conversion was his arresting FBI officer, Richard Beasley, and subsequently they became close friends. Ponder also founded an outreach organization called Hope for Prisoners. (There was no mention of whether the likes of Paul Manafort, Michael Cohen, Rick Gates, or Roger Stone have enrolled in the program.) Trump met Ponder and Beasley when the president presided over an awards ceremony and gave degrees to some ex-prisoners in Hope's program.

This was a feel-good moment, with hugs and tears, especially when Trump gave Ponder a full pardon for his crimes, and it positioned Trump as the star of criminal justice reform, unless he's hearing the footsteps of New York District Attorney Cyrus Vance Jr. and wondering how they do lunch at Club Fed.

Rand Paul Cuts Trump's Lawn

The last time we heard from Senator Rand Paul (R-KY), his neighbor was beating him up in his front yard, in a dispute about brush near their joint property line.

In Republican politics, Paul is a wildcard, and for a while Democrats thought he might vote to convict Trump on impeachment charges or vote against Brett Kavanaugh. Since then, Democrats have learned not to expect too much from anyone named after Ayn Rand.

At the RNC convention, former doctor Paul got misty-eyed as he recalled businessman Trump aiding one of Paul's charitable missions to Central America. (*"I was planning a medical mission trip to Guatemala to perform charity eye surgeries, and we needed money to fund the trip. Donald Trump offered to help and immediately came through for us. . ."*) Deficit Hawk Paul decided not to say anything about Drunken Sailor Trump's give-away economics or the $24 trillion national debt.

The President Serves Up Lobster

A raft of small business operators, conveniently from swing states, all spoke in Mellon Auditorium about how Obama, Biden, federal regulations, and the Chinese threatened to put their companies into bankruptcy, which only the coming of Donald Trump averted. (*"I felt like Trump is definitely pushing more for the steel mills, the fishermen, just us making our own products and bringing everything in. . ."*) One witness to this miracle was a Maine lobsterman whose livelihood has been saved, so he says, by Trump opening up Europe to tariff-free lobster rolls. (*"As long as Trump is president, fishing families like mine will have a voice, but if Biden wins, he'll be controlled by the environmental extremists. . ."*) The Trump handlers had him add: "He [Trump] keeps his word, like eliminating the European tariffs and moving the U.S. embassy from Tel Aviv to Jerusalem"—no doubt a development of vital concern to Maine fishermen even though the Old Testament has lobster on its no-fly list.

The Economic Miracle of Marked Cards and Tilted Wheels

If every speech at the convention had been as concise as Larry Kudlow's (he was a Fox anchorman and now broadcasts directly to Trump as his economic advisor), the convention might have been over in a few hours. Kudlow spoke for less than three minutes, and he presented a concise case for allowing the Republicans to manage the economy. He said:

A great bipartisan rescue also saved the economy. Right now, our economic health is coming back. With emergency spending and tax cuts, Americans are going back to work. There's a housing boom, there's an auto boom, a manufacturing boom, a consumer spending boom. Stocks are in record territory. A V-shaped recovery is pointing to better than 20 percent growth in the second half of this year. Now looking ahead, more tax cuts and regulatory rollback will be in store, payroll tax cuts for higher wages, income tax cuts for the middle class, capital gains tax cuts for investment, productivity, and jobs.

It all sounded good, to the point that I almost wished it had been true. Unfortunately, casino economics depend on using other people's money, crooked wheels, marked cards, and unpaid loans. As Trump said in 2016, "I've made a fortune by using debt, and if things don't work out I renegotiate the debt. . . . You go back and you say, hey guess what, the economy crashed. I'm going to give you back half," which is about all that the American people should expect this time.

Far Right Poster Child Nick Sandmann

Nick Sandmann is the Covington, Kentucky Catholic high school kid who on a field trip (well, a March for Life) to Washington, D.C., had an encounter with Black and Native American demonstrators near the Lincoln Memorial. In early press reports, CNN and the *Washington Post*, among other outlets, reported that a smug Sandmann in a Trump MAGA hat baited participants in an Indigenous People's March. Sandmann sued various media outlets for defamation and libel, and eventually the case settled before going to trial. Sandmann was vindicated when video surfaced showing that he and his Covington classmates were themselves victims of racially abusive taunts (from what were called Black Hebrew Israelites)—not the other way around, as the media had first reported.

For standing tall on the right-to-life ramparts while wearing a MAGA hat, and for having sued and beaten the mainstream media, Sandmann has become a favorite son of the Trump set, who were eager to turn him into a convention mannequin. Speaking to the RNC, Sandmann said, in part:

> The full war machine of the mainstream media revved up into attack mode. They did so without researching the full video of the incident. . .without ever asking me for my side of the story. And do you know why? Because the truth was not important. Advancing their anti-Christian, anti-conservative, anti-Donald Trump narrative was all that mattered. And if advancing their narrative ruined the reputation and future of a teenager from Covington, Kentucky, well, so be it. That would teach him not to wear a MAGA hat.

Something tells me that it could well be Sandmann's fate to spend his life as a mouthpiece for larger, more powerful interests. (Forgive the Churchillian expression, but he looks more like a dummy than an organ grinder.) I wonder what's worse: getting slimed by the *Washington Post* and CNN or having to find work as a Trump dancing bear?

P.I. Lawyer Pam Bondi: "Help is just a phone call away. . ."

The Hunter Biden Ukraine mud file was given to a former Florida attorney general and Trump shill named Pam Bondi, who has a pedigree in Biden oppo and came to the convention floor with the street cred of having chanted "Lock her up" at Hillary during the last election.

Better yet, in 2018, while still the Florida attorney general, Bondi had dealings with Lev Parnas, one of the lowlifes (now under indictment) that Rudy Giuliani and Trump ("*I don't know who this man is. . .*") sent to Ukraine for some dirt-digging on Hunter and to smear the U.S. ambassador. One of the indictments against Parnas is for illegally bundling and funneling money to certain (unnamed) Florida politicians.

In her 2020 convention speech, however, Bondi was little more than perfunctory about the Ukraine bounty Hunter. ("*Yet he was paid millions to do nothing. He only had one qualification that mattered. He was the son of the man in charge of distributing U.S. aid to Ukraine. . .*"). Then Bondi changed gears to another Trump campaign obsession—that of smearing China, which, they insist, gave us Covid-19 and which owns both Bidens. (She said, "*. . .those Chinese communist bankers approved millions to go to Hunter's firm, and those bankers work for the Chinese Communist Party, which oppresses their people, cheated American workers for decades, and covered up a deadly virus.*")

Bondi is a Trump enabler, and has been since he donated $25,000 to one of her reelection PACs and (quite separately, I assure you) since she declined as Florida's attorney general to investigate that august body of higher learning, Trump University.

Miracle Cure-alls

We heard from Kellyanne Conway and others about how Trump has hired all sorts of women to senior key jobs. Then we had to sit through a heart-rending story, told by Mike Pence, who was standing in front of Abraham Lincoln's boyhood home, of a critically ill child whose life might be saved by the federal Right to Try bill, which allows doctors to administer long-shot medications that don't have federal approval, in cases of a terminal prognosis. Promoting the act also appeals to Trump's love of quackery and sticks it to the FDA for not letting him self-medicate the country with internet Covid cures. (*"I'm taking it. . . . What do you have to lose?"*)

What Wall?

We took a timeout from the convention so that Trump could preside over the naturalization ceremony of a group of five new citizens, including one from Sudan, which otherwise is on Trump's travel ban list. From his amiable chatting with the new citizens (*"As citizens, you're now stewards of this magnificent nation, a family comprised of every race, color, religion, and creed. . ."*), you might have come away with the impression that Trump spends much of his time encouraging immigrants to find paths to citizenship.

Tiffany Trump's Debutante Ball

I am not sure who dressed Tiffany Trump for her party speech, but she looked fresh from an ABBA concert, in an egg-shell blue suit with flaming, flared bellbottoms.

She has just graduated from law school and is presumably job hunting on Zoom, and she talked a little about those uncertainties before delivering what sounded like a high school commencement speech. (*"Because in America, your life is yours to chart. . ."*). There was little intimacy in what Tiffany said. I suppose it's possible that she wrote the speech herself. Or maybe an aide handed her a draft. She left me with the impression that in her life Trump is a distant abstraction.

Eric Trump's Air Kisses

It tells you what Trump thinks about his business that he left Eric in charge (along with Don Jr. who never seems to be in the office). In the same week that Eric spoke at the convention, his Aunt Maryanne (Trump's older sister) referred to him, on a secretly recorded tape, as a "moron."

Eric Trump doesn't speak so much as snarl. I sensed a chip on his shoulder the size of, well, Mt. Rushmore. Here's how he described the "radical Democrats":

> They want to destroy the monuments of our forefathers. They want to disrespect our flag, burn the stars and stripes that represent patriotism and the American dream. They want to disrespect our National Anthem by taking a knee while our armed forces laid down their lives every day to protect our freedom. They do not want the Pledge of Allegiance in our schools. Many of them don't want one nation under God. The Democrats want to defund and disrespect our law enforcement.

He went on in that flag-burning vein for about 10 minutes. I only started listening carefully when toward the end of his speech he direct-messaged his father, with expressions of love. ("*I miss working alongside you every single day. . . . I'm proud of what you're doing for this country. . . . Continue to be unapologetic. Keep fighting for what is right. You are making America strong again. . . . Let's go get another four years. I love you very much.*")

Secretary Mike Pompeo Zooms in from Jerusalem

From a hotel balcony overlooking the old city came Secretary of State Mike Pompeo, who was once described by an anonymous former U.S. ambassador as "a heat-seeking missile [headed straight] for Trump's ass." Pompeo's Zoom call from Jerusalem ("*this very city of God. . .the rightful capital of the Jewish homeland*") was hardly the result of his pressing diplomatic schedule, but a photo-op from Heaven (or as close as you can get) so that Mike could report how Trump had wiped out ISIS, brokered the new deal with the United Arab Emirates, and, kumbaya, brought peace to the Middle East. Pompeo violated diplomatic protocol, if not the 1939 Hatch Act, by involving the State Department in a partisan political event, but in the Trump administration breaking the law is part of the job description.

Melania Never Promised You a Rose Garden

Day Two ended with Melania Trump's catwalk through the replanted Rose Garden. She was dressed in the drab olive green and tunic of the Woman's Army Corps, either to make the point that this was a moment of national crisis and that she was doing her part by modeling an appropriately sensitive uniform, or, as First Hostage, to signal to the outside world that her husband is getting ready to declare martial law. No doubt White House carpenters (another violation of the Hatch Act?) had to work overtime to create a catwalk from the residence to the Rose Garden long enough to give Melania sufficient time to strut her goods in prime time. The poor Rose Garden (thanks, Melania) was hacked, cut back, and replanted in weird geometric shapes. It almost looks like a Nebraska field where someone has stamped out "Help Me!" from the corn rows.

Without this time plagiarizing from Michelle Obama, Melania managed to read through her speech in a morose monotone, which, as I heard it, reflected the tensions in the First Marriage. Clearly she wanted to talk about Covid sufferers, her trip to Africa and slavery, addiction, and bullying, while Trump's handlers insisted that her spiked heels toe party lines. Toward the end Melania said, "Total honesty is what we as citizens deserve from our president. Whether you like it or not, you always know what he's thinking, and that is because he's an authentic person who loves this country and its people and wants to continue to make it better."

If you ever want a frying pan launched in your general direction, try calling your partner or spouse "authentic." It sounded like a statement that Trump's divorce lawyer prepared for a settlement press release, and that she reluctantly agreed to sign.

Scaring Americans to Life

A LOT OF DAY-THREE TIME WAS SPENT (especially by Trump intimates and family members) trying to convince voters (or perhaps themselves?) that Don isn't the raving maniac that you know from Twitter but a loving, caring president, father, grandfather, father-in-law, boss, and colleague who loves God and country. The testimony sounded like those forced character letters sent to a judge about to sentence someone for having abused and fondled 22 women. But there was also airtime to put the boot into China and to remind suburban voters that Black and Latino people in swing states like Wisconsin and New Mexico are coming for their wives, sisters, and SUVs.

Go Ahead, Abe, Make My Day

The South Dakota governor, Kristi Noem, was dressed in neither Fox red nor suffragette white, but tasteful blue, and initially I thought she spoke well, but then she lapsed into the brainwashed cadences of a Trump True Believer. She talked up James Madison as the father of the Bill of Rights (only partly true; thank Patrick Henry) and Abraham Lincoln as a vigilante (Make-my-day Abe gave a law-and-order speech in 1838), and she tried to connect Lincoln's Republican Party (which got rid of slavery) to Trump's liberation theology in 2020. ("*In just four years, President Trump has lifted people of all races and backgrounds out of poverty. He shrunk government. . . . He has advanced religious liberty. He protected the Second Amendment. . .")* Noem took office in South Dakota in 2019, but only drew national attention in 2020 when she was at the forefront of Covid deniers, which included hosting in the state a virus-superspreader biker jamboree. She refused to shut down her state and curried Trump favor by talking up hydroxychloroquine. Think of her convention speech as an adverse reaction.

The Party's Over: No-Show Republicans

A logger from Minnesota talked up Trump as a great friend to lumberjacks, not quite along the lines of the Monty Python song, (*"He's a lumberjack and he's OK/He sleeps all night and he works all day. . ."*) but in that general direction.

Then Senator Martha Blackburn from Tennessee (an odd choice as she's not running for reelection in 2020) delivered what sounded like an animated cartoon to the convention. (*"If the Democrats had their way, they would keep you locked in your house until you become dependent on the government for everything. That sounds a lot like Communist China, to me. Maybe that's why Joe Biden is so soft on them. Why Nancy Pelosi says that China would prefer Joe Biden. Yeah. I bet they would. . ."*) Listening to the nonessential Blackburn, I decided to make a list of prominent Republicans who either refused to attend the convention or were not offered a speaking slot, and here are the names I came up with: Mitt Romney, George W. Bush, Dick Cheney, Henry Kissinger, James Baker, Colin Powell (he spoke to the Dems), Condoleezza Rice, Jeb Bush, Laura Bush, Megan McCain, Liz Cheney, Susan Collins, Lindsey Graham, Ted Cruz, Marco Rubio, Chris Christie, Pat Toomey, Paul Ryan, and Jeff Flake.

I am sure I have omitted many others. But we did get to hear from Tiffany and Eric.

War Is Hell and Good Politics

Without the heavy hitters from the Republican national security set, the convention featured the junior varsity, which included among others Texas Congressman and Navy Seal wounded war hero Dan Crenshaw (he made his pitch from the deck of the battleship *Texas*) and retired Lt. General Keith Kellogg (he's the national security adviser to Vice President Mike Pence).

Crenshaw talked about his Middle East deployment and the heroes who never came home, made references to sacrifice, and blessed America, but the closest that he came to mentioning Trump by name was when he said: "The defeat of ISIS was the result of America believing in our heroes, our president having their backs and rebuilding our military, so we'd have what we needed to finish the mission." I doubt someone as petty as Jared Kushner would have missed that sin of omission.

General Kellogg made the same case, reciting the litany about eliminating "the terrorist ISIS caliphate" and its leader, al-Baghdadi, "one of the world's most brutal terrorists." But Kellogg made the larger case that "President Trump is no Hawk." He went on: "He wisely wields the sword when required, but believes in seeking peace instead of perpetual conflict. . . . Ask yourself, has this president kept his promises to keep us out of needless conflicts and to pursue ending wars without end?" Actually, in the Middle East, Trump is running on a standing-tall narrative that he moved the U.S. embassy to Jerusalem, ripped up the Obama agreement with Iran (it was never a treaty), "took out" terrorists such as Qasem Soleimani (technically he was an Iranian government official), defeated ISIS, delivered peace to the region, and brought our boys home.

Another way to write that paragraph would be as follows: In the Middle East, President Trump has betrayed our long-standing allies the Kurds, backstabbed the Palestinians, and abandoned Syria to a lawless partitioned fate between Israel, Turkey, and Russia. He did not "eliminate" ISIS (credit the Obama administrations for most of that) but merely reduced its footprint. He's nowhere with Iran and has funded, via the Saudis (his private client), a brutal conflict in Yemen, which does nothing for the United States. He has no cards to play in any negotiations with the Taliban in Afghanistan, has little influence in Iraq, and is oblivious to the crisis in Lebanon.

Kayleigh McEnany Loves Her Voicemale

The White House press secretary told an emotional story of her genetic disposition toward breast cancer and her preventive double mastectomy, but only because President Trump called her after her surgery, which is proof of his empathy and enduring faith in humanity and that, by the way, "this president stands by Americans with pre-existing conditions." McEnany also made it clear that, in the Medici rivalries of the White House West Wing, her knives and vials of poison are wielded in support of Ivanka. (*"As I came out of anesthesia, one of the first calls I received was from Ivanka Trump. . ."*). Day Two was devoted to Ivanka product placement ads.

Mother Pence Rehearses Shakespeare

I warmed to Mother Pence, not because she delivered a compassionate speech about glassblowing war veterans, but because for whatever reasons I sized her up as one of the few on convention display who understands the sociopathic politics of the dysfunctional Trump family. Come 2024, Karen Pence, I am sure, believes her husband will deserve the Republican presidential nomination for his loyal service to the crazy king. At the same time, I sense (there was something in her body language) that she has an inkling that the Trumps will throw over Mike as if he were a gardener at Mar-a-Lago with a work permit problem.

In Trump World, American politics is just another a family business, and in 2024 Ivanka and Don Jr. will, as they have for their whole lives, compete for their father's favors, to be his worthy heir. It's a theme worthy of Shakespeare (in this case Lady McBeth vs. Hamlet, with Lear in the background on his cellphone), and something tells me that Karen senses the coming bloodbath, in which her husband will be run through with a sword.

Kellyanne Plays Family Politics

To hear Kellyanne Conway talk about life in the White House bubble, Trump isn't the delusional midnight rambler on Twitter, but is in office to comfort the afflicted and to afflict the comfortable, a cross between Mother Teresa and the Scarlet Pimpernel. (*"I have seen firsthand many times the president comforting and encouraging a child who has lost a parent, a parent who has lost a child, a worker who lost his job, an adolescent who lost her way to drugs. . ."*) All I could imagine when she spoke was that about half the members of the Conway house would be jumping up to change the channel. For Kellyanne, what's worse: Enabling Trump or having your 15 year-old daughter ask to be adopted by AOC?

Real Housewives of the White House: Lara Trump

Married to Eric, Lara Trump is one of the stars of *Real Housewives of the White House* (it helps to have long blonde hair and a few red dresses—Trump men have this thing about Fox anchors), and she used her airtime at the convention to talk up accomplished women ("*from Amelia Earhart to Rosa Parks and Sally Ride. . .*") and to express a gushing thank you to her famous father-in-law "for believing in me." Otherwise her bedtime story was a fairytale. ("*Never in a million years did I think that I would be on this stage tonight, and I certainly never thought that I'd end up with the last name Trump. . . .*").

Coach Lou Holtz Spins One for the Gipper

Former Notre Dame football coach Lou Holtz, slightly slurring his words through perhaps ill-fitting dentures, made a half-time speech for team Trump. ("*I used to ask our athletes at Notre Dame, 'If you did not show up, who would miss you and why?' Can you imagine what would happen to us if President Trump had not shown up in 2016 to run for president? I'm so glad he showed up. Thank you for showing up, Mr. President. . .*") Left out of this let's-go-get-'em-boys pep talk to the nation were Lou's words in 2008: "Ya know, Hitler was a great leader too."

Representative Elise Stefanik Gushes for Mr. Big

A Trump impeachment truther, Congresswoman Elise Stefanik (upstate New York) was rewarded for her stout House defense of the president with some prime-time love, although not before some Hollywood makeup artists brushed up her angry auditor image to make her look like an extra on *Sex and the City*. Stefanik said, "It's why more Republican women than ever are running for office this year. We understand that this election is a choice between the far-left democratic-socialist agenda versus protecting and preserving the American dream. President Trump is working to safely reopen our main street economy. . ." She should have quoted Carrie Bradshaw: "I like my money where I can see it—hanging in my closet."

Jack Brewer Takes It to Trump's House

You can see why Republican booking agents jumped for Jack Brewer, African American grandson of a Texas sharecropper, when they got his CV (*"I'm. . .a former three-time NFL team captain, college professor, coach, husband, son, and father. I'm also a lifelong Democrat, but I support Donald Trump. . ."*). Too bad he was charged with insider trading just before speaking. Still, the show must go on, although what went on stage could have been done with a little rehearsing. At one point Brewer said, "My early high school experience included fighting with skinheads and being a witness in an attempted murder trial, after my friend shot a skinhead in self-defense." I guess it was a call to arms, although perhaps not to those heading toward Kenosha with their guns?

Donald Trump's Chauffeured Freedom Ride

For a bit I enjoyed getting to know Clarence Henderson, who was one of the African Americans who asked to be served at a Greensboro, North Carolina, Woolworth's lunch counter in 1960, helping to turn the tide against segregation. (*"My friends had been denied service the day before because of the color of their skin. We knew it wasn't right. . ."*). He was one of the few speakers at the Republican convention whose voice was not dyspeptic. But when it came time to be served at the nation's counter, Henderson ordered Kool-Aid (*"Donald Trump is offering real and lasting change, an unprecedented opportunity to rise a country that embraces the spirit of the Civil Rights Movement of the '60s. . ."*).

Mike Pence Climbs the Stairway to Heaven

The backdrop to Mike Pence's acceptance speech was majestic Fort McHenry in Baltimore Harbor, where the bombs burst in air and the banner was yet waving at the dawn's early light. Another advantage of the location is that no War of 1812 national monument has ever been indicted for violating the Hatch Act.

In the preview biographical trailer that introduced the speech, Mike is shown coming of age in Indiana where he met his future wife "at a church service" and where his "foundation of faith in Jesus Christ was laid." (Sounds like quite a service.)

His career breakthrough was as a conservative radio shock jock (he was a minor league Rush Limbaugh), and that led to Congress and the Indiana governorship so that he could lead "in the fight to protect our time-honored values of family, faith, life, liberty, and limited government"—perfect training for someone to help preside over a $3 trillion budget deficit and the $1 trillion annually that goes to a standing army and spy agencies.

The word is that Melania liked the cut of his jib in 2016, which explains why Trump chose him to run as his apprentice. Trump also needed Pence on the ticket to assuage Conservatives and evangelicals who might not have been charmed by Trump's three marriages, abuse of women, or dalliances with Playmates and porn stars.

After three days of the RNC convention, and some eight hours of airtime, Pence's acceptance speech—a defense of conservative values and Trump—felt like the full version of "Stairway to Heaven." Where was Led Zeppelin when we needed them?

Succession Planning in 2024: Reading Trump's Will

On the American political spectrum, Pence falls somewhere between Richard Nixon ("*I don't give a shit about the lira. . .*") and

Barry Goldwater (*"Extremism in the defense of liberty is no vice. . ."*), but the bigger question is whether in 2024 the voters will buy into Pence's homespun prairie story and give him the Republican presidential nomination.

For the moment—judging by the speaker list at the RNC—those angling to succeed Trump would seem to be: Ivanka, Don Jr., Senators Tim Scott and Tom Cotton, Ambassador Nikki Haley, South Dakota Governor Kristi Noem, and Pence. If Trump and Pence lose in 2020, Pence is toast. If they win, his chances improve, although I have a hard time imagining Trump picking Pence over one of his children or even Nikki Haley.

Trump looks at the White House as one of "his properties" and views democracy as one of those suggestion boxes near the men's grill. To Trump, Pence is one of his casino managers, someone who keeps an eye on the dealers and hostesses, brings drinks to the high rollers, and is good about dropping off the winnings in the cage. I can't imagine that Karen Pence has any time for Trump any more than I can imagine that Ivanka wants to turn over the White House to a holy roller from Indiana.

The Trumps Drop By

Nevertheless, Trump and Melania made a surprise visit to the Pence acceptance speech at the end, coming in (while holding hands!) on yet another campaign catwalk, as if they were forcing themselves to drop in on a neighbor's (boring) cocktail party. Something tells me the Trump campaign has engaged a hand-holding consultant, to coach the first couple on such intimacy, given Melania's earlier slaps at Trump's wayward grip.

The Trumps' arrival prompted another round of the national anthem—country star Trace Adkins made it sound like a dirge—and then Trump, always gloomy when others are the center of attention, made the most of the photo-op, pointing and thumbing it up at the barricades, without either a mask or much distance from the cheek-by-jowl crowd. Trump is someone who would boast about being a superspreader. (*"I think I'm the best. . ."*)

All the President's Caddies

Day Four was all about waiting for Ivanka and Trump at the end of the evening, which may explain why the first hour of the program featured a dentist-congressman from southern New Jersey, Democrats who've turned Republican, a Billy Graham descendant offering up some prayers, veterans whom America has forgotten, someone who used to caddie for Trump at one of his golf clubs, and Senate Majority Leader Mitch McConnell (who caddies for him today).

Dan Scavino Humps Trump's Bag

Nominally, Scavino has the title White House deputy chief of staff for Communications and director of Social Media. In other words he's responsible (in some form) for Trump's tweets, which perhaps requires him to be on the job at 5:30 a.m. to stand at the foot of Trump's bed to send out messages about Sleepy Joe or all those "fine people on both sides" in Charlottesville.

His speech to the convention sounded like a letter to *Penthouse*:

When I was 16 years old, I got a part-time job at a golf course just outside of New York City. One day, I was cleaning golf clubs when a man pulled into the parking lot. There wasn't a single person who didn't know who it was. Everyone's jaws were on the ground. It was Donald Trump. All I could think was nobody will ever believe this at school tomorrow. I never would have imagined it at this moment, but I've now been at President Trump's side for almost 30 years. . .

Scavino's job this evening was to humanize his delusional boss—"President Trump is a kind and decent man. I wish you could be at his side with me to see his endless kindness to everyone he meets"—and to make the point that if everyone in the nation could carry his clubs, the country would recognize his greatness. (*He saw my potential even when I couldn't. He sees greatness in our country too and in each of you. He believes the world you dream about at night can be yours. He truly is a man of the people. . .*") Had Scavino served the French king Louis XIV, his title would have been "Gentleman of the Bedchamber."

Swamp Cat Mitch McConnell

It tells you something about Trump World that Scavino got more airtime than did the Senate majority leader, who in less than two minutes had to put the boot into Nancy Pelosi and the Democrats and make the pitch to keep the Senate in Republican hands. (*They want to pack the Supreme Court with liberals intent on eroding our constitutional rights, and they want to codify all this by making the Swamp itself, Washington, D.C., America's 51st state with two more liberal senators. We cannot undo the damage they've done.*") Actually the Swamp has been very very good to Mitch. In a lifetime of civil service and government jobs—a senator is paid $174,000—he's amassed a fortune reported to be worth between $30 million and $50 million. Marrying a rich second wife and inheritance helped, but don't discount the hard work of influence peddling.

Donald Trump's Corner Man

To introduce the next speaker, Dana White, the president of the Ultimate Fighting Championship (which is mixed martial arts, a bit like professional wrestling), the convention aired a trailer on "The American Athlete."

The purpose was to show Trump as another Miracle on Ice (which gave us the now Trumpian chant of "USA. . .USA. . ."). And there was a picture of Trump and a dark-suited Tiger Woods walking somberly around the White House, as if in deep conversation about a Cuban missile crisis (or perhaps Vegas chorus girls). The montage (Voiceover: *"Would you please rise for the playing of our national anthem?"*) was also to link the Democrats to unpatriotic players who kneel "disrespectfully" during the singing of "The Star-Spangled Banner." That said, at Trump rallies the only thing that gets the crowd to its feet is the playing of "Macho Man."

Then there was a long convention slog between the pro athletes and Ivanka Trump's Daddy Dearest tribute. The African American cabinet officer Ben Carson denied, in so many words, that Trump is a racist. His evidence: "In Palm Beach, Florida, Donald Trump led the crusade to allow Blacks and Jews into private clubs and resorts." Why can't the people of Portland and Kenosha be more grateful?

Rudy Giuliani and the Ghost of Roy Cohn's Past

To lead into Rudy Giuliani's call for law and order, the convention summoned to the lectern Pat Lynch, who is president of the Police Benevolent Association in New York City, where "we are staring down the barrel of a public safety disaster." Lynch evoked babies shot dead in their strollers and stray bullets killing innocent bystanders, and made the larger point that crime is rampant wherever Democrats are in power. "Democratic politicians have surrendered our streets. . .they've slashed police budgets. They have hijacked and dismantled the criminal justice system. . . . What they want is no policing. . . .You won't be safe in Joe Biden's America."

You do wonder what spell personal lawyer Rudy Giuliani has cast over his client Trump, such that, while under criminal investigation in the Southern District of New York and after his Biden huntering in the Ukraine caused Trump to be impeached, the former mayor was still asked to speak in prime time at the Republican convention.

In general, Trump has always been under the thumb of tough-talking lawyers (the odious McCarthyite Roy Cohn was another), who draft his prenuptial agreements, pay off demanding women, and give Trump the confidence that he's above the law.

Convention Rudy wasn't the paymaster running Parnas and Igor Fruman in Ukraine or sliming the U.S. ambassador in Kyiv, but he was back in the familiar role of the 9/11 New York mayor who was tough on crime, arresting all those turnstile jumpers. Here is Rudy's message:

> New Yorkers wonder, "How did we get overwhelmed by crime so quickly, and to climb so fast?" Don't let Democrats do to America, what they have done to New York. Again, the Democrats are urging you to vote for an obviously defective candidate. Biden has changed his principles so often, he no longer has any principles. He's a Trojan horse with Bernie, AOC, Pelosi, Black Lives Matter, and his party's entire left wing just waiting to execute their pro-criminal, anti-police, socialist policies.

I was surprised he didn't quote Senator Joseph McCarthy, "Today we are engaged in a final, all-out battle between communistic atheism and Christianity. . ." or announce that 205 members of the Obama-Biden administration had been card-carrying communists.

Senator Tom Cotton Spreads the China Virus

After Rudy's rant, Senator Tom Cotton of Arkansas picked up the theme of Biden as a wholly owned subsidiary of the Chinese. He said:

> Joe Biden aided and abetted China's rise for 50 years with terrible trade deals that closed our factories and laid off our workers. . . . Joe Biden allowed Chinese fentanyl to flood across our southern border. . . . Joe said Chinese communists aren't even our competitor, aren't bad folks, just months before they unleashed this plague on the world. President Trump is clear-eyed about the Chinese threat and he is making China pay.

I guess Cotton wasn't present at the meeting, described in John Bolton's book, when Trump begged the president of China, Xi Jinping to buy American soybeans and wheat in the run-up to the American 2020 election, so as to assure Trump's reelection.

Ex-Con Alice Marie Johnson: Orange Is the New Trump

Before the convention switched to the White House, the parents of an ISIS murder victim spoke, to imply that Biden's election would cheer the faithful in Raqqa. (*"The Trump team gave us empathy. We never received any from the Obama administration."*) Then the Trump campaign fawned over ex-con Alice Marie Johnson to trumpet criminal justice reform. (She said, *"But by the grace of God and the compassion of President Donald John Trump, I stand before you tonight, and I assure you I'm not a ghost. I am alive. I am well. And most importantly, I am free. In 1996, I began serving time in prison. Life plus 25 years. I had never been in trouble. I was a first-time non-violent offender.")*

For some time she's been a poster child for Trump's compassion for rehabilitated ex-cons. It didn't hurt her cause for clemency in 2018 that Kim Kardashian and Jared Kushner were pushing her case. Johnson was at one of Trump's State of the Union speeches, and a day after she spoke at this convention he issued her a full pardon.

I heard her described so many times as a "first-time non-violent offender," that it puzzled me what she had done to get a sentence of "life plus 25 years." Did she, like Irwin M. Fletcher, aka "Fletch," remove those tags from her mattresses? Then I discovered that her "first-time non-violent offense" was to operate an American distribution network of a Colombian drug cartel.

Ivanka's Coming-Out Party

Until the speeches of the president and his daughter Ivanka were delivered, the Republican national convention mostly took place at the rostrum of the Mellon Auditorium in downtown Washington, D.C. (near the corner of Constitution and Swamp). With Ivanka's speech, the stage scene shifted to the south portico and lawn of the White House, which were done over to resemble a Nuremberg parade ground, only this one flying American flags.

Looking at all the family and friends in the select White House audience that was seated on white wedding chairs, I felt that this was her speech at her coming-out party at a glitzy Trump hotel. The first daughter wore black (not white), and ostensibly her mission was to humanize her father. Otherwise she might not have mentioned the Lego replica of the White House that her young son made for his grandfather and which is still on display. Mostly, however, Ivanka was here to declare her own presidential candidacy, in four or eight years (or whenever she loses those exclusive trademarks to sell housewares in China).

Ivanka spoke with none of Don Jr.'s Red-Bull-in-a-shop animation. In fact, she's inherited her father's inability to read the prepared text of a speech. She spoke with slight traces of a Valley Girl-Kardashian accent (*'like, you know, our hearts are with ya'*), although mostly in an entitled monotone. Ivanka also inherited her father's runaway ego, and here and there throughout the speech she thought it important to emphasize that some acts of state in the last four years actually came from something that she had done on the job (other than model clothes each morning on her way to her limousine and earn $36 million in "outside income" while moonlighting with her husband Jared).

Here's one such humble brag sentence: "Four years ago, I promised that President Trump would support mothers in the workforce. In his first year in office, he signed into law the first-ever national paid leave tax credit. Today, eight million more Americans have access to this benefit."

Otherwise, Ivanka gave a speech that sounded like an interview with Oprah. (*"I've been with my father, and I've seen the pain in his eyes when he receives updates on the lives that have been stolen by this plague. I've witnessed him make some of the most difficult decisions of his life. I sat with him in the Oval Office, as he stopped travel to Europe."*) Although she spoke for 20 minutes, I would be hard-pressed to ascribe to Ivanka's text any coherent idea of government other than a rerun of *Leave It to Daddy*. (*"Four years ago, I told you I would fight alongside my father, and four years later here I am."*)

I suspect that Ivanka conceives of government as a franchise that the Trump family is happy to lease to you for the next four years. As long as you give the Trumps the management contract and 30 percent of the action, they are happy to let you keep your guns, pray in school, lower the cost of prescription drugs, move the embassy to Jerusalem, and maybe throw in some pool privileges.

The Rocky Trump Picture Show

By the time Donald Trump entered, the White House stage had the look of a Vegas casino in *Ocean's 11*. Flags were everywhere, as were garden spotlights, and near the front of the (socially un-distanced) audience there was a large jumbotron screen, as if maybe the A-list guests could stay on and watch a midnight showing of *The Rocky Horror Picture Show*.

These days Trump seems to walk like a determined bear or perhaps Frankenstein. While stomping out from the residence, he was holding hands with Melania, who in a bright forest green dress looked as though she had come to the party either with Robin Hood or Peter Pan.

Trump is a radio shock jock, not an orator, and reading his speech he sounded like a fourth-grader trying to recite the Get-tysburg Address. He paused for punctuation marks as if they were German umlauts. Had this been an honest-to-God Trump rally, his people would have shot T-shirts and MAGA hats into the crowd and the sound system would have pumped in "YMCA." Instead it was like a tycoon's birthday party at which all the guests had to hear him drone on about his life successes. ("*On this journey I was fortunate to have. . .*")

Trump Calls His Own Number, Collect

Does Trump have a vision of America? He might, but more likely he has a vision of Trump as the hero of every issue that is under discussion. Not that you need to be reminded of his achievements, but here is a summary: Trump, and Trump alone, withdrew the United States from the Trans-Pacific Partnership, approved the Keystone pipeline, abrogated the Paris Climate Accord, secured energy independence, cut taxes and regulations, stood up to China, eliminated human trafficking, built the Wall, ended illegal immigration, took on Big Pharma, provided for veterans, appointed conservative justices, reformed criminal justice, funded opportunity zones, wiped out ISIS, moved the U.S. embassy to Jerusalem, defended the Second Amendment, brokered peace in the Middle East, killed off terrorists, launched the Space Force, and, best of all, defeated "the China virus."

Trump achieved all this (mostly on his own—I guess maybe Ivanka helped some) while the Democrats were kneeling for the national anthem, removing the word "God" from the pledge of allegiance, shipping jobs off to China, having abortions, catching-and-releasing illegal aliens, funding looters, coming for your guns, promising Green New Deals, destroying the fossil fuel industry, signing unfair trade deals, gutting the military, coddling Iran, ignoring the Black community, failing women, killing off coal, cutting Social Security, burning down Portland, letting cops be killed, tearing down monuments of Jefferson and Lincoln, defunding the police, sneering at Israel, appeasing terrorists, and denying American exceptionalism. In a nutshell, that's the world according to Trump.

Washington's Monumental Ego

The evening, and the four-day Republican convention, ended with fireworks that exploded over the Washington Mall, eventually spelling out "TRUMP 2020" beside the Washington Monument.

I am assuming that Trump's fireworks, like his virus, came from China. I am also assuming that no one will indict the Washington

Monument for violating the Hatch Act, although if it happened, it would be convicted and might need the outreach programs of John Ponder and Alice Marie Johnson.

When the fireworks were done, everyone's attention shifted to tenor Christopher Macchio, who sang opera from the rear portico of the White House. His repertoire included Pavarotti's "Nessum Dorma" and Leonard Cohen's "Hallelujah," although when I heard the latter I started humming the lyrics to Cohen's "Chelsea Hotel" (*"I remember you well in the Chelsea Hotel/You were talking so brave and so sweet. . ."*), as it seems to speak more to Trump's other preoccupations. Cohen's estate later protested the use of his hit song for political purposes, but at least "Hallelujah" is about a failing relationship (*"And even though it all went wrong/I'll stand before the Lord of Song. . ."*).

As the party was winding down, Macchio switched beats and encouraged everyone to join him in singing "God Bless America," the words that had ended every speech during the four days of the Republican convention. Macchio started off briskly, but when the television cameras focused in on the president, to catch him belting out,

> *From the mountains to the prairies*
> *To the oceans white with foam*
> *God bless America, my home sweet home. . .*

what was clear was that Trump had no clue as to the words.

---★---

A Presidential Debate Primer

"In politics a community of hatred is almost always the foundation of friendships."

—Alexis de Tocqueville

---★---

Don and Joe Play Talk Radio

Yes, I have heard this week's presidential debate in Cleveland referred to as a shit show, clown car, clusterfuck, dumpster fire, and food fight, but now that I have heard, watched, and read the candidate exchanges three times—I know, Beam me up, Scotty. . .—I can say that it was something both less and more, although on many other levels this debate felt like a clinical trial between coke and Adderall.

The less you know. The more is that in the asides, insults, riffs, and streams of consciousness from the two candidates, we have a few more clues as to how each man conceives of the democracy or wishes to tear it down.

Part of the problem with events such as this one is that they are billed as "debates," with the expectation that Lincoln and Douglas will show up on stage in frock coats and declaim, using a lot of Latin phrases, on the meaning of representative government, perhaps with allusions to Dred Scott or Lecompton. In modern American politics, however, so-called debates were never modeled on those of Lincoln and Douglas, who—without the presence of a moderator—would speak for five hours and even take a break for dinner.

Since 1960, presidential campaign debates have been simulcast press conferences, in which moderators (from the obsequious Washington press corps) pose questions and set time limits for the scripted answers. In general, the debate winner has been the candidate who can most effectively recite the best pre-programmed lines (*"There you*

go again. . . . Where's the beef?. . .Senator, you're no Jack Kennedy. . .").
Technically speaking, there's never a lot of debating that takes place
in these forums, as candidates cannot really develop arguments or
pose their own questions ("*Sir, speak to your position on the Bulgar-
ian atrocities. . .*"). In the Trump era, however, demanding that the
president answer formal questions is asking a lot, which is why, on
his own accord, he's transformed the debate medium into talk radio,
in which the host can hang up on callers and riff on Hunter Biden.
("*He got three and a half million dollars from Moscow. . .*")

Maybe this most recent debate would have made more sense
if, instead of taking place on a colonial red-white-and-blue stage,
the candidates had ditched the moderator, worn those YouTube
headphones, and shouted their insults into oversized mics. Viewers
would then have understood that they were tuning into something
akin to *The Rush Limbaugh Show, Mike and the Mad Dog*, or *Howard Stern*, and that this was not an attempt to recreate the agora
in Periclean Athens. At least we all would have been spared this
week's national disappointment over the quality of the exchanges.

As political candidates, neither Donald Trump nor Joe Biden
has much to say. Nobody would confuse either of them with Henry
Clay or William Pitt the Younger. Neither of them is capable of
speaking in complete sentences. Here's one Trump answer: "I sent
in the U.S. Marshalls to get the killer of a young man in the middle
of the street and they shot him for three days Portland didn't do
anything." Biden said this: "The only way we're going to bring this
country together is bring everybody together."

Going into the election, all we have are these fragmentary
talk-show exchanges (less revealing than hieroglyphic inscriptions
found in an Egyptian cave) on which to gamble the future of the
republic. It's not much, I know. So use these notes as you might
the Rosetta Stone. As the *Village Voice's* Stan Mack used to write:
"Guarantee: All Dialogue is reported verbatim."

Ivanka's Perp Walk to Prime Time

The first presidential debate took place in the medical school at Case Western University in Cleveland. Inside, however, it had the feel of a democratic-themed funeral parlor, complete with paneled inscriptions from the Declaration of Independence, a Civil War recruiting banner (complete with an eagle) proclaiming "The Union and the Constitution Forever," and room behind two lecterns for a double-body viewing. About 10 minutes before the debate kickoff, $700,000 external consultant Ivanka Trump, sporting $95,464 worth of makeup and hairspray, led in the delegation of Trump family members, as if part of some stylish perp walk.

Ivanka was dressed in a creamy white outfit (it was hard to tell if it was a jumpsuit), and she sat socially distanced between Tiffany, Kayleigh, and Kimberly, who appeared to have come down from her party convention high. Eric was there in high glower, taking a break from the search for the Trump tax leaker to the *New York Times*. (Having read the stories carefully, my sense is that the leaker is an institutional player, with high-speed computers at its disposal, as the massive data dump to the *Times* isn't what would emerge from a file that a disgruntled Trump Organization secretary, tired of getting pawed at the Christmas party, would send to the paper.) Given all the pre-debate blather about how Joe Biden should take a drug test before appearing on stage, I was a little surprised that none of the Trumps showed up with a sniffer dog.

Melania Catwalks: Trick or Treat?

Melania only made her entrance (stage left) after the entourage of Trump defendants had taken their seats. She was wearing a dark gray pinstriped suit with wide lapels, as if for Halloween she is dressing up as a white-collar criminal defense lawyer. You do wonder if Melania is having some frissons about what she might collect in a post-presidency divorce. Before the tax leaks (which most years showed Trump paying no taxes) I guess she was thinking of laying claim to a billion or so, but now I think she'll be lucky to get out with a season skating pass to Wollman Rink.

Promptly at 9 p.m. the hapless moderator Chris Wallace, the Fox News anchor with less presence than a substitute algebra teacher, called the debate to order by meekly saying, "The audience here in the hall has promised to remain silent. No cheers, no boos, or other interruptions so we, and more importantly you, can focus on what the candidates have to say." Wallace divided the evening into six 15-minute segments devoted to Covid-19, the Supreme Court nomination battle, street violence and racial justice, climate change, the economy, and mail-in balloting.

He need not have wasted his weekend writing up a convoluted lesson plan, as both candidates used their allotted time to go off on tangents. And when they weren't speaking, they smirked, smiled, clowned, and growled as the other candidate spoke— American politics reduced to on-stage facial GIFs. For the most part Trump just snarled, a man with a permanent wedgie, while Biden had the slightly detached and bemused look of a greeter at Home Depot.

The Supremes. . .'never meant to be. . .'

Trump's take on shoving the nomination of Amy Coney Barrett down the throats of Senate Democrats is that he has the numbers to win. (TRUMP: "We won the election. Elections have consequences. We have the Senate, we have the White House, and we have a phenomenal nominee respected by all.") Biden didn't have much of an answer, as nowhere in the Constitution does it say, "The President shall nominate, and the Senate shall confirm, justices to

Supreme Court, unless, in an earlier presidential administration, Mitch McConnell made Barack Obama look like a bedwetter."

Biden did land a few blows on Trump's Supreme Court strategies by arguing that a court of Trump footmen (and women) would, as early as mid-November, overturn key features of the Affordable Care Act and strip millions of their health insurance. Biden also said that under a Trump health care plan (Take Two Aspirin and Call Me in Four Years?) many would be excluded from insurance coverage because of pre-existing conditions, including those who have recovered from Covid-19. It was a strong argument that Biden then muddled with this logic: "The deal is that it's going to wipe out pre-existing conditions. And, by the way, the 200,000 people that have died on his watch, how many of those have survived?"

Do I think—as I-Work-For-Nothing, Ukraine Muckraker, Personal Lawyer Rudy Giuliani suggested last week—that Biden has dementia? I didn't quite see that during the debate, although I did detect that some wires in his brain fail to connect, leading to sentence fragments and odd constructions. (To wit he said: *"And by the way, in terms of the whole notion of a vaccine, we're for a vaccine, but I don't trust him at all. Nor do you. I know you don't. What we trust is a scientist."*)

You can figure out what Biden is saying, but with all his sentences there's a moment of terror, about halfway through, when you think he's going to look up and say, "Now where was I?" And it tells you how bad Biden is at debate that he allowed Trump to get the better of the argument over the economy during the pandemic. Basically, the president's argument was that he was trying to balance public health and economic growth while saying that all Biden wants is to shut down the economy as a campaign tactic to defeat Trump. (That's a Fox News line on the shutdown.)

Biden failed to mention that the pandemic economic recovery (whatever it happens to be) is thanks to the money that the Congress approved (over Republican opposition), so that Trump could send out one of those Nigerian oil-minister chain letters to every American on the stimulus list. (*"I am writing to you as president of a great oil producing nation, and I need your help to spend $3 trillion. . ."*)

President Bernie Madoff

It took a little while for Trump to perfect his schtick, but after about 20 minutes of debate time he was in full shock-jock interruption mode, cutting in on Biden no matter what he said. (To be fair, Biden did the same, if to a lesser degree. Mostly, he just mimed for the camera.) My sense is that Trump did this deliberately, to rattle Biden into more pronounced stuttering, as it's hard for someone with a speech impediment to recover quickly from an interruption, and I am a little surprised more mention has not been made of this bullying, schoolyard cruelty on Trump's part.

Another Trump tactic that worked well (assuming you take some pleasure in rudeness) was that the president not only played the role of debate candidate but also supplied running Fox News snarky commentary, endlessly muttering asides about Biden into the microphone (*"Oh yeah, sure. . . . Forty-seven years, you've done nothing. They understand. . . . He doesn't want to answer the question. . . . That's wrong. . . . Why didn't you do it over the last 25 years?"*) The interruptions kept Biden from hammering home an argument (truth be told, Joe doesn't have much of a hammer), and on a few occasions—notably the questions over Trump's taxes—the interruptions allowed the president to shift the subject completely.

Only a few minutes of the entire debate focused on Trump's spurious tax returns, but during that time Biden failed to emphasize that Trump is most likely bankrupt, $400 million in hock to banks, loan sharks, Russian and Saudi bagmen, and foreign countries, and that, in terms of historical precedent, Trump is more an heir of Bernie Madoff than Abraham Lincoln.

Biden even let Trump reframe the economic discussion, moving it from the pandemic recession to Hunter Biden's board service in Ukraine and his clients in Russia. Here's one exchange:

> TRUMP: China ate your lunch, Joe. And no wonder your son goes in and he takes out billions of dollars. He takes out billions of dollars to manage. He makes millions of dollars. And also, while we're at it, why is it just out of curiosity, the mayor of Moscow's wife gave your son three and a half million dollars?
> BIDEN: That is not true.
> TRUMP: What did he do to deserve it? What did he do with. . .
> BIDEN: None of that is true.
> TRUMP: . . .to deserve $183,000?
> BIDEN: None of that is true.
> TRUMP: Oh really, he didn't get three and a half million?

Not exactly snappy rejoinders, and it went on in this vein for several minutes, with Biden issuing his rote denials, reminding me that throughout the 2016 campaign Hillary Clinton never developed coherent talking points to explain why all her State Department emails were routed through a home server located in her Chappaqua, New York basement. Nor, in response, did Biden bring up that during the first two years of his presidency, Trump took in, according to the New York Times, $73 million from his foreign operations (on which he paid that $750 in federal tax). Throughout the debate Joe remained the deer Hunter in the headlights.

Twelve Steps with Joe and Chris

Trump only answered the questions about African Americans and justice with allusions to urban violence and the police—the implication being that every Black American, in Trump's mind, is burning cop cars in Portland, Oregon.

Race for Trump is an abstraction, something he glimpses from his limousine on his way to MAGA rallies. He also seems stuck in a 1960s image of cities (Black and full of rioters) and suburbs (happy young white couples pushing baby strollers).

Trump said: ". . .if you look at New York where it's going up, like nobody's ever seen anything. The numbers are going up a 100 percent, 150 percent, 200 percent crime, it is crazy what's going on and he [Biden] doesn't want to say law and order because he can't because he'll lose his radical left supporters and once he does that, it's over with. But if he ever got to run this country and they ran it the way he would want to run it, we would have by the way our suburbs would be gone."

Over and over, on issues of race, all Trump could bring up was that he had more police union endorsements than Biden. (*"He doesn't have any law support. He has no law enforcement."*) Then they had this exchange:

BIDEN: That's not true.
TRUMP: He has almost nothing. Oh, really, who do you have name one group that supports you name one group that came out and supported you. Go ahead. Think we have time.
BIDEN: We don't have time to do anything.
TRUMP: No, no think right now. Name one law enforcement group that came out in support of you.
WALLACE: Now, gentlemen, I think I'm going to take back the bottom line.

Biden is lucky that Wallace jumped in to save him, or we might all still be in Cleveland, waiting for Biden to think of a police department that supports him. Biden is also lucky that forensic linguists haven't made more of the similarities between what he said during the debate to Trump (*"Will you shut up, man"*) and what he allegedly said in that Senate hallway when staffer Tara Reade rejected his romantic advances (*"C'mon, man, I thought you liked me"*).

The Boer Republic of Trump

A Black Lives Matter discussion led to Wallace asking Trump, "[Are you] willing tonight to condemn white supremacists and militia groups and to say that they need to stand down and not add to the violence in a number of these cities as we saw in Kenosha and as we've seen in Portland?" In responding, Trump tried to haggle with Wallace, and then Biden, who together sounded like a group therapy session trying to coax a confession out of a blocked member. (Wallace: *"Well, do it, sir. . ."* Biden: *"Say it, do it, say it. . ."*)

Trump didn't like being cornered at an AA meeting, which may explain why he bobbed and weaved until he uttered the words that may end his presidency: "Proud Boys, stand back and stand by. But I'll tell you what, somebody's got to do something about Antifa and the left because this is not a right-wing problem this is a left wing."

He made the Boys sound like his private army, which I guess they are. And if Trump loses this election, I sense that he might move to a camp in Wyoming and take up the cause of Western chauvinism. If he does, here are the four "degrees" of the initiation process:

1. Public declaration that you are a Proud Boy.
2. Being beat up by other members until you name five kinds of breakfast cereal. This degree also includes a vow to stop masturbating.

3. Getting a Proud Boy tattoo.

4. Engaging in physical violence with members of Antifa.

Let's hope the Boys have heard of Egg McMuffin and All-Bran; otherwise, Trump might find himself charged in the second degree.

Wallace then tried to get each candidate to speak about "why should voters elect you president over your opponent?" For a moment Trump spoke about fixing the VA, appointing all those Federalist Society judges, and the star-trekking Space Force, but when Biden answered to say, "Under this president, we become weaker, sicker, poor, more divided, and more violent," Trump switched the subject to Hunter Biden (*"Your son got three and half million dollars. . . . Once you became vice president he made a fortune in Ukraine, in China, in Moscow, and various other places. . ."*), and the cats were back in the bag.

Only Greenskeepers Can Prevent Forest Fires

When the subject turned to climate change, capping carbon emissions, and the Green New Deal, Trump and Biden sounded like two old guys in their 70s talking about the internets or how to connect their iPads to Zoom.

For Trump the issue of wildfires in the West comes down to "forest management" (*". . .the forest floors are loaded up with trees, dead trees that are years old and they're like tinder and leaves and everything else. You drop a cigarette in there the whole forest burns down. You've got to have forest management"*). He clearly wants the West to look like the gardens at Mar-a-Lago. Then Trump was off on something he called "forest cities" in Europe, the implication being that many European capitals are located in the equivalent of Sherwood Forest, except that in Europe—

unlike California and Oregon—they rake up their leaves. Trump said:

> In Europe, they live their forest cities. They call forest cities. They maintain their forest. They manage their forest. I was with the head of a major country, it's a forest city. He said, 'Sir, we have trees that are far more, they ignite much easier than California. There shouldn't be that problem.'

Trump sounded a bit like Truthbrary.org's Dr. Billy Wayne Ruddick (a Sacha Baron Cohen character), going on about climax change.

On the environment Biden wasn't much more lucid. (*"There's so many things that we can do now to create thousands and thousands of jobs. We can get to net zero, in terms of energy production, by 2035. Not only not costing people jobs, creating jobs, creating millions of good-paying jobs. Not 15 bucks an hour, but prevailing wage, by having a new infrastructure that in fact is green. . ."*). It led to this exchange:

> BIDEN: The Green New Deal will pay for itself as we move forward. We're not going to build plants that, in fact, are great polluting plants. . .
> WALLACE: So, do you support the Green New Deal?
> Biden: Pardon me?
> WALLACE: Do you support the—
> BIDEN: No, I don't support the Green New Deal.
> TRUMP: Oh, you don't? Oh, well, that's a big statement.
> BIDEN: I support. . .
> TRUMP: You just lost the radical left.
> BIDEN: I support. . .the Biden plan that I put forward.
> WALLACE: Okay.
> BIDEN: The Biden plan, which is different than what he calls the radical Green New Deal.

Welcome to the Mad Hatter's tea party that will be the Biden presidency.

Go Ahead, Make My Election

The debate saved its worst for last, in which we were treated to Trump's country club theories on mail-in ballots (". . .*it's a disaster*") and given an indication (don't say you weren't warned) that it will take a posse to root Trump out of his White House foxhole after he loses the election ("*This is not going to end well*").

In the world according to Trump, even though he won the election in 2016, the system was out to get him from the start. He explained:

> So when I listen to Joe talking about a transition, there has been no transition from when I won. I won that election. And if you look at crooked Hillary Clinton, if you look at all of the different people, there was no transition, because they came after me trying to do a *coup*. They came after me spying on my campaign. They started from the day I won, and even before I won. From the day I came down the escalator with our first lady, they were a disaster. They were a disgrace to our country, and we've caught them. We've caught them all. We've got it all on tape. We've caught them all. And by the way, you gave the idea for the Logan Act against General Flynn. You better take a look at that, because we caught you in a sense, and President Obama was sitting in the office.

Fast-forward to the impeachment (a "hoax") and now the 2020 election, which the Democrats are about to steal by papering the electoral market with duplicate ballots. ("*They're being sent all over the place. They sent two in a Democrat area. They sent out a thousand ballots. Everybody got two ballots. This is going to be a fraud like you've never seen.")* The fact that barcoded mail-in ballots have better tracing than levered votes in polling stations seems lost on the president.

Trump's solution to the mail-in ballot legitimacy issue is to deploy goon squads as "poll watchers" on Election Day. How poll-watching Proud Boys et al. in full open-carry regalia (Fred Perry polo shirts, lots of flags, mail-order riot gear) can assist or verify the counting of mailed-in ballots wasn't made clear. Trump said:

> I'm urging my supporters to go in to the polls and watch very carefully, because that's what has to happen. I am urging them to do it. As you know, today there was a big problem. In Philadelphia, they went in to watch. They're called poll watchers, a very safe, very nice thing. They were thrown out. They weren't allowed to watch. You know why? Because bad things happen in Philadelphia. Bad things. . .

Registered, pre-approved candidate poll watchers are one thing; vigilantes outside elementary schools are something else.

Trump Electoral College: *Vincere decipiat* ("Cheat to win")

Actually, the "fraud like you've never seen" is the coming Republican storm that, by challenging the legitimacy of mail-in voting, will attempt to tilt the presidential election into either the House of Representatives (where each state delegation gets one vote) or the Supreme Court (Trump's personal injury law firm).

How would it work? After the election, in a number of targeted swing states (Pennsylvania, Michigan, Florida, Wisconsin, North Carolina, Ohio, Arizona), Trump legal teams will contest the outcomes if Biden is deemed the winner and attempt to legitimize a second slate of presidential electors when the Electoral College meets in December to certify the winner of the presidential election. In some states that have a Republican majority in the state legislature, it might even be possible, during these arguments, for the legislature to overturn the popular vote and vote in Trump electors.

If that's not possible, the goal will be to use the alleged fraud of mail-in ballots to deny certification of any winner in the Electoral College, where 270 votes are needed to win. If Trump can tie up the returns in key swing states (the states listed above control 119 electoral votes), those numbers would be sufficient to deny Biden a 270 majority in the Electoral College.

That outcome would throw the election into the House of Representatives, where at the moment Republicans have a majority in 26 state delegations. (Some of those delegations could turn in the 2020 election, notably in Pennsylvania, which at the moment is even.)

If that's not a gloomy prospect, consider this: While the House is deciding who should be president, with each state delegation casting one vote until a candidate emerges with at least 26 votes, the Senate would have to choose a vice president from among the two candidates who received the most votes in the Electoral College (Mike Pence and Kamala Harris). In the event that the House cannot choose a president by January 20, 2021, that Senate-elected vice president would serve as acting president until the House chooses the next president.

It means that Mike Pence could become acting president on January 20, 2021, if by that date the Electoral College and the House of Representatives have yet to choose a president. (While in office, he could pardon Trump and Ivanka for their crimes.) And if those reelection gambits failed, to stay in power Trump could always invoke the 1807 Insurrection Act and surround the White House with Proud Boys. The Insurrection Act reads:

[I]n all cases of insurrection, or obstruction to the laws, either of the United States, or of any individual state or territory, where it is lawful for the President of the United States to call forth the militia for the purpose of suppressing such insurrection, or of causing the laws to be duly executed, it shall be lawful for him to employ, for the same purposes, such part of the land or naval force of the United States, as shall be judged necessary, having first observed all the pre-requisites of the law in that respect.

We know they are a militia, "standing by," and I am sure that Attorney General William Barr and the acquiescent Supreme Court would sign off on the precedent. In the first presidential debate, when Trump said, "And I am urging my people. I hope it's going to be a fair election. If it's a fair election. . ." Wallace pushed back: "You're urging them what?" To which Trump responded: "I am 100 percent on board. But if I see tens of thousands of ballots being manipulated, I can't go along with that."

Pence v. Harris Debate:
Synchronized Robocalls

By now, as regards to the vice presidential debate between Mike Pence and Kamala Harris, you have heard that "not much was said," "no one made a mistake," and that both candidates "held their own." You may also have heard that it was more "civilized" than the presidential debate between Donald Trump and Joe Biden and that the moderator, Susan Page from the Washington bureau of *USA Today*, managed to keep the candidates "in line."

What you might have missed, especially if you only saw a few highlights on the fly, is that the so-called debate (it had all the depth of synchronized robocalls) had almost nothing to do with history, politics, economics, or the 2020 election and everything to do with 2024, for which Pence and Harris begin as the frontrunners.

According to the debate libretto, Pence was supposed to be the doltish faith healer from Indiana, with his hands on the radio, while Harris was the hard-charging prosecutor, the debate champion (okay, leave out her 2 percent polling in the Democratic primaries) who is good on her feet and can talk to a jury. But for much of the evening Harris preferred to sing songs of herself, which allowed Pence to deliver endless messages "from our sponsor"—government of the casino, by the casino, and for the casino, in which he's a piano player.

The Colonial Air of a Brooklyn Liquor Store

The debate was held at Kingsbury Hall on the campus of the University of Utah in Salt Lake City. On a retro-colonial, founding-father, red-white-and-blue stage set, the Commission on Presidential Debates (it could also be called A Convenient Front Company Owned by the Two Major Parties So Things Don't Get Out of Hand) arranged three gray metal desks in a triangle, as though after the debate the candidates could get down to the serious business of selling life insurance. In between the desks some health-and-safety consultant placed plexiglass dividers that gave the stage the stale air of a Brooklyn liquor store more than that of a hydroxychloroquine safe house.

Moderator Page spoke like a Sunday school teacher. (*"The two campaigns and the commission on presidential debates agreed to the ground rules for tonight. I'm here to enforce them. . . ."*) I am sure her virtuous presence was comforting to the Pences, especially as Mike would be spending the evening on stage with two women who were not his wife (or wives, as, after all, this was Utah).

Page drafted nine thoughtful, multi-part questions about Covid, the economy, China, and the Supreme Court, etc., but she need not have bothered, as both candidates spent the evening ignoring the questions, occasionally speaking over each other, and giving pre-recorded service announcements, not unlike those at Amtrak stations. (*'Now leaving on track seven. . . . I am speaking, Mr. Vice President. . . . Senator, you're entitled to your own opinion; you're not entitled to your own facts. . .'*)

Take Some Bleach and Call Me in the Morning

The challenge for Harris, in responding to the Covid question, "What would a Biden administration do in January and February that a Trump administration wouldn't do? Would you impose new lockdowns for businesses and schools and hotspots, a federal mandate to wear masks?," was not to be personally disrespectful of the convalescent Trump while at the same time conveying the message that he is a negligent superspreader who has killed off some 200,000 Americans.

If you believe that only Trump and Pence hold the copyright on ineffective political ideas when dealing with Covid, think again, as here, in full, is how the Biden-Harris administration will bring the virus to bay, as per Kamala:

> They still don't have a plan. Well, Joe Biden does. And our plan is about what we need to do around a national strategy for contact tracing, for testing, for administration of the vaccine, and making sure that it will be free for all. That is the plan that Joe Biden has and that I have, knowing that we have to get a hold of what has been going on, and we need to save our country.

Given the vagueness of that, I might take my chances with some candyman's steroids and a little bleach.

In trying to explain away the virus, Pence hit the high notes from Trump's Hallelujah Chorus: It was China's fault, we did all we could, banned all those flights from Wuhan, saved millions of lives, etc.—all standard fare. But her comeback on this, although she turned full-on to the camera when speaking, was to say, "So I want to ask the American people, how calm were you when you were panicked about where you were going to get your next roll of toilet paper?"

Vice President Mike Drebin, Police Squad

Pence looks a lot like the actor Leslie Nielsen (*Naked Gun*, *Airplane!*). He was wearing the standard Trump-issue red necktie and spoke gravely, even when blaming "the American people" for the absence of masks and distancing at the Rose Garden infection jamboree for Amy Coney Barrett. (*"Many of the people who were at that event. . .actually were tested for Coronavirus, and it was an outdoor event, which all of our scientists regularly and routinely advise. The difference here is President Trump and I trust the American people to make choices in the best interest of their health."*) So far some 215,000 Americans have made some pretty bad choices.

At Trump rallies, Pence is a warm-up band, bouncing around stage and doing the phallic thumb gesture for the MAGA crowd. When he speaks, it comes out as one long grovel, in which every phrase begins, "With Donald Trump as your president. . ." Pence also resembles a character who has escaped from a Sinclair Lewis novel, which, if you have missed them, are set in the Midwest and describe narrow-minded fundamentalist preachers, politicians, and businessmen.

In *Babbitt* Sinclair Lewis writes: "There's no stronger bulwark of sound conservatism than the evangelical church, and no better place to make friends who'll help you to gain your rightful place in the community than in your own church-home!"

Pence Mails In His 2020 Vote

Pretty early on in this debate, I came to the conclusion that Pence had written off a win in 2020 and that his only shot at redemption was to position himself for the nomination in 2024. The biggest tell, as they say at poker tournaments, was when he said, "So let me just say, I think we're going to win this election," while shaking his head "no."

Based only on C-SPAN observations, my sense is that Mother Pence is disgusted with the Trump reality show and wants Mike out of the den of iniquity and back to leading Bible study classes in Indiana. Led into the temptations of power, Pence, however, would love to think of himself as Trump's political heir. But when you bet on an inheritance, you often wind up paying for the funeral.

Are You Ready for a Foreign Affair?

What surprised me about Kamala Harris was how little feel she has for world politics. I figured that as a fact-finding senator she might have picked up some vibe about Kosovo, Nagorno-Karabakh, or Transnistria, but apparently she has not. Harris's background is as a career prosecutor, first in the office of the district attorney for San Francisco and later as attorney general for California, which may explain why during the debate she kept referring to "dead bodies" from the virus. Maybe it's a CSI expression?

During the 90 minutes of this debate, Harris said almost nothing about foreign affairs other than "I serve on the Senate Intelligence Committee where I've been in regular receipt of classified information about threats to our nation in hotspots around the world. I've traveled the world, I've met with our soldiers in war zones." When she spoke about China, I got the feeling that she was reading from the *World Book Encyclopedia*.

During the debate Harris curried favor with her boss by passing on the nugget that Joe's one great truth about foreign affairs is that it's "about relationships," making international politics sound more like Ashley than James Madison. (*'Mature imperial power seeks good safe menace in the Middle East for movies, concerts, and to try out Pentagon hardware. . .'*) Otherwise, Harris's world views seem lifted from a Davos handout.

Harris Paints the Economy by Numbers

How was it possible for Pence, speaking on behalf of Trump's casino capitalism, to get the better of Harris when the discussion turned to economic issues? I guess the answer is that Harris has little feel for business or economics (it's not really a DA thing), and all she could do was to memorize some talking points and recite them, as if a Miss America contestant in the question round (*"Who is the person you look up to the most?. . ."*). How's this for a pageant answer: "Joe Biden's economic plan. . . Moody's, which is a reputable Wall Street firm, has said [it] will create seven million more jobs than Donald Trump's." (I know Moody's blessed all that subprime debt in 2008, but it cannot be that stupid, can it?)

Unless I am missing something, Trump and Pence have reduced the American economy to a variation on some Vegas or Atlantic City spin cycle, in which the federal budget and national debt are used to launder losing hands (the cards held by most Americans) into the accounts of the syndicates that own the roulette wheels (roughly the 1 percent). Yet when the debate turned to economics, Pence still managed to back Harris into the you'll-raise-taxes corner and to paint the Green New Deal as somehow un-American, for which she only had sputtering answers.

For the benefit of swing state voters, especially in Pennsylvania, Pence turned the entire economic discussion into a referendum on fracking, stating that Biden and Harris would be coming for your wildcat drills. Heck of a job, Kamala.

Harris did take a few swings at Trump's pathetic taxable income and net operating losses, and she chanted the mantra about creating new jobs by investing in infrastructure, but Pence quickly brushed her aside, saying:

But America, you just heard Senator Harris tell you, on day one, Joe Biden's going to raise your taxes. . .right after a time where we're going through a pandemic that lost 22 million jobs at the height. We've already added back 11.6 million jobs because we had a president who cut taxes, rolled back regulation, unleashed American energy, fought for free and fair trade, and secured $4 trillion from the Congress of the United States to give direct payments to families, [and] save 50 million jobs through the Paycheck Protection Program. We literally have spared no expense to help the American people and the American worker through this. Joe Biden and Kamala Harris want to raise taxes. They want to bury our economy under a $2 trillion Green New Deal, which you were one of the original co-sponsors of in the United States Senate.

You know it's going poorly in a debate when you have to say, as Harris did, "That is absolutely not true." And she had to say about three times that "Joe Biden will not ban fracking." In politics, getting your opponent to issue a denial is always a winner. (Bill Clinton: "*I did not have sexual relations with that woman, Miss Lewinsky. . .*")

After some more cross-talking, Harris tried to remember her lines about China and the trade war, presumably to make a play for some farm and rustbelt votes (for whom China's exports are a subsidized lifeline), but something got lost in translation. She said to Pence:

The president's trade war with China. You lost that trade war. You lost it. What ended up happening is because of a so-called trade war with China, America lost 300,000 manufacturing jobs. Farmers have experienced bankruptcy because of it. We are in a manufacturing recession because of it.

Normally, in a U.S. election, it's the Republicans who campaign for cheap imports and free trade, while the Democrats curry favor with unions by talking up tariffs and trade protection. But in this election Biden and Harris are running as Walmart Republicans, while Trump is running from the law.

Joe Has a Plan

You would think in 2020, with the West on fire, that a discussion about climate change might favor the Democrats, but in this instance Pence succeeded in making Biden and Harris look inconsistent on the Green New Deal (Biden says he's against it, Harris was a co-sponsor in the Senate, and both start tap-dancing at the mention of the words), which in any case, according to the vice president, "would crush American energy, would increase the energy costs of American families in their homes, and literally would crush American jobs."

To hear Pence tell the story, Biden and Harris want to eliminate fossil fuels, redistribute wealth, mount the electorate on eBikes, and force windmills and solar panels on just plain folks. (If only they did, except that Scranton is anthracite coal country.) Pence added, ". . .the climate is changing. We'll follow the science." (The word "science" has taken on mystical importance in modern politics, maybe because so few in office understand it.) But he didn't stop there and went on to make the point that it's the free market, corporations, and "innovation" that are cleaning up the environment. Who knew? I thought they were flooding the market with plastic bottles that take 1,000 years to decompose and fleets of SUVs, which contributed 700 million tons of carbon dioxide to the atmosphere from 2010 to 2018.

In response, all Harris could say is that "Joe is about saying we're going to invest that in renewable energy, which is going to be about the creation of millions of jobs. We will achieve net zero emissions by 2050, carbon neutral by 2035. Joe has a plan. . ." Maybe Joe's plan is that black binder stage prop you see him carrying off his campaign plane, as though his entire career has been built on "the science" and not PAC money from Wilmington credit card companies. Harris's warm embrace of fracking and her social distancing from the Green New Deal were only part of her pivot to re-brand the Democrats as the Democratic-Republican Party (ironically, its name in the 1790s, when Thomas Jefferson founded it).

Without ever mentioning Franklin Roosevelt, John or Robert Kennedy, Lyndon Johnson, Bernie Sanders, or Elizabeth Warren (among many others), she said:

> Joe and I are particularly proud of the coalition that we've built around our campaign. We probably have one of the broadest coalitions of folks that you've ever seen in a presidential race. Of course, we have the support of Democrats, but also independents and Republicans. In fact, seven members of President George W. Bush's cabinet are supporting our ticket. We have the support of Colin Powell, Cindy McCain, John Kasich. Over 500 generals, retired generals, and former national security experts and advisors are supporting our campaign.

So much for the Trump-Pence insinuation that Harris is a fellow traveler—unless it is with the administration of George W. Bush.

The Great Oval Office Death Watch

It's not hard for me to imagine that either Pence or Harris one day will be president, although I cannot see either of them getting into office through the popular vote. Succession would seem to be the more probable route. Neither strikes me as having, as was said of Franklin Roosevelt, "a first class temperament." (The full quote by Oliver Wendell Holmes was that FDR had *a second class intellect, but a first class temperament.*") Both are hard-wired, calculating, and humorless. Pence also has the soul of a footman, while Harris speaks as though the entire electorate were bored members of a homicide jury (and maybe they are).

In terms of political lineage, Pence is descended from Richard Nixon, someone willing to say or do anything to advance his career. Pence may not have Nixon's vindictiveness, but his evangelical embrace of Trump's groping criminality suggests a certain suppleness to his Main Street conservative values. As Sinclair Lewis wrote of George Babbitt: "Just as he was an Elk, a Booster, and a member of the Chamber of Commerce, just as the priests of the Presbyterian Church determined his every religious belief and senators who controlled the Republican Party decided in little smokey rooms in Washington what he would think about disarmament, tariff, and Germany, so did the large advertisers fix the surface of his life, fix what he believed to be his individuality."

Harris is, likewise, hostage to the fortunes of ambition. In this presidential race, she's Everywoman—someone who can console African Americans or lock them in jail; someone who can march with Black Lives Matter or ride the limos of the *Fortune* 500; someone who can excoriate American interventionist foreign policy and still pose for selfies with troops out on the Afghan wire.

President Charles Ponzi

Pence's path to the presidency is harder than Harris's, even though he's the sitting vice president and the president, as I write, seems to be chasing the dragon around the White House. Under several end-of-days election outcomes—some involving the presidential race being decided in the House of Representatives—Pence could remain in office past 2020, although I think he's done once Trump is smoked out of his hole.

When the two are out of power, and Trump is exposed as the political and financial heir of Charles Ponzi, Pence will be seen as having driven one of the getaway cars, which cannot help his chances in 2024.

Assuming Biden is elected president, Kamala Harris would have two good chances to move to the top job: one is as the vice president of a 78-year-old pre-existing condition who seems to be shrinking before our eyes. (Is it just me or does he seem diminished in press pictures these days, a little old man in a baseball cap?)

The other way forward for her is through the Democratic nomination in 2024, when the likes of Elizabeth Warren and Bernie Sanders will be out of the picture, although on her own in 2020 Harris was a 2 Percenter. And if a Biden presidency has the feel of an extended Irish wake—think of Woodrow Wilson's last year in office—Harris would share blame as one of the pallbearers who delivered the "body" to the White House.

Harris Walks a Thin Blue Line

Harris used up some of the question-and-answer time over the Supreme Court nomination of Amy Coney Barrett to clean up her Personnel file. She tried to erase the impression that, as the San Francisco DA, she was vigorous in locking up every street pharmacist selling a little cheeba, and would like everyone to forget that in 2010 she campaigned against legalizing the personal use of marijuana. She said, "We will, on the issue of criminal justice reform, get rid of private prisons and cash bail and we will decriminalize marijuana."When it was his turn to speak about criminal justice, Pence waved the flag over the thin blue line (*"And I want everyone to know who puts on the uniform of law enforcement every day, President Trump and I stand with you. . ."*) and Swift-boated, so to speak, the liberal ex-prosecutor Harris for having failed to support a Senate bill on police reform.

In turn, Harris rounded on Pence (*"I will not sit here and be lectured by the vice president on what it means to enforce the laws of our country. . .the only one on this stage who has personally prosecuted everything from child sexual assault to homicide. . ."*), but the exchange dug at the Achilles' heel of Harris's political persona, which vacillates between Inspector Harry Callahan (*"Go ahead. Make my day. . ."*) and family advisor Al Sharpton.

The Supremacist Court and People of Praise

As a U.S. senator, Harris sits prominently on the Judiciary Committee—her bully pulpit, so to speak. At the Brett Kavanaugh confirmation hearings, she was a flagellant in the agonies of Christine Blasey Ford (more so than she now buys into the confessions of Tara Reade). Presumably, the Democrats want Harris to headline the Senate opposition to Amy Coney Barrett, although something tells me that some besotted Democratic senators may have caved in after Amy's blue-dress charm offensive.

In opposing the Barrett confirmation, Harris slipped in a little homily from the life of Saint Abraham (Lincoln), saying that he had delayed nominating a Supreme Court justice until after the 1864 election. But she invented the quote (*"But Honest Abe said it was not the right thing to do. . ."*) and ignored the fact that Lincoln nominated Salmon Chase to the court just after the election. (In his way, Kentucky lawyer Lincoln was as wily as Kentucky Senator McConnell.)

Instead of calling Lincoln as a character witness, Pence flipped the tables on the Democrats for opposing the Barrett confirmation timetable (before the election) and asked Harris, "People. . . are voting right now. They'd like to know if you and Joe Biden are going to pack the Supreme Court if you don't get your way in this nomination." It led to a concise Pence argument (court packing as a political sin worse than rushing through the Barrett nomination) that seemed to catch Harris off-guard, although Biden himself has repeatedly waffled in answering the court-packing question. The vice president said:

> You know the people deserve a straight answer, and if you haven't figured it out yet, the straight answer is they are going to pack the Supreme Court if they somehow win this election. Men and women, I got to tell you people across this country, if you cherish our Supreme Court, if you cherish the separation of powers, you need to reject the Biden Harris ticket come November the third, reelect President Donald Trump, and we'll stand by that separation powers in a nine seats Supreme Court.

Point to Pence, but just as Harris stumbled over the Supreme Court exchange, the vice president had no cogent answers for why Donald Trump is endlessly fawning over white supremacists. (He mumbled, *"No. Not true. . ."*) It led to Harris's strongest pitch of the night, when she said:

> And the reality of this is that we are talking about an election in 27 days where last week the president of the United States took a debate stage in front of 70 million Americans and refused to condemn white supremacists. . . . And it wasn't like he didn't have a chance. He didn't do it. And then he doubled down. And then he said, when pressed, "Stand back, stand by." And this

is a part of a pattern of Donald Trump's. He called Mexicans rapists and criminals. He instituted as his first act a Muslim ban. He. . .on the issue of Charlottesville, where people were peacefully protesting the need for racial justice, where a young woman was killed. And on the other side, there were neo-Nazis carrying Tiki torches, shouting racial epithets, anti-Semitic slurs. And Donald Trump when asked about it said, "There were fine people on both sides." This is who we have as the president of the United States, and America, you deserve better.

In this campaign Harris should be prosecuting Trump, but instead Biden's handlers have her talking about job creation and China.

The Last Temptation of Donald Trump

The vice presidential debate ended, as did the presidential debate the week before, on the simple question of whether, if Trump loses, he will "accept the outcome of the election" and leave office without the assistance of handcuffs or a taser. From what Pence said—adding to what Trump said and didn't say the week before—the answer is "no." As Trump did, Pence went off on the Democrats for attempting "to overturn the results of the last election." He said:

> I mean, there were documents released this week that the CIA actually made a referral to the FBI, documenting that those allegations were coming from the Hillary Clinton campaign. And of course, we've all seen the avalanche, what you put the country through for the better part of three years, until it was found that there was no obstruction, no collusion, case closed. And then Senator Harris, you and your colleagues in the Congress tried

to impeach the president of the United States over a phone call. And now Hillary Clinton has actually said to Joe Biden that, in her words, under no circumstances, should he concede the election.

It was only after the vice presidential debate that Trump publicly, more than once, called for the arrests of Barack Obama, Hillary Clinton, and Joe Biden, which borrows directly from the plot of another Sinclair Lewis novel, *It Can't Happen Here*, about a fascist takeover of America after the 1936 election. In the novel Lewis writes:

> "More and more, as I think about history," he pondered, "I am convinced that everything that is worth while in the world has been accomplished by the free, inquiring, critical spirit, and that the preservation of this spirit is more important than any social system whatsoever. But the men of ritual and the men of barbarism are capable of shutting up the men of science and of silencing them forever."

Unfortunately, it has already "happened here."

Democracy's End

"Politics, as a practice, whenever its professions, has always been the systematic organization of hatreds."

—Henry Brooks Adams,
The Education of Henry Adams, 1907

Trump's Reichstag Fire

AN URBAN LEGEND IS BEGINNING TO SPIN: Come January 20, 2021, President Donald Trump will wall himself into the White House, with a few of those gilded sofas wedged up against the Oval Office door, and refuse to come out when the Joe Bidens come calling for the ceremonial ride to the Capitol and the presidential inauguration.

Remember the scene four years ago, when Don and Melania showed up gripping that eggshell blue box from Tiffany & Co. (*"Can't we just give them that platter we got last year?"*), with Trump leaving his wife behind to struggle with the limousine door while he did his bear-walk toward the waiting Obamas and, more to the point, White House power?

I have to say that I am indifferent as to whether Trump stays or goes on the morning of January 20, since barricading himself in the Oval office will simply add to the criminal charges that will come his way that afternoon or in the days that follow.

Mercifully, political power in the United States is based on faith, not the keys to the White House panic room, and I suspect that a few Washington Mall park rangers, experienced at handling trespassers mumbling to themselves that they are president, can remove him from office (once Comcast has cut his cable subscription).

Nor do I think that anyone, other than perhaps Eric and Don Jr. (Ivanka and Jared will have left on a ski trip), will answer the *coup d'etat* bell, should Trump choose to ring it. But since the specter of a Trump *putsch* (he is German, after all) is at least under discussion, let's review whether if where there's smoke, there's fire.

The White Noise of the Recount Drama

For starters, ignore all the Twitter noise about vote recounting in places like Pennsylvania or Georgia as changing the outcome of the presidential election. It was never the intention of Trump and personal lawyer Rudy Giuliani to claw their way into the White House on the back of some national recount, which is just a smoke-and-mirrors exercise to lay their entitlement claims before the court of public opinion.

If Trump were serious about his various state recount lawsuits, he might have organized better evidence than the affidavit of the convicted child sex offender/Trump poll watcher who saw some questionable ballot-counting practices in Pennsylvania, or he might have had a better plan than to send Rudy to the microphones in front of that Philadelphia dildo store (a "coals to Newcastle" exercise, I must say).

As a Reichstag fire, the great vote recount hoax isn't very convincing. Even if a case or two lands in front of the wholly-owned Supreme Court subsidiary, none of them has any chance of overturning anything more substantial than those 53 contested votes in Georgia. So those gas cans, in the lobby of American democracy, will fail to ignite.

Trump's Certifiable

Slightly more promising would be for Trump's hole-in-ballot-box gang to persuade some friendly state legislatures, in states where Biden has won, to intervene in the vote certification process and to appoint an alternative slate of Trump electors to make the case that they are the "real" electors when Congress counts the presidential votes on January 6, 2020.

The problem with this strategy, for example in Pennsylvania, is that while that legislature has a Republican majority, the governor is a Democrat, Tom Wolf, who appointed the secretary of state, Kathy Boockvar, who has the job of auditor-in-chief of electoral fairness (something she takes seriously, as do thousands of other vote-counting officials across the country).

Without knowing either Wolf or Boockvar, my guess is that they would lie down in the streets of Harrisburg before they would allow the Republican majorities in the state legislature to vote in an alternate slate of Trump electors that would turn up in Washington with phony credentials. For Trump and Giuliani, that leaves only Georgia and Arizona among the swing states where Biden has won or is winning the popular vote and that have a "trifecta" of the governor and both state legislatures under Republican control.

On paper anyway, those states could be susceptible to the appointment of rogue electors, although in Georgia and Arizona the legislatures would be breaking their own states' laws if they were to ram through electors (11 in Arizona; 16 in Georgia) for Donald Trump (still not enough to turn the election).

Here's the pertinent clause in the Constitution:

Each state shall appoint, in such manner as the Legislature thereof may direct, a number of electors, equal to the whole number of Senators and Representatives to which the State may be entitled in the Congress. . .

And the legislatures in Georgia and Arizona have "directed" that a popular vote will decide who is chosen as a presidential elector.

As I said, it would be against the law to send in Trump-cloned electors (if the popular votes have been tabulated otherwise), but keep in mind that three of the current members of the U.S. Supreme Court (Roberts, Kavanaugh, and Barrett) worked for Bush on *Bush v. Gore* in 2000, which shut down the recounts in Florida, gifting the presidency to George W. Bush. That case also left open the question of whether state legislatures have absolute authority, according to the "original intent" of the U.S. Constitution, to appoint presidential electors, which might give Trump some hope here.

Hail Mary Pence

The reason why fiddling with presidential electors is more promising for a Trump *putsch* than recounting votes in Wisconsin is because it is a joint session of Congress on January 6, with the unctuous Vice President Mike Pence presiding, that opens the electoral envelopes from each state, counts the votes, and resolves any disputes.

If the issue of electors (and their credentials) cannot be resolved by the House and Senate, then the House of Representatives (one delegation, one vote) would determine the election (in Trump's favor). It would be a Hail Mary for the God-fearing Trump, but perhaps one worth some genuflection, if the alternative to staying on in the White House is a stretch at Attica Correctional Facility.

Georgia on Mitch's Mind

Here's another dilemma for Trump's Three-Card Monte recount strategy: any attempt to strongarm the Georgia legislature would probably doom the two Republican senatorial candidates in the special runoff elections in Georgia, scheduled for January 5,

2021 (the day before the electoral votes are counted in Washington, D.C.).

If Trump tries a sleight-of-hand game in Georgia, he would find himself fighting not only Biden and the Democrats, but also, ironically, Mitch McConnell, as the Senate majority leader needs to carry at least one seat there for Republicans to maintain their (and his) grip on senatorial power.

I don't know whether you noticed it, but when Mitch gave Trump a high-five to chase after fraudulent votes, he limited his enthusiasm only until the states "certify" their vote totals. Here is what McConnell said in prepared remarks on the floor of the Senate:

> Obviously, no states have yet certified their election results. We have at least one or two states that are already on track for a recount. And I believe the president may have legal challenges underway in at least five states.
>
> The core principle here is not complicated. In the United States of America, all legal ballots must be counted and illegal ballots must not be counted. The process should be transparent or observable by all sides, and the courts are here to work through concerns. Our institutions are actually built for this. We have the system in place to consider concerns, and President Trump is 100 percent within his rights to look into allegations of irregularities and weigh his legal options.

It sounds fairly anodyne (blah, blah, blah. . ."*all legal ballots. . .*"), and matches what Rudy was saying in front of the lawn, garden, and vibrator center. And Mitch is correct to say it is within Trump's rights to ask for recounts and the like. But his upbeat comments draw a line in the sand at certification (December 8, 2020), after which, when Trump's court appeals will have failed, Mitch will be the top Republican dog in Washington, first in line to water down whichever fire hydrant he pleases.

Don't Let the Door Hit You on the Way Out

In the Senate runoffs in Georgia, Mitch is walking a fine line (although, I must say, he is doing it better than the Democrats, who decided the best way to win control of the Senate was to devour their own and blame Alexandria Ocasio-Cortez for the losses in Congress).

What Mitch wants to do in Georgia—in order to retain his and Republican control in the Senate—is to turn out Trump's base in the runoff election by saying loudly, "Hell, ya, we wuz robbed." That's the red meat (okay, beef jerky) served up to Georgia's MAGA Republicans. Hence all the orchestrated Republican comments—from the likes of senators Lindsey Graham and Ted Cruz—that imply Trump was cheated. Actually all of them know that Trump is going down for the count in the presidential election, but they need the juice of his suicide mission (". . .*all legal ballots*. . .") to help Republicans turn out in Georgia.

Going forward, many Republicans are happy to live their lives without Trump and to take their chances with Mitch lording over the Senate, Supreme Court, and Joe Biden, who loved nothing more than his racist colleagues in the Senate (see Thurmond, Strom, eulogy thereof).

Parscale Signs Off on Trump's Expenses

Another reason why Trump's recount endgame is doomed to failure is that he's broke and cannot pay for the multimillion-dollar legal strategy that Rudy and Eric were blathering on about in the adult store parking lot.

For the last few years, Trump has treated the finances of the Republican Party as if they were just another Deutsche Bank overdraft; for example, dipping into the reelection campaign fund to spend $80 million on personal legal expenses (all of his pussy-grabbing lawsuits, etc.). The remaining campaign funds were spent, in part, on Trump vanity indulgences, such as ads on Fox in Washington, D.C., so that the president (while lying in bed with a few burgers) could bask in the glory of his reelection spots (in a city that would vote 93 percent for Biden).

Given that Trump was able to siphon off $80 million of Republican Party money to pay his sexual assault defense lawyers, I do wonder what was the role of Brad Parscale (of late on suicide watch) in running the Trump reelection campaign. Was he put there as a Trump tap on Republican campaign money?

When recently Parscale's wife called the cops to their Florida home (Brad was threatening to hurt her or himself), the campaign boss was surrounded by enough new cars, TVs, and boats to look like the winning contestant on a TV game show ("*You, Too, Can Run a Presidential Campaign. . .*"). My take on the front-lawn swag is that it was the vigorish from the Trump gang for turning a blind eye to their own looting of party funds.

I saw Parscale in person at a Trump rally in Iowa, where his contribution to American politics was to shoot Trump T-shirts into the delirious crowd (as if it were a Heat-Raptors game). Something tells me that T-shirt shooting, however well done, isn't exactly the ticket to the Florida good life.

Let's Make a Trump Legal Deal

Now that Trump has been schooled in the presidential election, I would imagine that he's lost his drain on party funds, and that Mitch McConnell and other Republican hierarchs are telling him that he can hunt all the fraudulent votes he wants, so long as he (Trump) is paying for the dogs. Even in Trump's fictional world of wealth, there are limits on the number of $25 million legal bills that can be paid, and my guess on the voter-fraud-recount pageant is that it would cost millions, if done on an expedited basis using big-time law firms.

At the same time I suspect these firms, unlike personal marital-aid lawyer and *Borat Subsequent Moviefilm* extra Rudy Giuliani, are not willing to work for free, and that the most interesting conversations these days in American politics are those between Eric or Don Jr. and law firm partners, who in calm, rational voices are telling the Trump brothers that they would "love to help out" in Wisconsin, Arizona, Pennsylvania, or Georgia but that a retainer of $10 million will be needed "up front" to cover some "incidentals" that come with the stealing of an election. I don't believe that the vibrating Trumps have an extra $10 million at hand, which may explain why in Nevada the Trump campaign quietly dropped its lawsuit in a case involving alleged fraud over the counting of mail-in ballots.

The Nevada Supreme Court ruled against the Trump campaign, which declined to appeal the ruling, an indication that Trump's pockets are probably not as deep as he once might have implied to Miss America contestants. I have read all the stories about how Trump is planning to run again in 2024, how he's the future of the Republican Party, and how any day now he will launch his own dog-whistling cable network that will rake in millions, but my guess is that when the history of the Trump presidency is written, it will be as a Ponzi scheme of epic proportions, in which Russians, Saudis, Deutsche Bank, and the Republican Party, among others, were played on a Madoff scale. Add in the recount claim to this world of illusion.

The Lost Art of the Steal

WHAT'S THE MATTER WITH DONALD TRUMP and the Republican Party that they are making such a hash of stealing an election? Why are they making such a mockery of our finest political tradition? Have they no sense of history?

In 2000, even the hopelessly inept George W. Bush ("*Is our children learning?. . .*") figured out how, after 18,000 residents in Palm Beach County mistakenly cast their votes for Patrick Buchanan, the Supreme Court could deny an accurate recount of the errantly dimpled chads ("*for the sake of our democracy. . .*") and grant him the presidency, as if part of an inheritance. In 1960, John F. Kennedy decided that to win the presidency he would need, among his vote counters, Chicago Mayor Richard M. Daley ("*vote early and vote often. . .*") and Texas Senator Lyndon Baines Johnson (running as JFK's vice president).

In Cook County Chicago in 1960, Kennedy got almost 400,000 more votes than did the Democratic candidate in 1956, who was the former popular governor of Illinois, Adlai E. Stevenson II. Yes, I know: hard to imagine. Kennedy won Illinois in 1960 by a margin of 8,858 votes. In Texas, Kennedy won by 46,266 votes. As JFK's father liked to joke, imagining a telegram to his son: "Dear Jack: Don't buy a single vote more than necessary. I'll be damned if I'm going to pay for a landslide." Presumably, 46,266 was in line with LBJ's budget. And then there was the time, in 1876, when 101 percent of the residents in South Carolina voted in the presidential election. In 2020 is Trump even trying?

When Voter Suppression Paid Off

In the 2020 election Trump adopted a strategy that pinned all of his comeback hopes on post-electoral lawsuits winding up in the Supreme Court, where presumably Brett and Amy would do him a solid. In 2000, that ploy only worked as the election came down to the winner of one state, Florida, where the vote differential was less than 1,000.

Trump also put his reelection faith in the great game of voter suppression (purging the rolls in places such as Florida and Georgia), but it just made people angry. The last time voter suppression paid off in a presidential election was in 1888 (Grover Cleveland vs. Benjamin Harrison). In that contest both sides employed what were called "repeaters" (people who voted more than once in the same district) and "floaters" (they cast their second, third, or fourth votes elsewhere).

President Cleveland won the popular vote in 1888, but lost in the electoral college, largely because Harrison won in New York state. How did Harrison, an Indianapolis lawyer, win New York, Cleveland's home state? Harrison's agents cleverly threatened Tammany Hall supporters with jail sentences if they were to cast "doubtful" votes, which "suppressed" the Democratic turnout. The pious Harrison (his nickname was "The Human Iceberg") said after the election: "Providence has given us this victory," to which one of his political operatives quipped, "Providence hadn't a damn thing to do with it."

Trump Applies for Legal Aid

Money, or more precisely the lack thereof, is another reason why Trump has been unable to steal the 2020 election, as at the moment the golfing-obsessed Trump is looking financially tapped out. Coming into the home stretch of the election, the Biden campaign brought in $952 million while Trump raised $612 million, a gap that not even Deutsche Bank could bridge. That cash differential not only edged Trump off the airways in several swing states (notably Michigan), but after the election it has forced Trump to implement his steal-it-on-the-cheap strategy.

In Wisconsin, for example, Trump is only recounting the votes in two counties (Milwaukee and Dane, for which the cost is $3 million) instead of recounting the entire state (for which the price tag was $7.9 million, paid up front, a bit like ransom money). Part of the reason Trump lagged behind Biden in fundraising, I am sure, is because he can't open his mouth without telling people that "I am really, really rich. . ." Who during a recession wants to send $250 to a candidate who says he's worth billions?

Trump's lack of liquidity, however, may explain his refusal to concede, as in the meantime he can bleed his base for more donations. In theory the money now being raised is to be used for challenging the election results (*"This is a case where they're trying to steal an election. . . . They're trying to rig an election, and we can't let that happen."*) But in reality, if you read the fine print of the pleadings, the new money can be used to re-float the otherwise sinking *Good Ship Trump.*

Now that Trump has lost the election, the Republican Party wants nothing to do with picking up his padded expenses (all those jets for Eric and Don Jr., and expense money for Kimberly Guilfoyle and Lara Trump), especially for what it views as a lost cause.

Maybe if the electoral margin had come down to one state that was close (say, Georgia), Mitch McConnell and the Republicans might have stumped up per-diem vouchers to pay for some recount lawyers. But as Trump needs to turn at least three states (if not more), the costly recount game isn't worth the candle (at least not to Mitch), which explains why Trump is relying on The Legal Aid

Society (Rudolph Giuliani, Esq., representing its indigent client) to press his long-shot cases.

The White Shoes Walk

Nominally the reason that many large law firms (Porter Wright among them) withdrew from Trump's recount and certification claims is because they were getting pushback from their clients and partners, and because (this was unstated) they were worried about getting disbarred for advancing arguments they knew to be false. A more logical reason for these law firm withdrawals might be that Trump is refusing to pay them, probably because he has no money.

When Porter Wright dropped Trump as a client in Pennsylvania, it left the file with a Federalist Society lawyer, Linda Kerns. About a week later she was fired or quit so that Trump could pin his reelection prospects on Marc A. Scaringi, Esq., a Harrisburg "business and corporate" lawyer who "represents for-profit, nonprofit and not-for-profit businesses and their principals, owners, directors and officers."

In working for Trump, Solicitor Scaringi (who is also a conservative morning talk show host) would seem to be drawing on his not-for-profit experience. Since without Pennsylvania Trump cannot hope to overturn the 2020 election, you do wonder why he's betting on a morning talk-show lawyer who handles divorce cases. (I guess maybe Rudy's his ventriloquist.) No sooner did Scaringi take the Trump mandate than he was writing to his Twitter followers that, actually, the Pennsylvania cases were hopeless (as, I am sure, are his prospects of getting paid for his time in court).

At least when George W. Bush needed to steal an election in Florida, he had the good sense to retain presidential chamberlain and super lawyer James Baker. (Vice President Al Gore countered with Warren Christopher, who approached the Florida recount knife fight as if it were an academic symposium.)

The Postman Always Votes Twice

You do wonder which very stable genius in the Trump universe (I have some ideas) came up with the strategy of contesting mail-in ballots—especially after election day—to somehow secure Trump's reelection. Not only did the rantings about mail-in ballots discourage Trump voters from voting remotely, but it forced them, during a deadly spike in a pandemic, to vote in person, which not everyone wanted to do. Who knew that the greatest suppression of Republican voters would come from Republicans?

When it comes to stealing a presidential election, what works best is power and money, generally distributed, and having something to trade for off-balance sheet votes. In the election of 1896, in which William McKinley defeated William Jennings Bryan, power broker Mark Hanna, flush with cash from corporate trusts (who feared Bryan and his silver platform), judiciously bought votes in a number of swing states, most of which went for McKinley, who otherwise (a bit like Harrison) would have thought that providence had delivered his victory.

In 1876, another contested election, it was Republican control of the Congress that allowed Rutherford B. Hayes (aka "His Fraudulency") to defeat the New York Governor Samuel Tilden, who had won the popular vote by several hundred thousand. When it came time to send electoral votes to be counted in Washington, Republican governors in a number of southern states (then under federal military occupation) sent electors for Hayes, even from states where Tilden had won, resulting in the same kind of deadlock that today is Trump's only hope for stealing the 2020 election.

It's the scenario in which Republican legislatures go rogue and send in Trump electors, even though Biden will have won the popular vote in those states. And then it's Vice President Pence who would preside over the resolution of the deadlock.

Trumpff unter allen

In 2020, what does Trump have to offer Georgia, Pennsylvania, Nevada, and Arizona in order to overrule the popular vote in those states and send electors for Trump to Washington? The answer is: not much. For one thing, for all his spin, Trump doesn't "do deals." He runs scams, in which he alone is the winner.

Actually, the Republicans in Pennsylvania might be happier with the current results, in which, after getting rid of Trump, they get a conservative Supreme Court, a Republican majority in the Senate, and a corporatist, pro-fracking president who grew up in Scranton.

The so-called Compromise of 1877 worked because each side had something that the other wanted (Republicans wanted the presidency and the Democrats wanted the South), but in 2020 all Trump has to trade is bluster and unpaid legal bills, and nobody seems to want either.

America Installs a Pope

CAN SOMEONE EXPLAIN TO ME WHY, when a mob carrying spears and wearing Davy Crockett hats breaks into the Capitol, "our democracy is under assault" by insurrectionists and seditionists, while when another group takes over the Capitol with the likes of A-Rod and Bill Clinton, and lines the streets of Washington with storm troops, our democracy has suddenly been "restored"?

Yes, I watched most of the Biden inauguration, although somehow I missed Lady Gaga singing the national anthem. I did catch the aerial jumbotron shots of the Trumps slipping out of Washington and the 21-limo salute that new President Biden got on leaving the Capitol, and my take is that America has chosen a pope—not elected a chief magistrate. The pageantry had it all, lacking only white smoke coming out the chimneys of the Senate.

The day featured the return of Hillary Clinton to the national feel-good club (although her outfit looked like a home uniform of the Minnesota Vikings), culturally sensitive stage props (200,000 American flags?), and enough black Chevy Suburbans to warm the heart of any GM executive cutting a Super Bowl ad. At the center of it all was humble Father Joe, selected by the Electoral College of Cardinals, to serve as the American pope, in office to deliver daily benedictions for the salvation of the nation's soul.

The National Pardon Fantasy League

Before the swinging White House doors hit Trump on his way out of town, Mafia Don figured out one last way to define his presidency as little more than a variation on the rackets—by issuing a pardon or commutation to every small-time swindler or con man in the federal prison system who had bilked funds out of city contractors, Medicare patients, political slush funds, or MAGAistas mailing in $3 to help Mexico pay for the Wall.

I put the Trump pardons into two groups: those who at some later date can help Trump (at a Palm Beach fundraiser for the new Patriot Party?) or those who could hurt him (Bannon singing to the Feds about how the Trump presidency was just one large Ponzi scheme with Don and Don Jr. having set up a drain on GOP campaign funds). I have no memory from my youth of January 19 at the end of each administration being National Pardon Day, but now it's turned into an event, not unlike Cyber Monday. Given some time, I am sure the networks will figure out a way to promote it.

It Takes a Village People

Was I the only American watching President Trump and his wife Melania fly away to the soundtrack of "YMCA"? What happened to that cease-and-desist order issued by the Village People? Did the Trump 2024 campaign pay up for the rights so that the president could hear their consoling words of advice on his way out of town? At Trump rallies "Macho Man" is standard fare (it's his walk-on music), and other rally songs include Elton John's "Saturday Night's Alright (For Fighting)," Michael Jackson's "Beat It" (presidential historians, call your office), and "You Can't Always Get What You Want" (the Rolling Stones).

For the Trump farewell at Joint Base Andrews (not many supporters got up at 5:45 a.m. and dragged along five friends for the presidential goodbye at 8 a.m.), the Air Force or some imagineers in a console feed room capped "YMCA" with Frank Sinatra's "My Way" as *Air Force One* did its takeoff roll. It was the perfect Trump recessional. As the presidential jet lifted into the Maryland sky, I couldn't help but wonder how David St. Hubbins (*Spinal Tap*) would have seen Trump off. Would he have remarked, "It's such a fine line between stupid, and. . .clever."

The Bourbon Restoration of Democrats

With Trump and his family—until the end they looked like the cast of *Dallas*—heading into Florida exile (real estate hunting in a state that exempts multimillion-dollar houses from bankruptcy creditors?), the camera angles could return to the live studio audience on the Capitol platform, last used to film that gritty Netflix blockbuster, *Taking Nancy*.

Except for the hyphenated It couple, J. Lo and A-Rod, it was a Bourbon Restoration of Democrats, with the odd Bush and Senate leader tossed in to goose the ratings in rural America. Earlier that morning, many of them (including the GOP congressional leadership) were at mass with Father Joe. At the Capitol they were escorted to their seats of honor, which had enough safety glass to kit out a Bronx liquor store. The guests were socially distant and appropriately masked, giving the occasion the look of a national bank robbers' convention—as Butch Cassidy liked to say, "A small price to pay for beauty."

Bernie Broods

Bernie made it to the inner sanctum platform, as if dropped off on a snowmobile. He was wearing a thrift shop parka and idiot mittens that might well have had his name stitched inside by his mother, "BERNARD SANDERS, BROOKLYN." He seemed to be sitting alone (with the slouch of someone bored in traffic court), and I wondered what he made of all the references by Master of Ceremonies Amy Klobuchar to democracy's renaissance in the shadows of the defaced Capitol. In her opening remarks, the senator said:

> Two weeks ago, when an angry, violent mob staged an insurrection and desecrated this temple of our democracy, it awakened us to our responsibilities as Americans. This is the day when our democracy picks itself up, brushes off the dust, and does what America always does. Goes forward as a nation under God, indivisible, with liberty and justice for all.

When Bernie heard this, did he think?:

> I had this one in the bag until Obama reached you, Amy, and Pete too, and all the others, and you hosed me by dropping out of the race before Super Tuesday so that Chuck, Nancy, and the rest could anoint a has-been like Joe to save the 1 percent from my wealth taxes and to keep me from towing away their Audis. Who voted for Joe in the Democratic primaries in Iowa and New Hampshire? About five union guys with lunchpails, that's who. Who voted for Kamala before she dropped out? About 2 percent. And now they're up there taking a victory lap with J. Lo, and I'm back here freezing my buns off, waiting for some staffer to tell me over Zoom that climate change is "off the front burner" until Joe, Chuck, Mitch, and Nancy figure out how to dress up another corporate bailout as a Covid-19 relief package. Some democracy, Amy. . .

Biden Heals the Faithful

Biden's inaugural speech was more a sermon than a statement of political goals or concrete plans for the future. It was a homily on American faith (*"We come together as one nation, under God, indivisible, to carry out the peaceful transfer of power as we have for more than two centuries. . ."*), and an encyclical to the patriarchy promising that a government leadership of men and women in their late 70s and 80s will somehow, magically (fishes, loaves, and a few bailouts?), come up with solutions to problems that they did so much to create. Biden said:

> My fellow Americans, in the work ahead of us we're going to need each other. We need all our strength to persevere through this dark winter. We're entering what may be the toughest and deadliest period of the virus. We must set aside politics and finally face this pandemic as one nation, one nation. And I promise you this, as the Bible says, "Weeping may endure for a night, but joy cometh in the morning." We will get through this together, together.

Biden used the word "unity" more often than the Village People intoned "YMCA" at Joint Base Andrews. (*"To overcome these challenges, to restore the soul and secure the future of America, requires so much more than words. It requires the most elusive of all things in a democracy; unity, unity. . . . History, faith, and reason show the way, the way of unity. . . . Not of personal interest, but the public good, and together we shall write an American story of hope, not fear, of unity, not division, of light, not darkness."*)

In this utopia (one part Saint Augustine, the other part a gated community on the ocean?), Biden expects Trump to disappear into a Florida swamp, the Proud Boys to stand down and get jobs at Walmart, Mitch & Co. to reach across the aisle and vote for climate change legislation, racism to disappear, masks to cure the spread of the virus, and the United States to return to the Elysian Fields of the late 1950s, when the country had the optimism of a Chevy convertible and the good feelings of the Everly Brothers (*"Wake up, little Susie, wake up. . ."*).

The Bull Market in Domestic Terrorism

The payday for the crowd gathered expectantly on the Capitol gibbet was all the invocations by Biden and other speakers to deal with "a political extremism, white supremacy, domestic terrorism. . . ." The task of such a "good, safe menace" is to ratchet up fears now that the threat from the Taliban and ISIS hardly justifies pumping $1 trillion annually into that biggest doorbell camera of them all, Homeland Security. (*"Uses facial recognition software to detect very good people on both sides. . ."*) Where are A. Mitchell Palmer or the young J. Edgar Hoover now that we need them? Can't the Space Force be brought back to Earth to knock down a few militia doors in Montana or West Texas?

No doubt when Biden reaches across the aisle to his good friend Mitch, one of the first palms he will fill (with billions in unmarked bills) will be that of yet another federal agency dedicated to marching the Trump crowd into re-education camps—to beat their spears and raccoon hats into plowshares, if not into box work for Amazon.

So Who's Winning the Civil War?

Wasn't there something a touch hollow in hearing all the tough talk about taking out "domestic terrorism" in a city that was under martial law and lockdown? With a Nuremberg field of flags across the national mall? With only troops in combat fatigues there to cheer on the heavily armed presidential motorcade as it crept along Pennsylvania Avenue? Looking at the many centurions on duty around Washington, D.C. guarding the new American emperor, I was reminded of a World War II diplomatic meeting, held somewhere in Berlin. As German Foreign Minister Joachim von Ribbentrop was delivering an upbeat assessment to the summoned audience on the outcome of the war, the ambassador cut him off to ask, "If you're winning the war, how come we're having this meeting in a bomb shelter?"

Candid C-SPAN Camera

At the inauguration, I did like the silent (at least on my feed) C-SPAN/PBS camera that moved effortlessly among the honored guests, as if that fly on Mike Pence's head during the vice presidential debate.

I liked standing at the elbow of Barack Obama while he chatted up A-Rod and J. Lo—an attentive Bill Clinton was drawn there too. All this came just after Biden had invoked the tear-jerking images of Americans struggling to pay their mortgages and of the need to "put people to work in good jobs," etc. (Maybe they can become A-list celebrities and buy houses on the Vineyard?)

The Capitol's Field of Dreams

In lieu of the traditional congressional lunch with the new president, there was a short ceremony in the Capitol (no one was pounding on a desk in celebration, saying, "Hey, let's call Trump!") in which a member of Congress asked the new president and his doctoral wife to view an American painting on display in the Rotunda.

The painting was "Landscape with Rainbow" by Robert S. Duncanson, an African American artist who painted it in 1859. The landscape is a bucolic field giving way to a lake and distant hills. Some cows are grazing in the middle distance, and the day is clear. Out of nowhere comes the rainbow—sadly not painted very well—that has the look of a postcard waterfall, if not God's wrath, perhaps directed at some domestic terrorists hiding in a militia's log cabin.

I understand the symbolism of an African American artist, on the eve of the Civil War, painting the hopeful scene of the American Eden, with a visitation of either a rainbow or the Lord to comfort the country at a time of peril. And I understand why Dr. Jill would have picked this painting to hang in the Capitol, to symbolize her husband's new presidency at a time of similar danger in American history.

That the painting isn't very good doesn't distract from the otherwise laudable initiative that our public officials should be required to spend a few minutes in their busy days with American landscape art, as they would learn a lot about the country (Frederic Remington's vision of the American West?) not always found in their briefing books.

Mike Pence's Second Act

The pinhole TV camera said goodbye to Mike and Mother Pence in the parking lot of the Capitol. The Kamala Harrises wished them farewell, and there seemed to be some good feelings between the two vice presidential couples, as if they were overlapping in a time-share and happy to make each other's acquaintance.

During the inauguration itself, Pence sat in gloomy reflection, perhaps uneasy that the hangman might still cometh. That morning he had blown off the Trump farewell disco ball at Joint Base Andrews. (Is it possible that Pence could not think of five friends to bring along to an 8 a.m. line dance?) His last conversation with the president, after Pence had evaded Trump's posse, apparently did not go well. Despite being a man who for the past four years bore any indignity for the greater glory of Trump, Pence did not warm, clearly, to being described as "a pussy."

So here was the Fugitive Pence ("*an innocent victim of blind rage. . .*") in the bosom of the enemy at its coming-out party (all those Democrats who stole the election by letting their domestic animals vote) and now shunned by the MAGA base that he hoped would joyride him to the White House in 2024.

Pence should have taken comfort from looking around at all the former American presidents, vice presidents, members of Congress, and cabinet types who had fought ruinous wars, bailed out endless failed corporations, pardoned grifters, gone AWOL from the military, run up trillions in wasted deficits, ignored the climate, pocketed millions in speaking fees and from ghostwritten books, and groped women with impunity. Yet here they were, on the national stage with the curtain up, getting ready for a return engagement.

Who Won the Impeachment?

IF YOU'RE DONALD TRUMP, watching the last act of your impeached presidency, you don't need a Weatherman to tell you which way the wind is blowing, which is in the direction of a District of Columbia courtroom, where you will either be convicted as an accessory to second-degree murder (*"an extreme indifference to human life. . ."*) or a runaway jury will award plaintiffs (the Capitol police injured or killed in the riot) $1.8 billion in damages (which, by the way, Deutsche Bank will not cover with another overdraft).

Technically, Trump "walked" in the impeachment trial, but that's because the Senate is the only courtroom this side of Putin's Russia where jurors hearing a case can conspire with defense attorneys (who, while we're on the subject, confused the trial with something that sounded like a rerun of *Judge Judy*). The final vote on the charge of "incitement of insurrection" was 57-43 for conviction, which fell 10 votes short of the two-thirds majority needed to find for the House of Representatives, which brought the charge against Trump.

According to "Leader" Mitch McConnell (who after the trial appeared as if one of the Chicago Seven and might well have said on the floor of the Senate, *"Martin's dead. Malcolm's dead. Medgar's dead. Bobby's dead. Jesus is dead. They tried it peacefully. We're going to try something else. . ."*), the reason the Senate had to exonerate the former president is that Congress cannot remove from office someone who has already left. (McConnell said, "*I believe the Senate was right not to grab power the Constitution does not give us.*") In his postgame remarks, however, McConnell all but invited prosecutors in the District and elsewhere to throw the book at Trump ("*We have a criminal justice system in this country. We have civil litigation. And former presidents are not immune from being held accountable by either one. . .*") and perhaps also to throw away the key.

Upon his acquittal, Mar-a-Don issued a bizarre statement, channeling Lincoln's second inaugural, saying:

> It is a sad commentary on our times that one political party in America is given a free pass to denigrate the rule of law, defame law enforcement, cheer mobs, excuse rioters, and transform justice into a tool of political vengeance, and persecute, blacklist, cancel and suppress all people and viewpoints with whom or which they disagree. I always have, and always will, be a champion for the unwavering rule of law, the heroes of law enforcement, and the right of Americans to peacefully and honorably debate the issues of the day without malice and without hate.

The way this is written, it sounds as if Trump also wants his party to be free to "denigrate the rule of law, defame law enforcement, cheer mobs, excuse rioters, and transform justice into a tool of political vengeance. . ." (I thought it already had that right?) So who won the impeachment?

Trump's Many Legal Lives

Cats only have nine lives, but Trump—at least judicially—has hundreds. What other citizen of the republic can grope countless women, defraud banks and investors, lie under oath, bleed companies under arcane bankruptcy laws, cavort with various Russian and Ukrainian bagmen, run Ponzi schemes, have his way with porn stars, obstruct justice, conspire to overturn elections, attack the Capitol and Congress with an armed mob, kill police officers, and still enjoy "the blessings of liberty" in a gilded Palm Beach hotel suite surrounded by trays of half-eaten cheeseburgers and Diet Coke?

In theory, Trump comes out of the impeachment trial under a halo of invincibility that will see him back on top of the Republican Party, in time to "primary" (kids, it's not a verb) all those renegade senators who voted to convict him in the Senate. Nor should anything, other than his own madness, prevent King Donald from running again for president in 2024, by which time Leader McConnell will have come to his senses and opposed every program proposed by President Biden (to deal with the pandemic, climate change, the economy, immigration, and inequality—all those "Democrat" red herrings). A Risorgimento must be the plan among those in the padded Mar-a-Lago bunker (Don Jr., Roger Stone, Kellyanne?) who until last Saturday would have been studying extradition laws in Argentina. So what could go wrong?

For one thing the Liz Cheney, Mike Pence, Mitch McConnell, and Nikki Haley wings of the Republican Party appear to be done with Trump. They might want his 74 million voters and his fundraising prowess for the 2022 election and beyond, but they don't want the boorish Trump himself, especially if his only platform—now that Twitter is gone—is a defendant's table in a series of lawsuits and criminal trials.

Pelosi's Hidden Agenda

Yes, Trump "walked" on the impeachment charges, but Pelosi's and Schumer's goals in the Senate trial were never to secure 67 guilty votes from the likes of co-conspirators Ted Cruz and

Lindsey Graham. At trial the Democrats were content to brand Trump and his ilk as a party of Proud Boys who if allowed back in power will yet again march on the Capitol, only this time with more guns. The only way for the Republicans in the Senate to have double-crossed the Democratic strategy would have been to have voted unanimously to convict Trump. If they had, they would now be starting over as a conservative party in opposition to Biden's AAA platform (*"acid, amnesty, and abortion"*—it's a '70s expression). Instead the Democrats won twice—they had their show trial on prime-time television and left the erratic Trump at the head of a weakened political party that has the air of a QAnon chat room. Ka-ching.

He's Biden's Problem Now

Joe spent the trial above the fray, watching the Super Bowl, heading to Camp David, too busy with pandemic stimulus legislation to watch even Trump's ambulance-chasing legal defense team get laughed out of the Senate. In case you are wondering, here's a verbatim description of Trump lawyer Michael van der Veen's areas of legal practice: "Animal Bites, Assault, Motor Vehicle Accidents, Personal Injury—Plaintiff, Slip and Fall, Wrongful Death, Dram Shop Laws, Construction Accident, Brain Injury, Sexual Abuse—Plaintiff, Trucking Accidents, Premises Liability —Plaintiff, Litigation, Restraining Order, Small Claims, Arrest & Arraignment, Assault & Battery, Criminal Fraud, Criminal Law, Drug & Alcohol Violations, Expungement, Failure to Pay Child Support, False Accusations, Felony, Juvenile Delinquency, Misdemeanor, Motor Vehicle Offenses, Murder, Parole, Probation, Prosecution, Sex Offenses, Tax Evasion, Theft, Traffic Violations, Criminal Domestic Violence. . ." No wonder Trump hired him; he needs it all.

Biden's trickier issue, coming out of the McConnell acquittal denunciation of Trump, is that his Justice Department is now on the clock to indict Trump for the Capitol invasion, which is how Mitch gets rid of his Trump problem—by letting Biden do the dirty work.

If Biden walks away from Trump's obvious criminality, well, then, don't blame McConnell and the Republicans for not doing more to save the Republic. Hey, they did their duty in the Senate by upholding constitutional procedures in an honorable way. As Mitch said afterwards, "We refused to continue a cycle of recklessness by straining our own constitutional boundaries in response. The Senate's decision does not condone anything that happened on or before that terrible day. It simply shows that senators did what the former president failed to do: We put our Constitutional duty first." Henceforward, Trump is Biden's problem.

If Biden pardons Trump or lets him escape prosecution for the Capitol murders, hotheaded Democrats will turn on the weak-kneed president, accusing him of imagining a reach-across-the-aisle America at a time when Republican goons are swinging baseball bats and hockey sticks. But then, if Biden lets his prosecutors seek justice for Trump's endless crimes, Biden will become the president who turned the United States into a banana republic, with the ex-president dispatched to a Bolivian-like jail.

Whither the Republican Party

For my sins I watched every minute of the impeachment trial, which lasted some 20 hours (as did the Super Bowl pre-game shows). For much of the five-day series (I did get a little tired watching that endless loop of Capitol super-cop Eugene Goodman saving all those innocent senators from the mob), I thought about the future of the Republican Party, and if it has one.

In American history political parties have come and gone. We no longer have Democrat-Republicans (it was one party in 1792), Federalists, Whigs, Know-Nothings, Greenbacks, Free Soilers, or the Anti-Masonic Party (against Freemasonry from 1828-38)—to name but a handful of political parties that have flashed in the pan of American politics.

The modern Republican Party came into being in the 1850s, as the Whig Party collapsed from the weight of its unwieldy pro-slavery and anti-slavery membership (the tent was too big). The first Republican candidate for president was the western explorer, John C. Frémont (his slogan was *"Free Speech, Free Press, Free Soil, Free Men. . .Frémont and victory"*).

Although Abraham Lincoln established the party's anti-slavery street cred in the 1860s, since then the Republicans have endorsed (depending on their mood) the gold standard (Ulysses Grant), the tariff (William McKinley), trust-busting (Teddy Roosevelt), isolation (Warren Harding), fiscal conservatism (Herbert Hoover), liberal internationalism (Thomas Dewey), imperialism (Richard Nixon and W), and corporate welfare (Ronald Reagan). But nothing lasts forever.

Is This the End Game?

Who's to say that the current Republican Party will not splinter among the wings loyal to Trump, McConnell, and the Lincoln Project (those Trump-hating Republicans who made all those attack ads). A lot is made of the 74 million Americans who voted in 2020 for the Republican candidate, Trump, which ought to ensure the future of a unified party.

What happens to a party that is marching behind the standard of a man, Trump, who might spend the next four years ensconced in a variety of criminal and civil cases, all of which show him as an enabler of Oath Keepers and QAnon, if not Charles Ponzi? Keep in mind, too, that only a gerrymandered House, voter suppression, and non-proportional representation in the Senate have kept the Republicans in the recent political game.

Republicans have lost five of the last six popular votes for the presidency, although Republican presidents have still appointed 16 of the last 20 justices to the Supreme Court, and often have controlled the Senate. Will it be Trump, Liz Cheney, Mike Pence, or Mitch McConnell who will lead the party in the 2022 midterm elections, in which control of the Senate will be on the ballot? If the post-impeached Trump is shunned by the party establishment in Washington, will he go through with his threat to create a Patriot Party and divide the Republicans into the fragments of his explosive ego?

If I had to bet on a scenario, it would be that Trump is angrier at Republicans than he is at the Democrats; nothing would give him greater pleasure than to destroy his own party. Keep in mind that the mob in camo gear and coonskin caps that stormed the Capitol was chanting, "Hang Mike Pence."

Impeachments 'R' Us

In case you only watched the highlights of the proceedings, the first day was devoted to the jurisdictional question (deadly from a ratings standpoint) of whether the Senate had the right to hear an impeachment case of a president no longer in office (it voted that it did).

The next two days, Wednesday and Thursday, were taken up by Democrats showing video highlights of the attacks (all those little evil red dots getting close to saintly orange blobs). On Friday (after Trump had pulled another of his lawyers), the defense presented its case, which was that Nancy Pelosi was as responsible as Trump for the Capitol riots. Saturday was given to closing arguments by both sides and the vote (never really in question).

The Democratic main trial man was Maryland Representative Jamie Raskin, a former constitutional law professor, who opened the case for the House prosecutors and who popped out of his seat to answer questions about the wording or meaning of clauses in the Constitution. (Trump's lawyers were on firmer ground handling questions about dog bites.)

Raskin grew on me. On the first day he was weepy and professorial, treating us all like first-year law students. After that he gained crisp confidence, especially when he figured out that his opposing counsel was Jacoby & Meyers. By the end of the trial, he was under the thin skin of the Screaming Dutchman (Trump lawyer Michael van der Veen), who seemed to be arguing a case about the due process of his client's breathalyzer test.

Parade's End

The rest of the House manager team, pressing the case against Trump, had the ethnic diversity of a platoon in a World War II movie—only a wise-cracking Italian from Brooklyn was missing. But they did an excellent job presenting the case against Donald Trump, not that it required Cicero.

I liked them all, especially the delegate from the Virgin Islands, Stacey Plaskett, who remained focused whenever called to speak and who didn't mind, as they say in baseball, throwing at the intemperate van der Veen's head. If anything, the strength of the House managers revealed a fatal flaw in the Democratic Party, which is that it's a Confucian gerontocracy when there are lots of capable leaders who are younger and sharper.

Biden, Pelosi, Schumer, Sanders, Warren, and the Clintons are all in their 70s (Pelosi is 80) while Jamie Raskin, the oldest of the managers, is 58, and it made a difference to hear and see Democratic politicians speak with energy and passion. Plus I like his hero, Tom Paine.

Mar-a-Lago's Beached Whale

In most trials the incoherence of Trump's defense team (one of his lawyers sought to represent pedophile Jeffrey Epstein; another declined, as a district attorney, to prosecute Bill Cosby) would have doomed his case. Except that here Trump could have sent out dancing bears and Senate Republicans would have acquitted him. But you do have to wonder how Trump will fare, as a defendant, when he goes up against a team more aggressive than a bought jury. Even before this trial, many top law firms were distancing themselves from Trump. (I presume he wasn't paying them.) After this dismal performance (even though nominally he won), Trump's legal management incompetence will embolden all sorts of prosecutors, plaintiff lawyers, class action groups, and bounty hunters to have a run at the beached whale stranded in Mar-a-Lago.

Here's a short list of cases that Trump might well be asked to defend in the coming years: the election tampering phone call in Georgia; the Manhattan district attorney's investigations into the Trump Organization; the inquiries of the New York State attorney general into various fraudulent financial matters; the charges against Individual-1 (Trump) in the Southern District of New York case that sent Michael Cohen to jail; back taxes sought by the IRS; sedition and insurrection charges in Washington, D.C.; civil cases brought by the victims of the D.C. riots; bank lawsuits for unpaid Trump debts; fraud claims of Trump investors; those 26 cases in his matters of sexual harassment; and, finally, the possibility that Melania (despite a prenup) will claim $3.5 billion in some divorce court—half of the $7 billion Trump has always boasted he is worth.

If Trump's team consists of bottom-feeding lawyers from Phil-adelphia (with personal injury ads on buses) and a few Epstein wannabe apologists, it could—as Yogi liked to say—get late early out there.

Deaf Ears for Kevin McCarthy

The videos of the Proud Boys and Oath Keepers attacking Congress were horrifying, and there was a Zapruder film quality to the grainy sequences that show Mike Pence, hustling down stairs, declining the invitation to his own hanging. Otherwise, the trial lacked drama, at least about its outcome, as the senatorial jury was in the bag.

To summarize the case of the House of Representatives, Trump orchestrated everything from "the big lie" (the theory of the stolen election) to the January 6 noon rally at the Ellipse, after which the great patriotic rabble set off to "take back" their country at the Capitol, where a joint session of Congress was scheduled to count the electoral votes at 2 p.m. and certify the winner of the 2020 presidential election. Once the attacks on the Capitol began, around 1 p.m., Trump did nothing to secure the besieged branch of government, except to send out a few tweets and at around 4 p.m. to tell the attackers and killers "we love you."

As described by Representative Raskin and his co-managers, Trump not only incited the insurrection against Congress, but then, in violation of his oath of office, failed to preserve, protect, and defend the government then under assault; and the reason he didn't send help to the besieged Capitol is because the president, back watching television in the White House, was taking delight in the mob violence. As testament to his state of mind, when the

House Minority Leader Kevin McCarthy frantically called Trump asking for help, the president replied, "Well, Kevin, I guess these people are more upset about the election than you are." Only a president who plotted such an attack would be so indifferent to a congressional plea for more police support.

Free Speech Über Alles

On the Trump side of the trial, his lawyers never denied either that the attacks were deadly or that Trump had addressed the mob beforehand with bombastic language. But they said that Trump, as president, was protected by the free speech clause of the First Amendment to say what he did to the crowd, which then, on its own, decided to head over to the Capitol and attack the joint session of Congress.

Trump's lawyers said there was no connection between his free speech and the deadly acts that followed. He could not be held responsible for the actions of the mob. (Not-to-so-fun fact: the legal case cited by Trump's lawyers arguing his right to unfettered free speech was *Brandenburg v. Ohio*, in which members of the Ku Klux Klan shouted vile statements at a rally, which a court later said was their constitutional right, as the denunciations of Blacks and Jews had not incited immediate violence.)

Second, the Trump lawyers argued (despite the Tuesday vote) that the Senate had no standing to try an impeachment charge against a president who had already left office or then to deny him the possibility of standing for public office in the future.

Trial and Error

Missing, however, from this trial (as with the first Trump impeachment trial) was the testimony of witnesses. Nor did the

House managers have the ability, as in most trials, to subpoena documents or witnesses. (Both Democrats and Republicans agreed on having a quick trial.) All they could do to present their case was to supplement their pleadings with on-air videos from the riot and excerpts from Trump's speeches and Twitter account.

What it meant was that no evidence was produced at trial that established any connection, other than tweets and the speech on the Ellipse, between the Trump White House and those who attacked the Capitol. Nor was any connection established between any of the attackers and reconnaissance tours taken the day before of the Capitol, in the company of members of Congress or their staffs.

If, for example, there are texts or emails between the Proud Boys or Oath Keepers and anyone in Trump's entourage—say Don Jr.—they were not presented as evidence at the trial. Nor did the House managers go into much detail about who in the Trump White House helped to plan the rally or what was conveyed—other than the big lie—to those who assembled in Washington for their day of rage.

Why go to the trouble of a trial and not call any witnesses? Why, if the democracy is on the line, rush through the ending on a Saturday afternoon, so that senators can enjoy the long weekend and then the following week off?

The Grand Wizard of Washington

In the end impeachment is an act of politics, not law, and the political calculation of 45 Republican senators was to acquit Trump on the insurrection charge. Did they do so hoping that in 2022 or 2024 Trump, as the shadow president, would lead the party back from the wilderness? Did they do so fearing that Mafia Don would punish them for voting with the Democrats? Was money promised to any senators to determine their votes? (I ask as the acquittal of Andrew Johnson, during his 1868 impeachment trial, was determined by a $10,000 bribe delivered by Secretary of State William Seward.)

The impeachment winners? In the end congressional Democrats and President Biden got their show trial (which was well done and struck me as "necessary and proper"), and Republicans got to vote for Trump's acquittal and, afterwards, to say, "Yeah, well, he was guilty." (Mitch likes to have his cake and eat yours, too.) And Trump remains, for now, at the head of the Republican Party. As they often say in Congress, "There's something here for everyone."

The trial loser? Clearly it was American democracy. How can the chief magistrate send a deadly mob into the Congress while it is counting electoral votes, murder and wound dozens of Capitol police, try to kill the speaker of the House and lynch the vice president, and then cite, in his defense, the First Amendment principle of free speech? To paraphrase lead manager Raskin, the Trump legal position defies "common sense," but at least those Ohio Klansmen in the *Brandenburg* case should be proud of their boy.

Coda

"Dictators always look good until the last minutes."

—Thomas Masaryk

Trump Is Guilty,
Biden Should Resign

I REALIZE IT WAS DONALD TRUMP, NOT JOE BIDEN, who paid off the porn star and buried the hush money, not in her stocking but in what accountants call a suspense account. But I still think it's the president who should resign.

Before getting to the presidential resignation, let's review Trump's prime-time perp walk, accomplished without a raincoat draped over his shackled wrists, although I did notice that his Lion King mane is getting dangerously close to drummer dimensions.

Throwing the Book at Trump

For my sins I watched nearly all of CSI Trump, beginning with the arrival of his plane at LaGuardia Airport. Looking at the live feed, for a minute I feared we might be back to the dark era of the Trump Shuttle (1989–92), the short-haul airline that Donnie flew into the ground, costing banks several hundred million dollars in reneged debts.

On daytime television Trump's booking rose to a level of O.J.'s Bronco Chase, with a helicopter following the motorcade to Trump Tower on Monday afternoon. Then on Arraignment

Tuesday, the choppers followed the black SUVs down to Manhattan Criminal Court at 100 Centre Street, where the likes of Marjorie Taylor Greene (she had access to an amplified bullhorn) and George Santos were padding out the Trump claque; Q remained Anon.

I have no idea what it cost to put on this episode of *The Defendant* (a bit like *The Apprentice*, except the studio is a holding pen and the guests are named Rocko), but it had to be way more than the $130,000 that was forked over to silence Stormy.

Many Manhattan roads were closed for the motorcade, Centre Street was blocked off, and inside the court building hundreds of beefy cops were paid to stand around barriers on the off chance that Trump decided to leg it out of there and hole up in a Lower East Side single-room occupancy, Trump Less Than Grand.

The Trump Perp Walk

Given that Trump has been using his indictment to refill his slush funds—a few are selling T-shirts with a fake mug shot—it seemed a little rich on the part of the presiding judge, Justice Juan Manuel Merchan, to keep cameras out of the arraignment court on the grounds of decorum. Trump himself must already be in negotiation with Netflix to sell the rights to his impending stretch in the big house.

All that the studio audience at home got to see was Trump passing through a distant set of doors, and then turn abruptly to enter the courtroom, where the only permitted images were a few still photographs. (The innocent Central Park Five—who Trump wanted to send to the chair—had to get by with courtroom sketches.)

On the feed I was watching, a body language expert was consulted to decipher if Trump was angry, embarrassed, or thrilled that he was getting Q-ratings equivalent to those for *Monday Night Football*.

To me Trump had the look of a cornered Madoff or Weinstein—a deer (actually, more a hyena) caught in judicial headlights.

Cooked Books

I realize that District Attorney Alvin Bragg, Jr. has several degrees from Harvard, but I cannot say that his case against Trump pays the correct homage to the ex-president's lifetime of criminality, in which he started out scamming banks, chump investors, and Atlantic City high rollers until he moved on to election stealing, insurrection, bogus fundraising, and fronting for the Putin gang. (Vlad, just in case you've forgotten, was offered a gratis $50 million penthouse in the Trump Moscow building that was never built).

Bragg's case is built around accounting fraud, in the belief that Trump failed to properly record on his corporate income statements and balance sheets the hush money payments paid to a porn star (and others) during an election. (Given Trump's ego, I am sure he credited his unprotected sex with Stormy to goodwill rather than debit the golf-tournament quickie as a sunk cost.)

Cooking the books in Manhattan is a misdemeanor (and as prevalent as jaywalking), so Bragg's biggest challenge, in order to convict Trump of the felony charges, will be to prove beyond a reasonable doubt to a jury that Trump's accounting sleights-of-hand covered up the larger crime of election tampering and campaign finance violations. By the way, the amount in question is roughly $130,000—in a city where the market capitalization of the New York Stock Exchange is $39 trillion.

The Long Rap Sheet

I am not saying the charges ("*falsifying business records in the first degree...*") against Trump in New York are the equivalent of charging Al Capone with tax evasion, but to think that the only crime Trump has committed in recent years relates to errant accounting posts for porn-star hush money or "catch-and-kill" payments is absurd.

Just from a casual reading of the newspapers, I can believe that Trump has drained millions from public companies, defrauded any number of banks, sexually abused dozens of women, consorted with murky Russians, dispatched lowlifes to shake down Ukraine's president, obstructed justice (in many cases, including those with Manafort, Bannon, Mueller, and Comey), purloined state secrets and stuffed them in a Mar-a-Lago pool room, lied on just about every form he's filled out, used campaign contributions to float his own boats, engaged in election fraud (Georgia, fake electors, et al.), hired mobs to settle scores with enemies including the U.S. Congress and Electoral College, and caused injury and death to members of the United States Capitol Police. Despite such a rap sheet, all the cops can get him on is deceptive accounting? Admittedly, Trump goes through more lawyers than Jacoby & Meyers (I guess it would help if he sometime paid their bills), but in this case I am not sure he will need to retain the services of Perry Mason, Esq., to beat the rap.

Whoever handles this case will cite the inalienable right of candidates to pay off porn stars—citing precedent in the John Edwards case (he paid off his mistress/baby mama with campaign funds and walked)—the accounting of which is best left to the little people.

Nor will the prosecution take much pleasure in having fixer Michael Cohen, adult film actress Stephanie Clifford (aka

Stormy), or *National Enquirer* publisher David Pecker as its star witnesses.

Copping a Plea to the Press

After the arraignment, it was thought that Trump would give an angry press conference on the steps of Manhattan Criminal Court (I wonder if it gave Representative Santos a bit of frisson to be there?).

Given how few of the MAGA mob-for-hire showed up, Trump ducked the doorstop cameras and flew to Palm Beach, where an identical fleet of black SUVs was waiting to speed him to the Ball Room at Mar-a-Lago, so that he could cop his plea to a friendlier audience that included the likes of dirty trickster and pardoned felon Roger Stone.

Normally, at his rallies, Trump enters to the Village People sounds of "Macho Man" or "YMCA," although given the serious nature of these charges, in this instance he walked on to David Bowie's "Rebel Rebel" (*"Rebel rebel, you've torn your dress/Rebel rebel, your face is a mess. . ."*) and some Johnny Cash (not "Folsom Prison" but "Ring of Fire," which presumably speaks to Donald's impending martyrdom).

Trump no longer makes any pretense that he's interested in anything political other than The Importance of Being Donald. He speaks in what sounds like a confessional whisper, refers to himself as "Trump," and recites a litany of endless grievance about the slights and "Democrat" arrows that have been launched to bring down the Immaculate Conception of Himself.

In between these politics of bathos, there's a lot of sighing (to gin up applause) and sniffing (as if maybe he left Lower Manhattan with some blow). Otherwise, you know the rant: he won the election, made a "perfect" call to Brad Raffensperger, would have kept Putin out of Ukraine, hates Letitia James, Bragg, Jack Smith, and all of his tormentors, and believes that everything evil in the non-Trump world can be found on Hunter Biden's hard drive. Here's an excerpt:

> The millions of votes illegally stuffed into ballot boxes and all caught on government cameras. And just recently, the FBI and DOJ in collusion with Twitter and Facebook in order not to say anything bad about the Hunter Biden laptop from hell, which exposes the Biden family as criminals in which according to the pollsters, would've made a 17-point difference in the election result, and we needed a lot less than that, like about 16.9. . . .

If this was a warm-up for his testimony should he decide to take the stand against Bragg, the jurors will let him off on the grounds of insanity.

So if Donald Trump sounds like USS *Caine* Captain Philip Francis Queeg (*"Ahh, but the strawberries that's. . .that's where I had them. They laughed at me and made jokes but I proved beyond the shadow of a doubt. . ."*), why, in response, should President Joe Biden be the one to resign from office?

Despite unfitness for high office, Trump could well win the Republican nomination in 2024, and with that in hand he would have some chance (you calculate the odds) to win back the presidency.

I am not saying that the Bragg indictment (or others to follow) guarantees Trump the Republican nomination, but it does create a large sucking sound in American politics that will suffocate other Republican candidates and position Trump to run against Biden.

Biden's Resignation Speech

If there is the slightest chance that the race in 2024 would be a rerun of Trump vs. Biden, the president should step aside now so that Trump would find himself running against a non-octogenarian candidate.

How would it work? Biden should give a short address, along the following lines:

My fellow Americans: I have given long and hard thought to the question of whether any man or woman should serve in the office of the American president past the age of 80 years old. As you know, I turned 80 last November, and personally I feel more than up to the job of president.

At the same time, as we learned from George Washington when he declined to run for a third term, there may come a time when someone will hold this office past the age of 80 who is not fit to carry out its duties, and that, my fellow Americans, is not a risk the republic should ever have to take.

Therefore, I have decided, effective noon, after I have made a visit to Arlington National Cemetery, to resign from the presidency, so that Vice President Harris shall become president. I do this of my own free will and under pressure from no one.

I know that Vice President Harris can handle all the responsibilities of this office capably and professionally. At the same time, I am asking the leaders of the Democratic Party to hold vigorous and open primaries for the Democratic nomination in 2024, so that the best candidate might represent us in the next election. I am confident, with some time in this office, that Vice President Harris will win the nomination on her own, and she will have my support. At the same time I think the voters in our party should make the decision.

In closing, let me say that, should the members of the U.S. Senate so choose, I am prepared to serve under President Harris as her vice president until the end of the current term, so that the transition between us is seamless; but that's a decision for the Senate, not me.

Biden's resignation would achieve several ends, but notably it would drive a stake through the heart of a Trump restoration. It would also give Harris a chance to show the electorate whether or not she is up to the job of president, and at the same time it would require her to compete with other Democratic candidates for the 2024 nomination.

Presumably, in such a process, a candidate younger and more capable than Joe Biden would emerge to stand for the 2024 election, very possibly against the whispering Trump. Without Biden in office—sparing us more dog-whistling about Hunter's laptop—Trump's own candidacy becomes an exercise in madness.

The alternative of another Biden vs. Trump election is too great a risk for any democratic country to take. Even if the Bragg case is frivolous, Trump is both crazy and criminal. At the same time, at age 80, Biden is too old to remain in office for another six years.

What would happen if Trump were to beat his many raps and parlay his Palm Beach fascism back to the White House? If you want clues, watch his perp-walking Mar-a-Lago speech (it's on YouTube) and tell me that he would not impose martial law to silence the demons floating in his head and imprison his persecutors and prosecutors, both real and imagined.

MATTHEW STEVENSON was born in New York City and grew up on Long Island, attending Buckley Country Day School and Friends Academy. His university degrees are from Bucknell and Columbia universities, and he spent a year abroad with the Institute of European Studies in London and Vienna. He moved to Geneva, Switzerland, in 1991. He is a contributing editor to *Harper's Magazine* and has worked professionally in finance and investing. His essays and reporting have been published in many magazines, including, most recently, in *CounterPunch*. He is the author of many books, including *Reading the Rails, Appalachia Spring, The Revolution as a Dinner Party* (about China throughout its turbulent 20th century), and *Biking with Bismarck,* about the Franco-Prussian wars and the Treaty of Versailles. His last book, *Our Man in Iran*, explores his travels across the Islamic Republic. You can reach out to Matthew at:

matthewstevenson@sunrise.ch
www.odysseusbooks.com
www.matthewstevenson.com